CW00557441

A DARK HISTORY OF GIN

A DARK HISTORY OF GIN

MIKE RENDELL

PEN & SWORD **HISTORY**

AN IMPRINT OF PEN & SWORD BOOKS LTD
YORKSHIRE ~ PHILADELPHIA

First published in Great Britain in 2022 by
PEN AND SWORD HISTORY
An imprint of
Pen & Sword Books Ltd
Yorkshire – Philadelphia

ISBN 978 1 39907 051 5

Typeset in Times New Roman 11/13.5 by
SJmagic DESIGN SERVICES, India.
Printed and bound in the UK by CPI Group (UK) Ltd.

Pen & Sword Books Limited incorporates the imprints of Atlas, Archaeology,
Aviation, Discovery, Family History, Fiction, History, Maritime, Military, Military
Classics, Politics, Select, Transport, True Crime, Air World, Frontline Publishing,
Leo Cooper, Remember When, Seaforth Publishing, The Praetorian Press,
Wharncliffe Local History, Wharncliffe Transport, Wharncliffe True Crime and
White Owl.

For a complete list of Pen & Sword titles please contact
PEN & SWORD BOOKS LIMITED
47 Church Street, Barnsley, South Yorkshire, S70 2AS, England
E-mail: enquiries@pen-and-sword.co.uk
Website: www.pen-and-sword.co.uk

Or
PEN AND SWORD BOOKS
1950 Lawrence Rd, Havertown, PA 19083, USA
E-mail: Uspen-and-sword@casematepublishers.com
Website: www.penandswordbooks.com

Contents

Preface

Mention to anyone that you are writing a book about gin and the chances are that you will be met by the comment: 'Chuck the book, give me the gin any day'. But gin has a fascinating history – and an exciting future. I mean to say – who would have thought that a supermarket would celebrate the run-up to Easter by promoting 'a Hot Cross Bun Gin Liqueur'? It is described as being a 'sensational spicy gin, infused with nutmeg, cinnamon, cloves and ginger flavours.' You can get gin with the flavour of apple crumble, or lemon curd, or flavoured with any of many hundreds of different botanicals. You can google just about anything, adding the word 'gin' to the search and it will come up with exotic suggestions. You want gin truffles, rhubarb gin and custard humbugs, gin and tonic marshmallows, or pink gin fudge? It's out there. You want a gin advent calendar, a gin apron, a gin-and-tonic cracker set? It's yours for the asking. Hungry for Gin & Tonic popcorn? Or gin-flavoured cheese? But of course, just remember to add the cost of postage.

You can join Gin Clubs, there is a Gin Guild, you can attend any number of Gin Schools, and there is hardly a city in the country which doesn't have its own gin distillery. In modern literature it is associated with sophisticated settings and Beautiful People – think James Bond naming the Vesper Martini in Casino Royale. Ian Fleming was believed to favour Gordon's Export, Booths, Boodles and Beefeater gins but did not necessarily specify the particular brand of gin to be used by the character he created.

Gin drinkers were cool and glamourous. But gin was also the star of the cocktail age – it is hard to imagine Art Deco and Jazz without also thinking of sophisticated 'young things' knocking back a Pink Lady or a Tom Collins. It is a drink associated with Prohibition speakeasies – but it is also the drink we identify with the Victorian era, with its brightly-lit gin palaces. It's a drink associated with the Royal Navy, but also with Officers in the Indian army knocking back their G &Ts while a *punkah wallah* gently fans the still air. Earlier, the eighteenth century is indelibly linked with the 'Gin Craze' being a convenient way of describing the appalling social conditions prevalent in London. The poverty, the inequality, the hopelessness and the squalid living conditions led thousands of urban poor to drink themselves to death in scenes that are irreversibly associated with images produced by William Hogarth. Gin has certainly come a long way from being the cheapest way to get drunk quickly, transitioning to a drink that is sufficiently expensive to demand that it is taken seriously.

Gin was historically a drink associated with apothecaries – and earlier, with alchemists. If the distillation process could enable an alchemist to turn a fermented beer mash into a knock-out spirit such as gin, why couldn't that same alchemist turn base metal into gold? Alchemy was the basis of modern medicine and of modern chemistry, and the history of gin is therefore tied in with both branches of science.

I have enjoyed researching the journey from the excavation of distillery equipment in ancient Mesopotamia through to the modern-day use of shiny copper stills producing limited-edition gins to mark special occasions – and if at the end you decide that you prefer drinking it to reading about it, well, where is the harm in that? Indeed, my wife who has kindly proofread the book, suggests that rather than 'knocking it back in one' (i.e. reading it from cover to cover) readers may prefer to dip into it for an occasional swig...

As an introduction, have a look at some of these quotations made about gin over the past couple of centuries – some are rather contrived witticisms, some are spontaneous, some are sad, but all of them reflect the importance of a drink which has really 'come of age' in the twenty-first century. Cheers!

***

'An Oxford comma walks into a bar. Orders a gin, and tonic.' (Eric Jarosinski)

Dorothy Parker, who notoriously loved spirits but hated gin, was asked by the barman: 'What are you having?' Her response: 'Not much fun.'

'When a man who is drinking neat gin starts talking about his mother he is past all argument.' (C. S. Forester)

When asked why, if he didn't have a drinking problem, he bought 300 cases of gin immediately before Prohibition started, W C Fields replied: 'I didn't think it would last that long.'

'Of all the gin joints in all the towns in all the world, she walks into mine.' (Humphrey Bogart in the film *Casablanca*)

'I don't know what reception I'm at, but for God's sake give me a gin and tonic.' (Denis Thatcher)

'The only time I ever enjoyed ironing was the day I accidentally got gin in the steam iron.' (Phyllis Diller)

'The wages of Gin is Debt.' (Ethel Watts Mumford)

'Gin and drugs, dear lady, gin and drugs.' (T. S. Eliot)

'I work for three or four hours a day, in the late morning and early afternoon. Then I go out for a walk and come back in time for a large gin and tonic.' (J. G. Ballard)

'Zen martini: A martini with no vermouth at all. And no gin, either.' (P. J. O'Rourke)

'Little nips of Whiskey,
Little drops of Gin,
Make a lady wonder,
Where on earth she's bin'. (Anon)

'I exercise strong self-control. I never drink anything stronger than gin before breakfast.' (W. C. Fields)

'Gin-drinking is a great vice in England, but wretchedness and dirt are a greater; and until you improve the homes of the poor, or persuade a half-famished wretch not to seek relief in the temporary oblivion of his own misery, with the pittance which, divided among his family, would furnish a morsel of bread for each, gin-shops will increase in number and splendour.' (Charles Dickens)

'Bond ordered a double gin and tonic and one whole green lime. When the drink came, he cut the lime in half, dropped the two squeezed halves into the long glass, almost filled the glass with ice cubes and then poured in the tonic. He took the drink out onto the balcony, and sat and looked out across the spectacular view.' (Ian Fleming, in *Dr No*)

Ian Fleming in Casino Royale has James Bond say to a barman: 'Just a moment. Three measures of Gordon's, one of vodka, half a measure of Kina Lillet. Shake it very well until it's ice-cold, then add a large thin slice of lemon peel. Got it?' Bond then says to Felix Leiter: 'When I'm ... er ... concentrating I never have more than one drink before dinner. But I do like that one to be large and very strong and very cold, and very well-made. I hate small portions of anything, particularly when they taste bad. This drink's my own invention. I'm going to patent it when I think of a good name.' (Later, he names it Vesper, after the character Vesper Lynd)

'The gin and tonic has saved more Englishmen's lives, and minds, than all the doctors in the Empire.' (Winston Churchill)

'There is something about a Martini,
Ere the dining and dancing begin,
And to tell you the truth,
It is not the vermouth—
I think that perhaps it's the gin.' (Ogden Nash)

'A good heavy book holds you down. It's an anchor that keeps you from getting up and having another gin and tonic.' (Roy Blount, Jr.)

'Work is the only answer. I have three rules to live by. One, get your work done. If that doesn't work, shut up and drink your gin. And when all else fails, run like hell!' (Ray Bradbury)

'A lonely man is a lonesome thing, a stone, a bone, a stick, a receptacle for Gilbey's gin, a stooped figure sitting at the edge of a hotel bed, heaving copious sighs like the autumn wind.' (John Cheever)

'You can no more keep a martini in the refrigerator than you can keep a kiss there. The proper union of gin and vermouth is a great and sudden glory; it is one of the happiest marriages on earth and one of the shortest-lived.' (Bernard DeVoto)

Lord Byron, giving advice to his friend the author Thomas Medwin: 'Why don't you drink, Medwin? Gin-and-water is the source of all my inspiration. If you were to drink as much as I do, you would write as good verses: depend on it, it is the true Hippocrene.' (The Hippocrene was a fountain sacred to the muses, and a source of poetic inspiration)

'Personally, I believe a rocking hammock, a good cigar, and a tall gin-and-tonic is the way to save the planet.' (P. J. O'Rourke)

'A perfect martini should be made by filling a glass with gin, then waving it in the general direction of Italy.' (Noël Coward)

'I've tried Buddhism, Scientology, Numerology, Transcendental Meditation, Qabbala, t'ai chi, feng shui and Deepak Chopra - but I find straight gin works best.' (Phyllis Diller)

'To the question, "When were your spirits at the lowest ebb?" the obvious answer seemed to be, "When the gin gave out."' (Sir Francis Chichester, solo round-the-world yachtsman)

'You'd learn more about the world by lying on the couch and drinking gin out of a bottle than by watching the news.' (Garrison Keillor)

'My main ambition as a gardener is to water my orange trees with gin, then all I have to do is squeeze the juice into a glass.' (W. C. Fields)

'On Friday, March 30, I dined with [Samuel Johnson] at Sir Joshua Reynolds's ... Mr. Eliot mentioned a curious liquor peculiar to his country, which the Cornish fishermen drink. They call it Mahogany; and it is made of two parts gin, and one part treacle, well beaten together. I begged to have some of it made, which was done with proper skill by Mr. Eliot. I thought it very good liquor.' (James Boswell, 1781)

'I sleep badly except occasionally in the morning. I get up late. I try to read my letters. I try to read the paper. I have some gin. I try to read the paper again. I have some more gin. I try to think about my autobiography, then I have some more gin and it's lunchtime. That's my life.' (Evelyn Waugh)

'Besides, when not hard at work with this research, I'm actually conducting a side experiment on how cigarettes and gin increase charisma. As you might guess, the results are looking very promising.' (Richelle Mead)

'I really need a gin and tonic.' (Attributed to Camilla, Duchess of Cornwall)

Chapter 1

The Humble Juniper Berry

If it's not made with juniper berries, it ain't gin …

You can get London Dry Gin, Plymouth Gin, pink gin and gin flavoured with hundreds of different botanicals, but unless the drink is made with juniper berries it isn't gin – it is simply a type of flavoured spirit. On the other hand, if juniper berries are part of the distillation process, then it is still a type of gin whether it is made using alcohol derived from grapes, or grain, or sugar cane juice. Juniper berries are therefore the starting point of any examination of gin, which is ironic because they aren't berries at all – they are female seed cones in which the fleshy scales have combined to give a berry-like appearance.

Juniper is a coniferous bush with sharp needle-like foliage found in many parts of the world – including Canada and North America, as well as around the northern Mediterranean and throughout large parts of Europe. Juniper bushes can be found across the Middle East and as far east as the Himalayas. There are in fact some forty different species of juniper, varying from low-lying bushes to trees which can grow to a height of seven or even eight metres, and some of them produce berries that are toxic to humans.

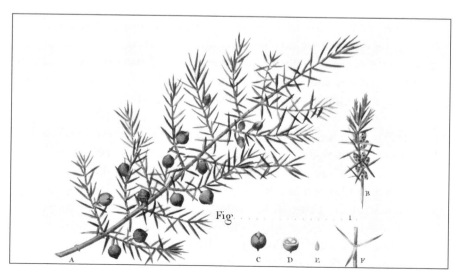

Fig. . . . . 1.

The most common variety, and the one most often used in cosmetics, aromatherapy and in drinks, is *Juniperus communis*. It seems unlikely that it has ever flourished in the Southern Mediterranean countries such as Egypt, which makes it surprising that juniper berries have been located in some of the pharaonic graves – a reminder of a trade with Greece where the berries were long-renowned for their cleansing and purifying qualities. Or put another way: their pungent rich aroma was popular with Egyptian embalmers and tomb workers because they disguised the less savoury aromas of decomposition ...

The berries take eighteen months to mature, starting off brown and moving through to a deep purple colour and because of the maturity time, the same bush can exhibit berries at all different stages. Picking them is always done by hand and this can be a prickly occupation unless the harvester places a tarpaulin on the ground and then shakes the shrub vigorously, causing the berries to fall off, ready for collection. When ripe, the berries have a blue-to-black waxy coating and they have long been considered to have medicinal properties. The Greek doctor Hippocrates, who lived between 460 and 370 BC, used the berries in preparations for relieving pain and reducing the chills after childbirth, and for treating 'female hysteria.' A few years later Aristotle was writing to extol the beneficial health-giving qualities of the berries, while Ancient Egyptians mixed up the berries with a concoction of cumin, frankincense and goose fat to produce a treatment for migraines and headaches.

In time the Romans exploited the fact that juniper berries could be dried and made into a powder to make a tea, or added to wine to make a flavoured drink, or crushed so as to produce aromatic oils. They used it in cooking in lieu of black peppers if the seeds of the pepper tree were not available. However, they appear to have stopped short of adding it to distilled wine and therefore never actually created gin. They did however appreciate its medicinal qualities and when Pliny the Elder was writing, in the century after the birth of Christ, he listed some of the properties:

> The juniper, even above all other remedies, is warming and alleviates symptoms; for the rest, it resembles the cedrus. Of it there are two species, one smaller than the other. Either kind when set on fire keeps off snakes. The seed is beneficial for pains in the stomach, chest and side, dispels flatulence and the feeling of chill, relieves coughs and matures indurations. Applied locally it checks tumours; the berries taken in dark wine bind the bowels, and a local application

Ironically, the plague doctors often had no medical qualifications and because the masks made them look like a duck this appearance gave rise to the expression 'quack doctor'. It is still used today to describe a charlatan or peddler of fake remedies.

In one book, entitled *A Treatise of the Plague* by the Welsh philosopher and alchemist Thomas Vaughan, writing under the pseudonym of 'Eugenius Philalethes', the advice was given to anyone wishing to go outdoors that they should first 'take a Piece of Bay-leaf, or Orange-peel, or Juniper Berries, which being bruised and soaked in a little Vinegar, pour upon a red-hot Iron, hold your Head over the Fumes, receiving them into your Mouth, Nostrils, and every Part of your Body and Cloaths'. The same book advised anyone worried about contracting the plague to 'Purify your Chamber and your Cloaths with clear Fires made of Juniper' and also recommended making sweet candles, to ward off 'the plague and all pestilential distempers'. Your candle was to be made with a catalogue of ingredients, including 'Frankincense, Roses, Cloves, Juniper Berries, Musk and Amber together with finely powdered charcoal'. These were then to be mixed up with 'Rose-water, and Gum Tragacanth, and put over a Fire, till they are reduced into a Paste, of which make small Candles, and let them dry gently.' The same writer urged people at risk to chew half an ounce of juniper berries as part of 'an antidote to be taken inwardly.'

It is easy to see how it was just a small step from saying that the berry had great medicinal properties to suggesting that those same properties were transferred to any distillates which were flavoured by those same berries. The ground had been prepared for what was regarded as a basic truth: gin was good for you. Not that the word 'gin' had been invented at that stage, the early drink being known as genever (from the French *genévrier*). In Holland, it was known as 'jeneverbes' and by the time the word had been Anglicised, it was variously spelt 'genever' or 'Geneva' (perhaps in the mistaken belief that it had something to do with the Swiss capital). The first mention of 'geneva' in print in England would seem to have been in 1623 when Philip Massinger wrote his tragedy called *The Duke of Milan*. In the opening scene, the playwright uses the words:

> …and if you meet an officer preaching of sobriety, unless he read it in Geneva print, lay him by the heels.

In this context 'read in Geneva print' means 'to be drunk' and 'lay him by the heels' meant 'put him in the stocks'. Massinger deliberately puns the word for the drink (Geneve) and the place (Geneva) because 'Geneva print' originally meant the small roman typeface used to print the early Puritan bibles – more specifically the 'Geneva Bible' which first appeared in 1560. The pun on 'Geneva' had developed to the extent that 'Geneva' was already a slang word used to describe what was otherwise called 'Hollands' – i.e. genever.

In time the English proved too lazy to pronounce the whole word and when in 1714 the Anglo-Dutch physician and satirist Benjamin Mandeville published his notorious 'Fable of the Bees' he was able to comment that: 'the infamous Liquor, the name of which, deriv'd from Juniper in Dutch, is now by frequent use and the Laconick Spirit of the Nation, from a Word of middling Length shrunk into a Monosyllable, Intoxicating Gin.'

Slowly, the word 'genever' fell into disuse in England and when Jonathan Swift wrote about the spirit in his *Journal of a Dublin Lady in a letter to a Person of Quality* in 1729 he used the word 'gin' – as did Alexander Pope in his *Epistle to Satires* written a decade later. Nowadays, genever is regarded as a separate drink, distinct from gin, and with its own *appellation*. This arose after 2008 when the Dutch government obtained A.O.C status for the drink, applicable solely to a spirit made in a certain way in specific areas of Holland, Belgium, Germany and Northern France. The *appellation* specifies two distinct types of genever, *jonge* and *oude*. '*Jonge*' or young genever is made with no more than 15% malt wine and ten grams of sugar per litre whereas the '*oude*' or old genever has a minimum of 15% malt wine and is allowed to contain up to 20 grams of sugar. They both contrast with what is termed 'London Dry gin' because for a gin to be 'dry' it must have absolutely no extra sugar added at all. The 'old' and 'new' definitions have nothing to do with the age of the spirit and merely reflect the historic nature of the drink. The *oude* spirit was always sweeter and nowadays is enjoying a consumer revival.

One other thing deserves mention – the work of the great British herbalist Nicholas Culpeper. In 1652 he brought out a book called *The English Physithian*, relaunched a year later as the *Complete Herbal*. He had much to say about juniper berries, claiming that they 'stay all fluxes, help the haemorrhoids or piles, and kill worms in children'. They were great for curing flatulence because a dose could 'strengthen the stomach exceedingly, and express the wind. Indeed, there is scarce a better remedy for wind in any part of the body, or the cholic than the chymical oil drawn from the berries.' Users were advised that 'such country people as know not how to draw the chymical oil, may content themselves by eating ten or a dozen of the ripe berries every morning'. Culpeper reckoned that juniper berries were excellent when used to make a tea, because the infusion was good for gout and arthritis, writing: '… [the berries] are excellently good in all sorts of agues; help the gout and sciatica and strengthen the limbs of the body'. He also spoke of the diuretic qualities: 'they provoke urine exceedingly, and are therefore very available to all dysuries and stranguaries [both, types of painful urination]'. There seemed to be no end of its virtues: 'It is so powerful a remedy against the dropsy, that the very lye made of the ashes of the herb being drank, cures the disease. It provokes the terms, helps the fits of the mother. They are admirably good for a cough, shortness of breath, and consumption, pains in the belly, ruptures, cramps, and convulsions. They give safe and speedy delivery to women with child, they strengthen the brain exceedingly, help the memory, and fortify the sight by strengthening the optic nerves.' If that wasn't enough, the plant was described by Culpeper as being 'an admirable solar shrub' which was 'scarce to be paralleled for its virtues'. He went on to say that 'a lye made of the ashes of the wood, and the body bathed with it, cures the itch, scabs and leprosy. The berries break the stone, procure appetite when it is lost, and are excellently good for all palsies, and falling-sickness'.

Culpeper also tells the reader that juniper berries are 'a most admirable counter-poison, and as great a register of the pestilence as any growing; they are excellent good against the bitings of venomous beasts'.

A final point before leaving the study of juniper and moving on to the actual production of a distilled spirit: the fact that for much of the seventeenth century in England the juniper berries were used primarily as a flavourant, and as a medicine. When Christopher Wilkinson published a book in 1682 entitled *The Natural History of Coffee, Thee, Chocolate and Tobacco* he included a *Tract of Elder and Juniper Berries in our Publick Houses*. The anonymous writer made no mention of distilling, but emphasised that 'the simple decoction … sweetened with a little fine Sugar Candy will afford liquors so pleasant to the eye, so grateful to the palate that I cannot wonder after all these charms they have not as yet been courted and Ushered into our Publick Houses.' The method of production was described: '…[the juniper] berries which are so common, and cheap, that they may be purchased for little or nothing; one ounce of the Berry well-cleansed, bruis'd and mash'd will be enough for almost a pint of water; when they are boyl'd together the Vessel must be carefully stopt; after the boyling is over, one spoonful of Sugar Candy may be put in.' The tract helpfully states where the juniper bushes could be found – 'upon many hills in Oxfordshire and upon Juniper Hill near Hindlesham in Cambridgeshire' as well as in other parts of the country. As for harvesting the berries, 'the Astrological Botanists advise us to pull them when the Sun is in Virgo'. The writer explained that the berry was a particular favourite amongst the Danes and Norwegians as a means of getting rid of kidney stones. Apparently, 'the Learned Mr Evelyn' extolled them in 'the Wind Collick, and many other Distempers'. The book quoted other writers who commended the berries for 'Dropsies, Gravel, Coughs, Consumptions, Gout, Stoppage of the monthly courses, in Epilepsies, Palsies and Lethargies'. It's an impressive list! The user merely needed to 'Take one spoonful of the Spirit of Juniper Berries, four grains of the Salt of Juniper, three drops of the Oyl of Juniper well-rectified; mix them all together, drink them morning and night in a Glass of White-wine and you will have no contemptible Medicine in all the aforementioned Diseases.' Anyone doubting the efficacy of the decoction was advised to read the works of Benjamin Scarffius and John Michael who 'have publish'd in Germany two several Books of the Juniper and you may meet with far more persuasive arguments than I can pretend to offer you'. The significant omission from the book was any idea that the berries were to be added to the production of a distilled spirit, suggesting that the consumption of 'genever' in public houses was not particularly widespread, and that the medicinal properties of the berry were paramount.

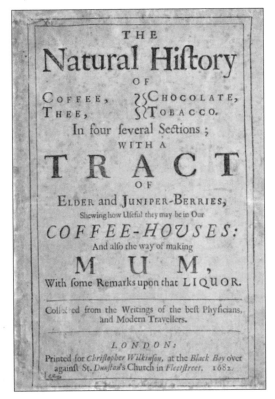

The front page of the 1682 book, including a tract on Juniper Berries.

Chapter 2

The Advent of Distilling

Turning to the production process: central to distillation was the pot-still, otherwise known as the alembic still. This was the basic tool of the alchemist, with origins dating back at least as far as 790 A.D. with the Arabic physician-cum-alchemist Abu Musa Jabir ibn Hayyan, otherwise known as Al Jabir. He called the still *al-'ambiq*, meaning to distil, from *ambix*, the Greek word for a cup. From this, the modern word 'alembic' is derived. Al Jabir may simply have been using equipment that had been around for centuries – archaeologists have found versions of the alembic dating back way into pre-history. In its basic form, the still consists of three parts; the cucurbit, being the pot in which the material to be distilled is heated up; the head or cap which fits over the top of the cucurbit to collect the vapours; and a downward sloping pipe or tube leading to a vessel where the

Al Jabir's alembic still.

distilled spirit is collected. At a site in Slovakia (Abrahám) archaeologists have found parts of the three components in the same place suggesting that the three stages – boiling, condensing and collecting – were all being carried out in combination. The site is believed to be six thousand years old. Meanwhile, excavations at Tepe Gawra in the upper valley of the Tigris river, near Mosul in Iraq, have revealed pieces of ceramic, believed to be part of an alembic, dating back to 3500 B.C. There is nothing to suggest that they were used to make an alcoholic drink and were probably intended to extract oils used in cosmetics and medicines. Experimental archaeologists have carried out tests using replicas of the pots, linked by one-metre lengths of reed to carry the condensed materials. The experiments showed that it was possible to produce distilled oils from plants such as pistachio, Turkish pine and juniper. These plants (*pistacia mutica, Pinus brutia,* and *Juniperus oxycedrus*) were all indigenous to the area near Mosul. After an hour over the heat, sufficient condensed spirit was produced to flow down the reed 'pipe' into the collection vessel. The reeds themselves – *arundo donax* – are still commonly found in the area originally described as Mesopotamia and can have a diameter of six centimetres. Once cleaned, inside and out, they prove ideal for the task of acting as a conduit in the distillation process, particularly if wrapped in a damp cloth to prevent the reed from catching fire. Think 'flexible tube' rather than 'weedy reed'.

All of this supports the contention that distilling was carried out in Mesopotamia thousands of years ago, something supported by the frequent reference to medicinal drugs described in the many hundreds of clay tablets recovered from the palace in Nineveh. These date from between 669 and 626 B.C. but are themselves believed to be transcripts of earlier texts, some dating back to the Sumerian civilisation several thousand years earlier. Intriguingly, the archaeologists at Tepe Gawra found that perfumed waters, such as rose water, are still being produced today in Iraq using exactly the same techniques, and with similar equipment to the implements in use several thousand years earlier.

Moving closer to home, the discovery on Cyprus of the so-called Alembic of Pyrgos points to the possibility of the still being used to manufacture alcohol, since it was found next to grape seeds in a wine jar, suggesting the production of an early form of grappa. The time frame? Probably 1800 B.C. The site, dating from the Early Bronze Age and situated near Limassol, has revealed an industrial complex that produced wine, textiles and in particular, perfumes. It is thought that the perfumes were scented with extracts of lavender, bay, rosemary, pine or coriander and were kept in small translucent alabaster bottles. Just as important as the scents which have been found was the excavation of the area where the archaeologists found them – a 43,000 square foot perfumery factory. There they found at least sixty distilling stills, mixing bowls, funnels and perfume bottles. The discoveries are now on display at the Capitoline Museum in Rome and show that distillation had moved on from a cottage industry to a full-blown manufacturing process.

The oldest written record of the use of an alembic appears in a single-page manuscript known as *Cleopatra's Chrysopoeia,* held in the St Mark's Library, Venice. Dating from the second century BC it probably describes an apparatus used for the manufacture of balsams and essences and the name 'chrysopoeia' – which translates as 'transmutation into gold' – shows the ancient connection between distilling and alchemy.

Other alembic fragments have been found in Sardinia during excavations of the Nuragic culture of the second millennium BC. Further east, excavations at Shaikhan Dheri in the Peshawar Valley of Pakistan on a site believed to date from a hundred years BC, have revealed that the ceramic condensation chamber was immersed in an earthenware basin, thereby increasing the amount of distillate produced. There are also traces of distillation processes in India dating back two thousand years, probably linked to the production of a fermented beverage based on flowers of *madhu* or *mahu* from the tree *madhuca longifolia*. Slightly toxic in their natural state, the toxicity is removed during distillation, and there are apparently people living in the Bihar region of North-East India who still use the technique to make their own hooch.

What these very distinct and separate finds show is that distilling was taking place over a wide area of the Eastern Mediterranean, Middle East and the Indian sub-continent, probably quite independently. Some may have distilled spirit as part of a ritual, some to get inebriated, some to make essential oils for cosmetic purposes and some to make medicines.

In its worldwide context, rice wine was being distilled in China many hundreds of years ago, while there is evidence showing that when the Spanish conquistadors reached Peru in the fifteenth century they found the local Indians using distilling equipment which involved heating materials in a pot with a concave lid on its lower surface. Condensation took place on this surface and a collector, in the form of a spoon placed under the lowest point of the concave shape, drew the condensed droplets into a second, external, container.

The possible benefits of distillation were known to the Ancient Greeks, with Aristotle writing some four centuries before Christ that 'seawater can be made potable by distillation as well – and wine and other liquids can be submitted to the same process'.

Getting back to Al Jabir and his alembic still: even if he didn't invent it, Al Jabir experimented with it, using the still to make alcohol and also to separate out numerous chemical compounds, identifying a number of acids (hydrochloric, sulphuric and nitric). Among the 600 or so treatises attributed to Al Jabir were descriptions of the way that an inorganic compound – *sal ammoniac*, otherwise known as ammonium chloride – could be produced from organic material (plants, blood, etc) by chemical means. His vast literary output and the originality of his experiments gives rise to his reputation as the 'father of chemistry'.

The alembic still was central to his experiments: and he used copper piping to link the two chambers. Copper remains in use in traditional distilling because it is malleable, does not corrode, and is good at removing sulphuric compounds given off during the manufacturing process. It does not 'taste' the spirit and has the advantage that it heats up evenly across all surfaces. Early chambers were made of glass or pottery and easily cracked, but a great improvement was made in the late 1480s when a copper hood, called a rosenhut, was developed. The image below shows a rosenhut made from copper, in a woodcut dating to ca. 1500.

The tube linking the two containers is traditionally shaped like a swan's neck. In alcohol production, the liquid, known as the wash, would be heated in the first chamber. Historically this involved an open flame, and vapour would be produced. This would rise, pass through the narrow swan's neck where the copper would be cooled, usually by the use of cold water, causing the vapours to condense and fill the second container. The distiller would need to be able to remove the first quantity of spirits – the heads – and also the end of the batch – the tails – in order to get rid of impurities. The heads, sometimes known as the foreshots, have to be discarded because they may contain deposits left behind by the previous distillation, as well as the taste being influenced by toxic methanol or by undesirable chemical compounds

such as acetone. Similarly, the tails, sometimes known as 'feints', can be affected by sulphates and fatty acids that would give an unpleasant oily taste on the palate. The 'bit in the middle' – the heart – is what the distiller keeps and bottles.

A further development was called a Moor's Head – basically a bath through which the swan's neck was passed, filled with cold water, shown here in the detail from a painting of an alchemist at work and showing a still topped off with a Moor's Head, ca.1640.

The problem faced by the distillers was in removing impurities, and in coping with the problem of using direct flames to provide the heat. In unskilled hands, the liquid could easily burn and ruin the taste. An added problem was that the still could only be used on a batch basis – once one batch had been produced, the equipment would have to be dismantled, so that the dregs could be removed. It would then be cleaned and reassembled before the next wash could be added.

The distilling process worked on the basis that different substances vaporise at different stages. Alcohol has a lower boiling point than water and therefore it vaporises first and can be drawn off, condensed and then stored in a more concentrated form. Repeated distillation produces a stronger and purer spirit on each occasion. Distillers often used a mix of barley, corn, wheat and rye to produce a first distillate known as low wine. Rough in taste and low in alcohol it needed to be 'rectified' in a process involving a second and third distillation, in order to remove the impurities and to increase the strength.

The old manufacture of genever involved mixing the second distillate with a separate distillate made using a juniper berry-infused spirit. Sometimes a third distillate was added consisting of malted wine and botanicals. By the time the distillation process spread to England, the botanicals were not simply mixed after distillation had taken place, they were distilled with the base spirit to give a final spirit which was far too strong to be consumed, and would therefore be hydrated i.e. by adding water, to bring it down to an acceptable strength.

Barley was a traditional component. First, it had to be prepared by being malted, that is to say, it would be soaked in water until the point of germination was reached. The germinating process would then be halted by adding heat. This malting process acted as a trigger to get the other grains – rye and wheat – to start working so that fermentation could take place. The resulting grain-based alcohol would then be ready to be heated in the still, although in the modern production of gin the base is a neutral spirit.

This brief overview of the distilling process is given in order to explain some of the skills needed by the distiller. In some ways it is beautifully simple, in others it is highly complex and it is little wonder that in the early days it was a process used by pharmacists and practitioners of alchemy. Some might even argue that turning a watery porridge into gin is no less remarkable than turning base metal into gold!

Distilling wine to make aqua-vitae or 'water of life' was certainly commonplace in Italy in the Middle Ages, leading eventually to the production of grappa, by blending the distillate with crushed grape seeds, stalks and skins left over from the wine making process. The spirit was known as marc in England, although the name of 'pomace spirit' was also used. Italy was the centre of experimentation with distilling, in connection with its medicinal uses, particularly around Solerno where the 'Schola Medica Salernitana' (medical school) had been founded in the tenth century. In the Vatican Consilia Codex of 1276, the Florentine Taddeo Alderotti described in detail how aqua-vitae could be obtained from wine with double distillation and was the first to provide written evidence of the practice of immersing the coil, which was being used to carry the vapours away from the alembic, in cold water so as to speed-up condensation. A doctor from Padua by the name of Michele Savanarola published an early treatise on the subject of distilling aqua-vitae in the early years of the fifteenth century under the title of *De Conficienda Aqua Vitae*. By 1512 the artist Hieronymus Brunschwig was illustrating the book *Liber de arte Distillandi* with apparatus for making aqua-vitae, shown as Plate 1.

At that stage, there was a close link between distillation and medical research. Enter Catherine de Medici, a scheming, highly political creature whose offspring included three European monarchs. She was responsible for the St Bartholomew's Day Massacre of 1572 in which an estimated three thousand Protestants were slaughtered. Here was a woman who was greatly interested in poisons and herbal medicines – and when she wasn't experimenting with doses of toxins sufficient to kill her enemies she noted how aqua-vitae could help cure the plague. In her published *Experiments* she wrote: 'The perfect water to heal the plague and worms: A man is given a quarter litre, a modest person half a quarter, and a child an eighth. Take half a jug of aqua-vitae and add to it the undermentioned things: gentian, tormentilla, ditcamnus and carlina half an ounce; cooked and skimmed honey as required.' Presumably, if you were a man dying with bubonic plague you might well feel slightly perkier if someone poured a quarter of a litre of neat alcohol down your throat, with or without the gentian and other plant extracts. Mind you, she also advised adding 'the water of a healthy young virgin child' and if that wasn't unpleasant enough, she suggested taking 'some excrement of a ten to twelve year old boy, dry, and make it into a powder, then use the powder in the following way. Place not more than two spoonfuls in a glass of water of life and mix.' Perhaps if she had missed off all the other ingredients and just added juniper, she could have been known as 'Mother of Gin' instead of 'Madame Snake'...

The secret of distilling spirits had spread rapidly throughout Europe and by 1494 had reached the monastery in North-West Fife known as Lindores Abbey. The Exchequer Roll for that year shows that the Scottish King James IV had commissioned Brother John Cor from the monastery to turn 'eight bolls of malt' into aqua-vitae. That translated to just over a thousand gallons of malt – enough to make perhaps fifteen hundred bottles of 'ardent spirit' – the forerunner of today's whisky.

The identity of the man who first combined distillation with juniper berries is lost to history. There are fleeting references to what was called 'genever' in manuscripts from Bruges in the thirteenth century and from Antwerp two centuries later (*'Een Constelijck Distileerboec'*). The latter, written in 1552 by Philippus Hermanni, is claimed by some to contain the first written record of the recipe for what we might term gin today. Meanwhile, the Nationaal Jenevermuseum Hasselt in Belgium states without reservation that genever was created in the lowlands of Flanders in the thirteenth century. Others point to a Dutch book with the title *Om Gebrande Wyn ti Maken* which translates to *Making Burned Wine* published in 1495 and which refers to a distilled spirit made with a cacophony of flavours obtained from cardamom, cinnamon, cloves, galangal, ginger, grains of paradise – and juniper berries.

A significant improvement in the distilling process was reportedly made in 1526 by the Swiss alchemist-cum-physician with the grandiose name of Philippus Aureolus Theophrastus Bombastus von Hohenheim – otherwise known as Paracelsus. It has been suggested that he came up with the idea of placing the condensing unit in a bath of cold water, in order to speed up the distillation process.

In 1582 Casper Janszoon Coolhaes, shown on page 16 in a portrait from the time, published a book entitled *A Guide to Distilling*. In it, he stated that genever made from a grain-based distillate was called Korenbrandewijn and was 'in aroma and taste almost the same as brandy-wine'. The book said that this distilled spirit was 'not only named brandywine but also drunk and paid for as brandywine'. In its early guise, genever may well have been recommended for its medicinal properties but the fact that it became so popular – popular enough for it to attract the attention of the tax authorities – suggests that it was being used for purely recreational purposes. By 1601

CASPARVS COELHASIVS. SS.
THEOLOGIÆ. PROFESSOR.

'genever water' was being taxed by the Dutch government, along with both distilled wine and 'fennel and anise water'.

For some reason which is not clear, credit has often been given to a man called Sylvius de Bouve for being the first to distil genever. Sylvius de Bouve was, for fourteen years, a professor at the University of Leiden and his research included distilling medicines with juniper berry oil, but none of his research papers contain any reference to genever.

De Bouve had been born in Hanau, Germany to a well-off family but he studied medicine at the Protestant Academy of Sedan, and in Leiden from 1632–1634. He went on to have a lucrative medical practice in Amsterdam. While there, he became interested in chemistry and in 1658 was appointed professor of medicine at the University of Leiden. He became the University's Vice-Chancellor in 1669 and carried out research into stomach and kidney disorders. This involved treating patients with a variety of juniper-based compounds. He also researched the circulation of blood in the human body and examined the way in which the human brain worked. He became successful enough to be recognised as a leading scientist of the time, and one whose name was given to a number of anatomical discoveries – including the Sylvian fissure and the Sylvian aqueduct in the brain. Nowadays he is looked on as one of the founders of medical biochemistry. The point is: he was famous, he was successful and it may well have suited distillers to give him credit for an invention that was actually made many years earlier, just so as to add caché and respectability. But whereas it is the case that de Bouve may well have experimented with genever, he certainly cannot be said to have invented it – how else could it possibly have been subjected to taxation before de Bouve was even born? But there are always counter-theorists at work and some people have argued that there were *two* professors at Leiden, serving eighty years apart, both sharing the identical name. According to these theorists, the first Professor de Bouve was actively selling genever in 1595. The truth is impossible to ascertain because names were often somewhat flexible. After all, the man called Sylvius de Bouve was actually born Franz de le Boë and also went by the name Franciscus Sylvius. It is not impossible that another man, with a somewhat similar moniker, flourished in the previous century in the same field of excellence.

What is undeniable is that by the end of the sixteenth century, alcohol derived from grapes was being distilled and flavoured with juniper. The breakthrough came when distillers from what is now Belgium and Holland started to use malted grain as the alcohol base, rather than grape juice. Genever was originally produced by simply distilling malt wine ('moutwijn' in Dutch) to what was termed 50% ABV. ABV, standing for 'alcohol by volume', is still the measure used to describe the strength of the spirit. The malt wine was produced by triple distilling a blend of rye, wheat and corn. The resulting spirit was not very palatable – it was bitter, and therefore distillers added juniper berries and sometimes other herbs and spices in an attempt to disguise the flavour. It quickly caught on and was particularly favoured by Dutch sailors; there was apparently a popular saying in Dutch which translates as 'A sailor's best working compass is a glass completely full of genever'. Sea voyages from Holland out to the Dutch East Indies could take not just months but years and it was more economical for the captain, in terms of space on board the cramped ships, to carry genever rather than wine.

As for the soldiers, they liked to have a swift snorter before going into battle. The Low Countries were at that time part of the Spanish Empire and had become a political football, part of the ongoing religious schism which split Europe into Catholic and Protestant divisions. In what became known as the Eighty Years War, between 1568 and 1648 the inhabitants of the Low Countries fought to throw off Spanish control. In 1585, the English Queen Elizabeth had sent 6,000 men to the Low Countries to provide support for those involved in the Dutch independence movement, but they arrived several months too late to be of any use. Independence was finally gained – at a price – with the country split into two and with the formation of the United Provinces of the Netherlands (then known as the Dutch Republic) controlling the north while the southern section, corresponding nowadays to the countries of Belgium and Luxembourg, remained under Spanish control until 1714.

In 1618, the continent of Europe became engulfed in religious conflict, with the outbreak of what is known as the Thirty Years War. The newly-independent Dutch fought for the Protestant cause, against the Catholic forces of Spain, the Habsburg Monarchy and the Electorate of Bavaria. During the course of the conflict, some 50,000 English troops joined the

Protestant armies, fighting alongside the Dutch troops. This gave the English soldiers the chance to observe the Dutch army in action and they became familiar with the sight of their Dutch colleagues having a quick swig before combat. It gave rise to the expression 'to take Dutch courage' and in time both the phrase and the drink found their way back across the English Channel. There is some evidence that 'taking Dutch courage' caught on with the British army, and by 1720 when Benjamin Mandeville was writing about gin, he commented on 'the Advantage we received from [gin] abroad, by upholding the Courage of Soldiers, and animating the Sailors to the Combat; and that in the two last Wars no considerable Victory had been obtain'd without.'

Throughout the sixteenth and seventeenth centuries, genever became increasingly popular. The Dutch were competing to become the greatest carriers of the world's goods: in 1602, the Dutch East India Company was incorporated and in 1652, Cape Town was established as a Dutch colony at the tip of Africa so that ships could re-provision there en route to Indonesia and the Far East.

The Dutch had trading posts set up by the VOC – the name given to the Dutch East India Company – across the Indian Ocean, to Ceylon, parts of India and over to Indonesia, where Batavia (modern-day Jakarta) became the centre of the trade in spices. Back home, Dutch traders were not ones to miss a trick: if they could add value to an alcoholic drink by making it stronger and more concentrated – in other words with a higher ABV – then it cost less to be shipped, and could be diluted prior to being consumed. Also, the Dutch levied tax on alcohol based on volume, not strength and therefore a barrel of gin had the same tax burden as wine, with the advantage that it could be easily re-hydrated for sale. Genever became a tradeable commodity across the continents.

One of the problems in using grain as a basis for the production of genever was that the authorities were worried that it would cause food shortages and hence put up prices, and by 1601 various areas had introduced a ban on distilleries. This, combined with the ravages of war, led to a constant flow of distillers from the Flemish heartlands in the south into what became the far more prosperous north, as well as down into northern France and eastwards into Germany. As the Spanish tightened their grip on the southern part of the country, many refugees took flight, some of them preferring the climate of religious tolerance which they could find in England. They brought with them their skills – most particularly as weavers and silk workers, but also as distillers.

One family of distillers driven out of Antwerp by religious persecution and the yoke of Spanish oppression were named Bulsius. They moved first to Cologne, then a haven for Protestant refugees. In time they headed back and settled in Amsterdam, opening their first distillery in 1575 in an out-of-town site by the banks of a stream, in a place called t'Lootsjie. The name meant 'the little shed' and the site was chosen because the Amsterdam authorities did not allow distilleries to operate in the central area of town because the distillates were highly inflammable. The family then changed its name from Bulsius to Bols and were soon producing spirits in a huge variety of flavours in its distinctive stoneware bottles. Bols still make gin and liqueurs nearly 450 years later and are the oldest distillery firm still in existence. Interestingly, they now make a drink sold as Damrak Gin. Bols describe it as being 'proud to be the Amsterdammer among the London boys. With its cheerful bottle and fresh citrus notes, Damrak is everything but a standard London dry gin'.

In part, Bols prospered because the Bols family became major shareholders in the VOC and earned themselves preferential rates on the herbs and spices brought back from the Far East, enabling the Bols distillery to produce over 200 differently flavoured drinks, of which genever was just one. Lucas Bols was born in 1652, the grandson of the founder, and he oversaw a rapid expansion of the company during his country's Golden Age. He died in 1719 and in the century following his death the family somewhat neglected the business and it only just survived. In 1818, the company was sold by the surviving members of the family – but with a proviso in the sale contract that the purchaser could use the Bols name in perpetuity.

Back in 1600-1700, the Dutch distilleries, including Bols, found a ready market in the VOC, where in time the sailors were granted a genever allowance of 150ml per person per day. Multiply that up for a voyage of many months, even years, and you would end up with each ship needing to carry at least 100 litres of spirits per sailor. In the seventeenth century a large Dutch East Indiaman of 700 tons would typically carry between 250 and 300 people There might be 140 sailors, 120 soldiers and perhaps a dozen passengers on each trip out to Batavia. That might mean carrying 25,000 litres of spirit, with each barrel holding around 120 litres. That makes 200 barrels before you start loading cargo – to think of the lumbering East Indiamen as floating gin palaces might be stretching things a bit far, but certainly it meant an awful lot of genever, all of it supplied by local distillers.

Books started to appear in English describing the distillation process, including one dated 1651 entitled *A description of new philosophical furnaces, or A new art of distilling* by Johann Rudolf Glauber. He was a German-Dutch apothecary and alchemist who researched the chemistry of wine production, as well as experimenting with distillation and producing new designs for distillation machinery. The book starts with the preface:

> I have hitherto reserved to myself as secrets, some peculiar furnaces and compendious wayes of distilling, which with diligent study and speculation I found out some few yeers since, by which many excellent works, impossible to be done by the vulgar art, may be performed; but now at last I have, considering with myself how advantagious it may be to the world, determined to conceale this art no longer, but for the good of my neighbour to publish it, by giving to Chymists a perfect and fundamental information of this new invented art, that they may no longer for the future spend their time, and expend their costs in long tedious operations, but may after a more easie way by the help of my furnaces be able to effect many excellent things.
>
> Now this book shall be divided into five parts, the first whereof shall teach how to build a furnace, in which incombustible things are distilled and sublimed, and indeed such things which cannot be done by retort or any other vessels, and how the Spirits, Flowers, and Oyles of Minerals, and Metals may by the help thereof be prepared, as also what their use, and vertues are…

Part Three was stated as containing 'a certain new invention hitherto unknown, of distilling burning spirits, as of Wine, Corne, Fruits, Flowers, Hearbs and Roots'. That section begins by stating:

> First, the seeds must be broken in a mill, flowers, hearbs, and roots cut small … upon which afterwards a good quantity of water (in which they may swim) must be powred [poured] for the maceration of them, so that when the distillation is ended there may remain some water, lest for want of water they be burnt in the distilling, and yeeld an oyl savouring of the *empyreuma,* and not sweet.

'Empyreuma' is an obsolete word given to describe the smell and taste associated with burning decomposing vegetable and animal matter. A warning was given not to pour too much water on the material and that one should only use:

> as much as shall serve to prevent the burning of the aforesaid vegetables in the distilling of the oyl thereof. And indeed fresh vegetables may presently without any foregoing maceration, being put with their proper waters into the distilling vessel be distilled. But they that be dry may for the space of some dayes be macerated before they be distilled. Also the water appointed for maceration must be salted, for the better mollifying, and opening the aforesaid materials, that they may the sooner yeeld their oyl. Now green and fresh need not any salt water, yet it wil not be hurtful to mix some therewith, because salt helps the boiling water, so as to make the oyl more easily to ascend. It also helps and furthers distillation as doth Tartar and Allome, if they be rightly mixed and ordered. Which being all rightly done, the materials that are macerated must be put by a funnel into the distilling vessel, and fire must be given as hath been spoken concerning the burning spirit, and the oyle of the seed ... will come forth in the coition together with the water. All the oyle being come forth (that which is perceived by the changing of the receivers) the fire is to be extinguished, and the remainder is to be taken out, which if it be of seeds, hearbs, or fruits, may being yet warm be fermented by the addition of ferment for the distilling of the spirit ... the water that is distilled together with the oyle, is to be set in a certain temperate place, until the oyle ascend, and swim upon the water, from whence it is to be separated with a funnel ... also there are some oyles which doe not ascend, but fall to the bottome, which are also to be separated with a funnel, and kept for their uses.

The book also set out ways of reducing the high cost of expensive distilling equipment, using substitute containers made of wood instead of metal, and clay instead of glass.

Finally, before leaving the history of distillation, a word about botanicals. An added bit of magic inherent in the production of gin involves the use of botanicals – seeds, herbs, flowers and other plant products to produce the blend of flavours needed to make the gin palatable. There are literally scores of different botanicals regularly used by distillers. Some use just half a dozen, some many more. Some add the botanicals individually, others combine them right at the start of the process. The easiest way is probably to macerate all the ingredients at the same time – in other words, crush them and leave the ingredients to soak in the base alcohol for up to 48 hours, before the infused spirit is re-distilled. That is known as the 'steep and boil' method. Another process involves placing the botanicals in a basket suspended inside the neck of the condensing tube, so that the vapour is forced through the flavourants. This is known as vapour infusion. A third way, favoured during the American Prohibition era and often associated with what was termed 'bathtub gin', is more properly called a cold compounded spirit. Here the botanicals are never actually part of the distilling process but are added afterwards when the distilled spirit is poured over the botanicals and left to soak. Unlike distilled gin, which is clear, the cold compounded gins are often straw-coloured and more usually will involve fresh ingredients rather than the dry-stored ingredients used in the distillation process.

The distiller needs the skill to know which flavours blend well with each other. The different oils and aromas in the botanicals come through the distilling process at different rates – the citrus flavours tend to come through first whereas some of the woody undertones may come out last. Leaving the distilling process too long may bring out those woody notes but also risks 'infecting' the taste with sulphur compounds – bad eggs and rotten cabbage come to mind. A look at the botanicals available to the distiller gives a mind-boggling choice, taking in a worldwide exploration of herbs and fruits.

After juniper berries, the most common plant extract is coriander seed, found particularly throughout the Balkans, in Russia but also in Morocco. It is used to give a complex citrus top-note to the gin. The root of the angelica plant is used because it helps bring the different notes together, as well as adding a woody flavour. The distiller has the choice of either using the angelica plants found in the Saxony area of Germany (smooth and mellow) or the more strongly aromatic roots found in Belgium. The angelica seeds have traditionally been used in many other drinks including Dubonnet, Chartreuse and Benedictine and are also occasionally used by gin distillers. Two other popular botanicals come from lemon and orange peel, usually obtained from southern Spain. The peel is used because that is where most of the aromatic oils are found. The orange growers in Seville take the bitter oranges – similar to the ones used to make marmalade – and peel the skin in long strips which are then air-dried in the sun. Much the same process is followed by the lemon growers of Andalucía.

For some distillers, an essential ingredient is orris, obtained from the corms of the bearded iris plant. It is prevalent in Northern Italy and in Morocco. The iris roots, or corms, are harvested in July and August and left to dry out completely for several years. The rock-hard root is then ground into a powdery substance which is highly perfumed and shares with angelica the ability to fix the various other flavours in order to give length and substance to the gin.

Cinnamon and cardamom are sometimes used, along with nutmeg from Indonesia. Ground up, these seeds and nuts add a spicy taste to the drink, while the pulverised root of the liquorice plant gives the drink a bittersweet, rounded, taste. These are just a few of the more commonly-used botanicals – the web page of the Gin Guild (a body representing the whole of the gin industry and supported by the major distillers such as Diageo, Bacardi, Chivas Brothers and William Grant and Sons) lists some 150 botanicals along with the names of the gin makers using them. If you want dandelion, rhubarb, galangal or lavender, you are certain to find someone, somewhere, who has used it as part of the distilling process.

Early Dutch pot-still linked to what was termed a worm-tub (a barrel containing a coiled copper pipe cooled by cold water) illustrated in *Een Constelijck Distilleer Boeck* by Philippus Hermanni, 1552.

Chapter 3

Distilling comes to London – Gin in the 1600s

By the time Queen Elizabeth died in 1603, there were three distinct types of distilling carried out in England. First, and often in country areas, there will have been cottage industries where small quantities of spirit were produced in homemade stills, infused with herbs and scented plants to produce a concoction that could be consumed for medicinal purposes. Secondly, and more likely to be found in cities such as London, apothecaries and alchemists alike will have been using stills to make spirits to serve a multitude of purposes. Thirdly, there were the Dutch emigres who had left cities such as Amsterdam, Haarlem, Delft, Dordrecht and Leiden – all of them distillery centres – and had settled in Britain in the previous quarter of a century. Here, they used their stills to distil malt wine (in other words a barley/grain mash) in order to produce genever, which would have been sold throughout the locality where the distillation took place. All three processes were likely to have been small-scale operations carried out from residential premises, but as the production using malt-wine increased, so did the concern of the government authorities. Elizabeth's chief minister Lord Burghley commissioned the City of London's Alderman Anthony Ratcliffe to prepare a report to look into a number of worries.

First and perhaps foremost, the government did not want to see any successful enterprise go un-taxed; secondly, there was a concern that 'unwholesome' impurities were being used. In 1593, William Phillip had published a book entitled *The Book of Secrets* setting out some of the procedures and ingredients used in the distillation process. Alderman Ratcliffe reported that when lees from wine production were not available the Flemish immigrants were not averse to adding to the fermentation process a variety of waste products from the beer-brewing trade. Normally the mash used by brewers after they had made their beer was fed to the pigs – but here it was being used in the distilling process. The production was largely unregulated and therefore in 1594 a patent was granted to a man called Richard Drake giving him exclusive rights to make what was called 'aqua

Cheers!

vitae, aqua composita and vinegar'. The grant of the monopoly to Richard Drake was intended to ensure that proper standards were maintained.

Aqua-vitae, or aquavit, was basically distilled wine and may well have originated in Italy several centuries earlier, when all the left-over materials from wine making – the grape skins, the seeds, the stalks – were distilled to make grappa. A variety of leftovers might be added, to produce a fiery spirit bearing very little resemblance to any wine.

Aqua composita was a catch-all phrase covering all manner of things made when the active or flavouring ingredients were distilled from alcohol rather than from water. Some definitely do not sound as if they were intended for the food chain. For instance, 'Aqua calcis minus composita' was made from water and quick lime, to which sassafras bark and liquorice were added. That sounds like one for the apothecary. On the other hand, 'Aqua juniperi composita' involved juniper berries and 'aqua seminum anisi composita' was made with aniseed.

As for vinegar, a distinction was made between true vinegar which was made from the produce of the vine, and what was termed alegar – or beeregar – made from beer. Both were made by distilling beer after the addition of enzymes to produce an acetic fermentation. The alcohol would then turn into acetic acid when left in contact with the air. In its dilute form (approximately 5% by volume) the result is a type of vinegar that could be used as a preservative, as in pickling, or as a flavourant to food.

The granting of a monopoly was a favourite way used by the Crown to boost its finances, but in the case of the grant to Richard Drake, the monopoly caused an uproar because the trade 'concerned so many poor men's livings' and in 1601 the grant was revoked. Fast forward a few years to the reign of King James I and he was desperate to raise finance, and in the same way, Parliament was desperate to control those same royal finances. Cue an almighty tussle that revolved around the grant of charters of incorporation, or patents, conferring legal powers to regulate specific branches of trade or manufacture. Throughout the 1620s and 1630s, the Crown granted monopolies affecting a huge range of businesses and in doing so the Crown was treading on the toes of the City of London, which had traditionally controlled the world of business through the various Livery Companies. The Livery Companies lobbied the City authorities and they, in turn, lobbied Parliament, so that when a parliamentary Bill was produced in 1621 'for the relief of distillers and sellers of Aquae Vitae, Aqua Composita and other strong and hot waters in London and Westminster', Parliament chucked it out.

The petition to Parliament in support of the Bill, as submitted by the distillers, gives an interesting picture of the distillery industry of the time: their distilled products were needed for 'those that be aged and weak in time of sudden qualms and pangs, and to help their old and decayed stomachs'. In other words, the distillers were stressing that what they produced was medicinal. But equally the distillers emphasised that their products were needed 'for use shipboard and for sale to foreign nations ... by way of merchandise to the advancement of His Majesty's Customs and to the great and public profit and benefit of this realm'. The same petition stated that there were over 200 families engaged in the distilling process in the London metropolitan area, while 'bringing up many apprentices without employing them in any other service...'.

The petition failed, but ten years later another application was made for a monopoly patent for distilling, this time endorsed by a number of prominent individuals – Sir Theodore de Mayerne, who had been appointed as First Physician to the King, Sir Thomas Cademan, Physician Ordinary to the Queen and the courtier Sir William Brouncker. The trio had the support of some ninety-nine distillers, who were fed up with being caught between two rival groups, both of whom had their own interests at heart, and not those of
the distillers. On the one hand, distillers could be members of the Grocers Vintners and Brewers Livery Company, or be a member of the Society of Apothecaries, founded in 1618. Both groupings had their own reasons not to want to lose control of distilling. In particular, they wanted to retain the membership fees which they levied on the distillers, revenue which they would lose if the distillers got their own incorporation.

Despite opposition, particularly from the Society of Apothecaries, King Charles I granted a charter of incorporation on 9 August 1638. The lengthy incorporation document set out the purposes for regulating the industry. It was to be 'for the benefit of our people, as well as by the use and expense thereof within our kingdom and dominions as for victualling and furnishing our ships for and in long voyages and for our plantations and colonies in foreign parts and otherwise in the way of merchandise in sundry parts beyond the seas.' The incorporation document set out the constitution and dealt with the way apprentices were to be trained. Specifically, it granted the company the power to carry out searches of a whole range of premises – brew houses, distilleries, or warehouses where 'any wort, wash or dreg' was prepared for distilling – and granted a right to seize and destroy any ingredients considered to be unwholesome. This covered all liquids, spices, seeds, herbs and fruits and meant that officers of the chartered company could turn up at a moment's notice at any premises within a twenty-one-mile radius of the Cities of London and Westminster, and stop any form of distillation which failed to comply with company rules and standards.

In the year in which the chartered company was incorporated, an official rule book was prepared by Sir Theodore de Mayerne and this led to the publication of *The Distiller of London* containing recipes and instructions for the production of over twenty different types of distilled spirits. Reprinted at thirty-year intervals throughout the century, it enhanced the Company's claim to be entitled to regulate distilling throughout the metropolitan area, but it was to be a claim challenged by members of the Society of Apothecaries who fought tooth and nail to protect their own interests. They petitioned the Lord Mayor and lodged a complaint with the Privy Council, claiming that the majority of distillers were unskilled and that they were producing wares which were 'most dangerous for man's health'. Branded as 'sailors, bawds, innkeepers, quack salvers, aliens – men and women whose honesty and skill are both of no value' the distillers were accused of using ingredients which came from the 'emptying of brewer's vessels, droppings of alewives' taps, and the washings of beer hogsheads'. They were condemned for 'dulcifying it with the refuse or dross of sugar, or the dregs of the filthiest remnants of the clarifying of sugar, which is fit only for hog's treacle'.

There were apparently no depths to which distillers might sink – they used lousy rags gathered in the streets or obtained from kennels [the channels running down the centre of the street] or from dunghills. Not only that but they supposedly used unfit alembic stills made from lead and other inferior materials – and hence were blamed for causing 'cancer, virulent agues, plague and madness'. The distilled drinks were unsafe, so the apothecaries maintained, to the extent that English sailors were dying in droves on board ships sailing to the East Indies.

The complaint is also interesting because it lists over thirty 'barbarous' names employed by distillers to promote their products – such as '*aqua mirabilis*'. There is no evidence as to what miracle '*aqua mirabalis*'

claimed to produce. A century and a half later a product by the same name was described by Samuel Johnson as consisting of a distillation made from soaking cardamom, cloves, cubed galangal, ginger, mace and nutmeg in wine spirit. The accusations against the distillers made no specific mention of genever, but clearly the Apothecaries wanted to rubbish the entire distillery industry. No matter that the distillers counter-petitioned, claiming that the allegations were mendacious and biased. Soon, the whole thing got bogged down in an almighty row about the powers of the monarch to raise money independently of Parliament. In particular, the City of London sided with the Apothecaries and refused to enrol the new charter, ostensibly because it infringed the rights of pre-existing Livery Companies. It would be twenty years before the City relented – twenty years in which the Distillers' Company was left totally in limbo.

The restoration of the monarchy in 1660 saw a new lease of life for the company. It set about exercising its powers by conducting its searches and making seizures with great enthusiasm, bringing proceedings against an intriguing cross-section of the community, which suggests that distilling was quite widespread. Former soldiers, widows, Huguenot refugees, Flemish immigrants, even Quakers, were all accused of failing to pay the appropriate fees and abiding by the Company rules. The distillers prospered as demand for genever grew and with wealth came respectability. In 1671, the Distillers Company was granted a livery – meaning that it had full rights to take part in civic elections. Its members could stand for high office, and join in with the pageants linked to the election of the Lord Mayor of London. They may not have had the kudos of the members of the Goldsmith's Guild or others in the 'Great Twelve' list of Livery Companies, but at least they had arrived.

For the consumer, their first introduction to the drink may have been because of its perceived medical qualities, hence Samuel Pepys was to confide in his Diary on 10 October 1663 that when he was suffering from kidney stones, constipation and urinary pains he 'chose to make shift to go to the office, where we sat, and there Sir J. Minnes and Sir W. Batten did advise me to take some juniper water, and Sir W. Batten sent to his Lady for some for me, strong water [i.e. distilled spirits] made of juniper.' He seemed to have enjoyed taking strong water – it is mentioned on two dozen occasions in the diaries, but apart from the instance just mentioned, never for purely medicinal purposes!

In 1687, the new king, James II, granted a further charter whereby the Company's powers of search and seizure were extended to thirty-one miles. This reflected the rapid expansion of the London conurbation, particularly after the Great Fire of 1666, and meant that Company officials could act as an early form of Trading Standards Officer – handing out fines for anyone using short measures or attempting to sell 'foul and weak wares'. The consumption of distilled spirits, of which genever was the most popular, started to go through the roof, especially after William of Orange came to the throne after the so-called Glorious Revolution in 1688. William was Dutch through and through and his coronation in April 1689 was to mark the beginning of a large and influential influx of fellow countrymen, all of them bringing with them an appreciation of 'strong waters' – in other words, flavoured spirits, cordials and genever. Ironically it was to herald a new era, one in which things got totally out of hand: the Gin Craze was about to envelop society.

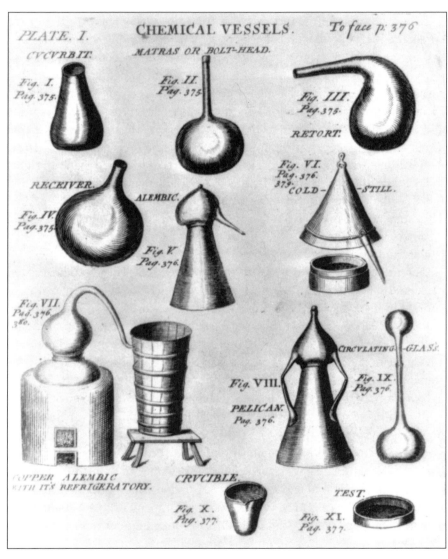

An illustration from a book published in 1727 showing a variety of different types of 'chemical vessels' used in the distilling process, including a 'cucurbit, matras or bolt-head, retort, an alembic, a cold-still, circulating glass, pelican, copper alembic with its refrigerator, and a crucible.'

Chapter 4

The Early Years of the Gin Craze, up to the first Gin Act, 1729

When William of Orange came to the English throne, bringing thousands of his countrymen in his wake, it marked a swing away from Roman Catholicism and allegiances with France. Anti-French feeling led to a ban on the import of French brandy, under the Distillation Act of 1690. To offset this, the government wanted to encourage home-brewing and home-distilling using malted barley, because this would boost the acreage of land under cultivation and increase national output. In 1695, Parliament passed 'An Act for Encouraging the Distilling of Brandy and Spirits from Corn'.

These two separate pieces of legislation had a double consequence. First, they led to a startling increase in the smuggling of cognac across the

Channel; and secondly, they resulted in an unregulated explosion in gin production. The idea of allowing distillers access to surplus grain stocks was understandable – several good harvests in a row had led to an over-supply and distilling seemed a way of helping farmers to offload their surplus. This is reflected in the preamble to the 1695 Act, which set out the reason for the legislation: 'For the Encouragment therefore of the makeing of Brandy Strong waters and Spirits from malted Corne and for the greater consumption of Corne and the advantage of Tillage in this Kingdome Bee it enacted ...'

The legislation imposed a sliding scale of duty payable, with the lowest rate of a penny per gallon being for spirits distilled using English-grown grain, increasing to eight pence a gallon if any foreign or imported materials were used in the manufacturing process. The legislation opened up distilling to everyone: 'Provided alwayes and bee it enacted and declared by the authoritie aforesaid That it shall and may be lawfull to or for any person or persons dureing the continuance of this Act to make draw or distill for Sale or to be retailed any Low Wines or Spirits from Drinke brewed from malted Corne...' It meant that anyone could open a distillery – all they had to do was to post a notice in a public place and wait for ten days. The legislation required distillers to make their premises open for inspection by the authorities and stated that no barrels were to be delivered to gin shops etc without first showing the number of casks to the Excise Officer, on payment of a £10 fine for non-compliance. In practice, the scale of operations meant that there was little or no possibility of supervision other than on a sporadic basis.

The growth of cheap spirits was to have catastrophic consequences. The figures speak for themselves – in 1700 the annual consumption of gin was around 1.23 million gallons. By 1714 it had crept up to just under 2 million gallons. By 1735 it had rocketed to 6.4 million gallons and by 1751 a staggering 7.05 million gallons were being produced. Undoubtedly, the population had grown significantly during the period of fifty years, but certainly not eight-fold, to match gin production levels. In London, where the gin consumption was at its highest, it equated to ninety bottles of gin for every single adult in every year – and of course, the consumption was not in any way even. As production increased, prices dropped. Distilled products were now cheaper than beer and this marked a tipping point: suddenly, the urban poor could turn their backs on beer and bury their sorrows in an affordable, mind-blowing, pain-numbing pint of gin. No matter that it was fiendishly strong or tasted absolutely vile, or that unscrupulous gin-makers adulterated their product with ingredients which were at best unpleasant and at worst seriously damaging to health. You want sulphuric acid with your gin? No problem. You want extra flavour? Try turpentine, or lime oil ...

The effect on the drinker of imbibing such strong liquor, with impurities, was instant and lasting. When Bernard Mandeville wrote his satirical and coruscating commentary on gin, in 1714, called *The Fable of the Bees, or, Private Vices, Publick Benefits*, he called it a 'liquid poison'. He describes some of the maladies created by gin, saying that it produced 'a fiery Lake that sets the Brain in Flame, burns up the Entrails, and scorches every Part within'. Gin, wrote Mandeville, 'has broke and destroy'd the strongest Constitutions, thrown 'em into Consumptions, and been the fatal and immediate occasion of Apoplexies, Phrensies and sudden Death'.

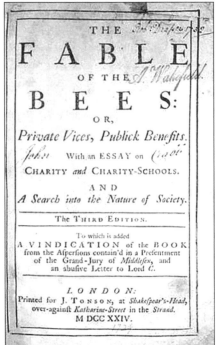

Mandeville observed that gin 'makes Men Quarrelsome, renders 'em Brutes and Savages, sets 'em on to fight for nothing, and has often been the Cause of Murder'. Not only that, but the user would often become the pusher: 'Among the doting Admirers of this Liquid Poison, many of the meanest Rank, from a sincere Affection to the Commodity itself, become Dealers in it, and take delight to help others to what they love themselves, as Whores commence Bawds to make the Profits of one Trade subservient to the Pleasures of the other.' Mandeville suggested that the actual gin shop workers were the most to be pitied, writing that he does not know 'a more miserable Shift for a Livelihood than selling gin at gin-shops'. Tongue in cheek, he listed the qualities required of a good gin-seller, saying that he 'must in the first place be of a watchful and suspicious, as well as a bold and resolute Temper, that he may not be imposed upon by Cheats and Sharpers, nor out-bully'd by the Oaths and Imprecations of Hackney-Coachmen and Foot-Soldiers'. Mandeville continues:

> … in the second, he ought to be a dabster at gross Jokes and loud Laughter, and have all the winning Ways to allure Customers and draw out their Money, and be well vers'd in the low Jests and Ralleries the Mob makes use of to banter Prudence and Frugality. He must be affable and obsequious to the most

despicable; always ready and officious to help a Porter down with his Load, shake Hands with a Basket-Woman, pull off his Hat to an Oyster-Wench, and be familiar with a Beggar; with Patience and good Humour he must be able to endure the filthy Actions and viler Language of nasty Drabs, and the lewdest Rake-hells, and without a Frown or the least Aversion bear with all the Stench and Squalor, Noise and Impertinence that the utmost Indigence, Laziness and Ebriety, can produce …

By 1725, the anti-social effects of rising gin consumption were starting to be noticed, with Sir Daniel Dollins, Chair of the Middlesex Quarter Sessions, remarking: 'The cry of wickedness, I mean excessive drinking gin, and other pernicious spirits; is become so great, so loud, so importunate; and the growing mischiefs from it so many, so great, so destructive to the lives, families, trades and business of such multitudes, especially of the lower, poorer sort of people; that I can no longer doubt, but it must soon reach the ears of our legislators in Parliament assembled; and there meet with … effectual redress.'

Daniel Defoe objected to any interference by the State in his 1728 *Plan of the English Commerce,* written before the worst excesses of the Gin Craze became evident. He felt able to write: 'As for drink, 'tis generally stout strong Beer, not to take notice of its quantity, which is sometimes a little too much'. He was happy to see 'Houses and Lodgings tolerably furnished, at least stuff'd well with useful and necessary household Goods'. It was his contention that, 'those we call poor People, Journey-men, working and pains-taking people do thus; they lye warm, live in plenty, work hard, and (need) know no wane'. He also remarked, possibly with some surprise, that 'the Distillers have found out a way to hit the palate of the Poor, by their new fashion'd compound Waters called Geneva, so that the common People seem not to value the French-brandy as usual, and even not to desire it'.

Two years earlier Defoe had published a short pamphlet with a long title – *A brief case of the distillers: and of the distilling trade in England, shewing how far it is the interest of England to encourage the said trade, as it is so considerable an advantage to the landed interest, to the trade and navigation, to the publick revenue, and to the employment of the poor.* In it, Defoe praises the efforts of the Company of Distillers, writing:

I take the Liberty to say, the Distilling-Trade in England, which is already so much improv'd and encreas'd, will in a very few Years conquer all foreign Importations, all the clandestine and corrupt Management of other Countries, who impose upon us, and even the smuggling and running of French Brandy itself.'

One suspects that Defoe was in the pay of the Distillers, because he continued:

> The Distilling Trade, considered in its present Magnitude, is one of the greatest Improvements, and the most to the Advantage of the Publick, of any Business now carried on in England. In former Times, the Distillers, like other incorporated Arts and Mysterys, work'd wholly for themselves and for their own Profit: now they, without a *Pun,* may be truly said to be publick spirited People; for they work for the whole Body, and that immediately and in a particular manner.

Defoe went on to explain that the distillers bought the grain produced by the landed gentry and therefore encouraged tillage and good husbandry. They provided a market for the crops raised by the tenant farmer; they encouraged the transport of goods across the whole country; they boosted the number of ships involved in coastal navigation, 'being the best Nursery of Able Seamen'; they gave employment to the maltsters; and they raised a small fortune for the Exchequer. Either Defoe had a subsequent change of heart – or he was paid by the opposition, because he later complained that drunken mothers were threatening to produce a 'fine spindle-shanked generation' of children.

It is worth pointing out that gin was not the only distilled drink on the market: arrack was a firm favourite especially amongst what might be called 'the more discerning drinkers' (as opposed to those who wanted to get drunk with the minimum of fuss and expense). Arrack, not to be confused with arak made from dates, was a drink brought back by the East India Company from its headquarters in Batavia – now in modern-day Indonesia. There, the natives would make a mash of fermented red rice, to which would be added a local yeast to give the brew a very distinctive flavour. This would then be diluted with the juice from sugar cane, distilled, put into teak barrels and shipped back to Europe where it became immensely popular. The lack of juniper berries in the infusion stopped it becoming a true gin, but it was often used in making punch in lieu of gin, brandy or rum and was popular because of its spicy tang. It was however a premium-priced spirit, consistently more expensive than all other spirits not least because it would have matured greatly on its six-month journey back from the Far East. James Ashley, who kept the London Punch House for thirty-five years until he died in 1776, was selling it for 16 shillings a gallon in 1740. That was around double the price of rum and cognac and vastly more than gin. His shop off Ludgate Hill was unmissable, with its

three iron punch bowls above and alongside the door, proudly displaying
the words:

> Pro Bono Publico, James Ashley 1731. First reduced the price of
> punch, raised its reputation, and brought it into universal esteem.

Ashley also deserves credit for possibly being the first person to promote
what was later to become known as the cocktail, since he was the first to
advertise that his barmaids could prepare an individual serving of punch,
flavoured to match the specific requirements of the drinker. At that stage, it
was described as being a 'rub', a 'sneaker' or a 'tiff'.

In Batavia, there were reported to be a dozen arrack distilleries in 1712
and possibly double that number by 1778. Visiting British sailors such as
Captain Woodes Rogers in 1710 were over the moon at discovering the
hooch, which sold in Batavia for a fraction of its retail price on the streets of
London. In his diary, Woodes Rogers remarked 'Some of [the sailors] were
hugging each other, others blessing themselves they were come to such a
glorious place for Punch'. Their return to England in 1711 helped develop the
popularity of Batavian arrack – especially when linked to the manufacture of
punch. Even the name was exotic, 'punch' apparently deriving from the Hindi
word for 'five' being the number of types of ingredients originally used to
make the concoction (sweet, sour, alcohol, water and spice). In 1773, Sydney
Parkinson, a crewman on Captain Cook's 'Endeavour', wrote excitedly to say
that the best grade of arrack on sale in Batavia cost a mere fifteen pence a
gallon—whereas he would have had to pay twelve times as much for the same
drink in London. Half a century later punch was still a symbol of hospitality
and convivial company, whether made from arrack or gin. The arrack base was
particularly enjoyed by the Prince Regent, later King George IV, and Regent
Punch combined a heady mix of arrack, rum, brandy and champagne – and
green tea. The full recipe for Regent Punch was given by Eliza Acton in her
book *Modern Cookery for Private Families* published in 1849:

> Pare as thin as possible the rinds of two china oranges, of two
> lemons, and of one seville orange, and infuse them for an hour
> in half a pint of thin, cold syrup; then add to them the juice
> of the fruit. Make a pint of strong green tea, sweeten it well
> with fine sugar, and when it is quite cold, add to it the fruit
> and syrup, with a glass of the best old Jamaica rum, a glass of
> Brandy, one of Arrack, one of pine-apple syrup, and two bottles
> of Champagne. Pass the whole through a fine lawn sieve until

it is perfectly clear, then bottle and put it into ice until dinner is served. We are indebted for this receipt to a person who made the punch daily for the prince's table, at Carlton Palace, for six months; it has been in our possession for some years and may be relied on.

However, arrack largely disappeared from English punch bowls when heavily-taxed imports from the Far East allowed rum from the West Indies to steal a march. No longer cost-effective to import, it reached the stage where the British East India Company banned arrack on board its ships, other than for consumption during the voyage.

In its heyday, punch involved arrack, but that is not to say that gin did not get a look-in, as evidenced by recipes from the nineteenth century such as Holland gin punch (using oude genever); Limmer's gin punch (named after Limmer's Hotel, where it was first developed); and Garrick Club punch, first described in 1835.

Back in 1729, the government had become alarmed at the increase in drunkenness and brought in the first of what would turn out to be eight pieces of legislation, collectively known as the Gin Acts. If one is being pedantic, they were not all separate Acts of Parliament (some were tucked in alongside other pieces of legislation, such as the one in 1737 where the provisions affecting the duty on gin appeared in legislation about tariffs on boiled sweets). All of the laws had names other than 'the Gin Acts', but the phrase is a convenient way of describing the collective efforts of Parliament, over a period of a quarter of a century, to tackle a major social problem that affected London worst of all, but which was by no means totally confined to the capital.

In this first Act, duty was raised to five shillings a gallon. Retail licensing fees were increased, but unfortunately this had the effect of hitting the responsible distillers hardest. The smaller back-street manufacturers of 'moonshine' using low-quality ingredients and impure water were simply not bothered: they carried on, in secret, regardless. Prosecutions were restricted because the Act only singled out spirituous liquors to which 'juniper berries or other fruit, spices or ingredients had been added'. The way around the legislation? Simply omit those extra ingredients – and make the resulting hooch so cheap and so strong that the person drinking it never noticed the vile taste. One of the main promoters of the new law was James Edward Oglethorpe and he was heard to say that he was optimistic that one side-effect of the new law would be that it would boost the export of distilled spirits, particularly to France and

Spain, claiming that this 'would destroy more people than the Duke of Marlborough had done'.

By 1730, a quarter of all government tax revenue came from the drinks trade in one form or another. On the one hand, the government did not want to kill off the goose that laid the golden egg, but on the other, they were worried about civil unrest and the possibility of rioting, linked to drunken behaviour. In 1729, an Act had been passed placing a duty of five shillings a gallon on all spirits and at the same time, it imposed a licence fee of £20 for anyone retailing spirits. Anyone caught hawking gin in the streets of London could be fined £10 – equivalent to perhaps £800 nowadays. The legislation marked a triumph for a coalition between magistrates, the Royal College of Physicians and the Distillers Company and it was noteworthy that the Act did not ban or tax the production of spirits, and dealt only with the retail trade.

An eighteenth-century distillery worker prepares the juniper berries for the distillation process, while the kneeling figure applies bellows to the flames beneath the still.

Chapter 5

Gin takes hold … despite the second Gin Act, 1733

The new law was widely disregarded and this led to its repeal in 1733, partly as a result of pressure from the landowners engaged in agriculture, who were reliant on the sale of grain to the distillers to keep prices high. Looking back, it is hard to see how the government could have got it so spectacularly wrong. Parliament wanted to deter the sale of gin by street hawkers, and therefore to bring drinking off the streets and into the public houses. In a sense, it failed so badly because it had a totally unforeseen side-effect – the conversion of literally hundreds, even thousands, of domestic residences into gin shops, otherwise referred to as dram shops.

The changes brought about by the 1733 Act led the Grand Jury of the City of London to express their concern about 'the late surprising Increase

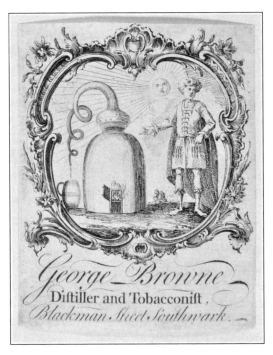

of Gin Shops and other Retailers of Distilled Spiritous Liquors'. They reiterated the facts produced some years earlier by the Royal College of Physicians and set out the effects of gin on 'those of the inferior sort': 'To this practice is chiefly owing that our lower Kind of People are enfeebled and disabled, having neither the Will nor Power to Labour for an honest Livelihood'. Meanwhile, the Grand Jury of the City of Westminster reported that, because gin was sold so cheaply, 'the meaner, though useful Part of the Nation, as Day-Labourers, Men and Women Servants and Common Soldiers, nay even Children are enticed and seduced to taste, like and approve of [gin]'. The result was that 'they are intoxicated and get Drunk and are frequently seen in our Streets in such a Condition abhorrent to reasonable creatures'. Further, they were 'often carried to a Degree of outrageous passion and become bold and daring in committing Robberies and other offences'.

An article in *The London Magazine, or, Gentleman's Monthly Intelligencer* reported that the County of Middlesex Justices had been commissioned at a former Quarter Sessions 'to make enquiry into the houses and places where geneva and other pernicious liquors are sold by retail'. The report stated that within Westminster, Holborn, the Tower and Finsbury divisions, but excluding the City of London and Southwark, '7044 houses and shops publicly sold liquors besides what is sold in garrets, cellars, back rooms and other private places'. Of that number 2,505 were said to be unlicensed and it was stated that geneva was 'being sold by above 80 other inferior trades, particularly chandlers, weavers, tobacconists, shoemakers, carpenters, barbers, taylors, dyers, labourers etc; there being in the hamlets of Bethnal Green upwards of 90 weavers who sell this liquor'.

There followed something of a pamphlet war, for and against controls. On the one hand, there was a pamphlet entitled *The Trial of the Spirits*, written anonymously in 1736, and arguing that it was wrong for a man to grow rich supplying a product that was detrimental to the prosperity of the country. As the author put it: 'No Body of men ought to get Estates at the Expence of the Poor, when that very Expence disables them from being Serviceable to the Community'. It continued: 'Gin, is sold very cheap so that People may get muddled with it for Three halfpence, and for three pence made quite Drunk even to Madness'. This suggested that it was the very cheapness of gin that lay at the root of the problem. Men could get drunk cheaply, and because they were drunk they forgot to pay their debts and failed to turn up for work, condemning their families to starvation. Worse, it led to 'desperate Attacks, Highway and Street Robberies, attended sometimes with the most Cruel and unheard of Murthers'.

One underlying concern was that the economy would suffer if labourers stopped labouring. When the London Grand Jury met at the Old Bailey to present its petition to the Lord Mayor it stated that its concern was at 'such publick Nuisances as disturb and annoy the Inhabitants of the City'. Its main complaint was that gin was robbing the 'lower kind of people' of their ability 'to labour for an honest livelihood, which is a principal Reason of the great Increase of the Poor'. To their way of thinking, drink caused poverty. Looking through the other end of time's telescope, we might say that it was the poverty that caused the drunkenness ...

The same Grand Jury submission made the link between gin drinking and crime: 'Most of the Murders and Robberies lately committed have been laid and concentrated at Gin Shops' and blamed alcohol because, 'being fired with these Hot Spirits, they are prepared to execute the most bold and daring Attempts'. Whatever the reason, the results were stark and the records of the Old Bailey for the eighteenth century show some 1,120 criminal cases where gin consumption was identified as an underlying factor.

A look at the Proceedings of the Old Bailey Online reveal a litany of crimes committed by men and women who lived in a twilight world of 'outrageous Crimes, in Whoring, Drinking to excess, Cursing, Swearing and Blaspheming, Picking of Pockets, Pilfering and Thieving, Robbing in the Streets and House-breaking'.

Interestingly the records of the Old Bailey first start referring to 'gin-shops' in 1726, but the product sold there was invariably described as 'geneva' and had been since at least 1707. In 1726, it was reported that 'Jenny Crommy and Black Bess had robbed an old Gentleman of a guinea and seventeen shillings'. A constable was directed to a gin-shop in White Horse Alley, where 'he heard the Prisoner and another quarrelling about dividing a Booty'. The evidence was sufficient to justify the death penalty for Jenny Crommy, who was described as 'swearing and jumping as if she was mad' when she was taken into custody. Rather more fortunate was Ann Ingram, charged with stealing seven guineas from one John Howorth. According to her, they met in a gin-shop where 'he asked me to drink, I told him I hoped he would do me no harm, and he said he would not, but he made me drunk and put me to bed, and when I awaked and found myself locked in, I was frighted – And next Day he charged me with [stealing] seven Guineas'. She was acquitted.

On another occasion, a woman by the name of Hannah Donolly was charged with stealing a bundle of clothes. In her defence, she claimed 'I am sure I know nothing of the Matter: I was very much in Liquor, and was very Sick with Drinking some out-of-the-way nasty Stuff. O Pray burn me, burn my Hand off, but don't send me away; I'll never go into a Ginshop any more, if you won't send me over Sea'. That appeal to the justices was to no effect and she was sentenced to transportation either to the American colonies or the Caribbean islands – one of thirty prisoners given the same sentence on 7 September 1737.

The same fate of transportation befell Sarah Hudson. One Sunday night, at 10 or 11 o'clock, 'William Hopkins went into a Brandy-Shop in Drury-Lane, and finding the Prisoner there, he treated her with a Quartern of Geneva'. That was a quarter of a pint of neat spirits, at roughly double the strength of modern gins. Before long his thoughts 'turned to the amorous' and inspir'd by this he went with her into a Back-Room where Sarah allegedly picked his pocket. On realising what had happened he 'shew'd his Resentment by changing his Passion from the Amorous to the Outragious'. Hopkins admitted that 'he knew the House to have a very ill Name, which render'd him more inexcusable, that could on a Sabbath-Day at Night get Drunk, and fall into such a Place and Company, where, in all Probability, it was impossible for him to escape without falling under some unhappy Dilemma, or committing some Extravagance'. Nevertheless, the court decided that his 'vicious Inclinations would not excuse her Actions' and the Jury found Sarah Hudson guilty. The amount stolen? Ten pence, and for that Sarah was shipped out to the Caribbean for seven years.

Another interesting case involved Thomas Cox, charged with bigamy. 'The Prisoner denied his second Marriage, and said that he came Home drunk, and his Landlady gave him half a Pint of Geneva: that he found himself in his own Bed; that the next Day the Lodgers wisht him Joy, at which he was surprized; and that he was drunk two Days together with Geneva.' During his mammoth drinking spell, he apparently went through a form of marriage, bigamously, but recalled absolutely nothing of the event. He was found guilty, and branded on the hand.

Other cases show that it was often the person who was worse for wear after imbibing too much geneva – the principal witness – who was the victim of crime. Eliza Sewett was perhaps a tad fortunate when she and a friend were picked up by Henry Smith and enticed into a gin-shop in order to 'share a quartern of Geneva'. She allegedly snatched money from his hand when he tried to pay for the round of drinks. Urged on by her companion, Miss Sewett deftly swallowed two golden guineas – and ran off. By the time she was apprehended, there was 'no Evidence against the Prisoner' other than from the victim and that as it appeared that he was 'in drink' the Jury acquitted her!

On another occasion, in 1728, Martha Potter, Elizabeth Bell and Jane Aubry of St. Margaret's, Westminster, were charged with stealing £4 from

Richard Wager. He got so drunk with them that they 'drank to the Tune of fourteen Quarterns of Geneva, when he fell asleep till Three in the Morning'. That meant that each of the quartet had knocked back nearly a pint of gin. Perhaps not surprisingly the court decided that his allegation that the girls had robbed him of all his money, every farthing, was unproven. 'His Drunkenness and Extravagance being considered, the Jury acquitted them'.

Sometimes it was the strong liquor itself that was stolen. One case showed the volume and variety of spirits available, when Robert Catheral and Jane Price were charged with 'stealing one Ten Gallon Vessel, value 12 pence, nine Gallons of Brandy, value 22 shillings, sixty Gallons of Geneva, value £6, five Gallons of Anniseed Water, value 12 shillings, five Gallons of Mint Water, value 15 shillings, five Gallons of Carraway Water, value 12 shillings and five Gallons of Usquebaugh, value 12 shillings.' They were both acquitted on the basis that there was no evidence of felonious intent. Less fortunate was William Worgan who was charged with stealing six gallons of gin from Mr Leader, who appears to have been his employer and was a dealer in gin. Explaining how the gin was stolen, Mr Leader informed the court: 'suppose a Woman sends for a Gallon of Gin, they took it in a two Gallon Runlet, which they filled, delivered the Gallon to her, and sold the rest'. The charge does not appear to have been substantiated, but Worgan was found guilty of stealing ten pence – enough to send him off for seven years' transportation. The same treatment was meted out to Joseph King in a case where six quarts of gin were valued at eight shillings.

Take the case of William Burroughs, twenty-two years old, charged with assaulting one Edward Allen and stealing from him a few pence – and his hat. The court heard that he 'drove hackney Coaches, and by that means fell into that dreadful Society of Gin-drinkers, Whores, Thieves, House-breakers, Street-robbers, Pick-pockets, and the whole train of the most notable Black guards in and about London'. He was found guilty of theft, sentenced to death and was executed at Tyburn on 16 June 1731.

A random look at any of the cases that resulted in hangings is almost bound to turn up cases involving strong drink. An example would be Viner White, twenty years old, and charged with robbery. He admitted that 'he was not long wicked, but only falling in with bad Company, he turned a Drunkard, and they carried him out with them to Street-Robberies, when he knew not what he was doing'. Found guilty, he too met his Maker at Tyburn, 9 October 1732.

The same fate on the same day was doled out to Benjamin Loveday, alias Lowder, charged with theft and extortion. He was '17 Years of Age, of mean Parents, who gave him no Education at School, so that he could neither read or write, and scarce knew any thing of Religion'. The court heard that 'his Chief Work was to do Mischief, having been one of the most mischievous, wicked, and profligate poor Black-guard Creature ever was born'. The court was told that 'from his Childhood he was taken up in nothing but Thieving, Stealing, and picking of Pockets, &c. He was a constant Drinker of Geneva'. He admitted that he was 'a most wicked, profligate, debauch'd Boy, and that he was very much taken up with Whores, Drinking, and all those different Vices, to which such Wicked dispos'd People are addicted'.

He was accompanied to the gallows that day by Edward Perkins, aged seventeen, whose parents died when he was young. By the age of thirteen, he grew weary of being apprenticed to a pin-maker and left the trade, and started going out at nights. He 'became acquainted with the Black-guards in Geneva Shops, which prov'd his speedy Ruin' and led him to try his hand at highway robbery. For that he was sentenced to death.

Accompanying him in the cart taking him from Newgate to Tyburn that day was John Vaughan, who 'owned that he was one of the most profligate young Fellows in the World, in Whoring, Drinking, Gaming, &c. but that he committed no more Highway-Robberies, save the one for which he died; and that his doing so was nothing but the Effect of Drink'. In all, eighteen young men, and one woman, were sentenced to death by hanging, on that one occasion. In nearly all the cases drink played a significant part in their downfall.

The woman was 'graciously pardoned by His Majesty' along with three of the men. That left fourteen to pay the ultimate price and year in, year out, the courts heard the same sad stories and came up with the same harsh penalties. It was small wonder that the courts were active in calling for reform of the laws relating to strong liquor and at times it must have seemed as if the whole fabric of society was being undermined by gin-soaked criminality.

But there was one case more than any other which shocked the nation: the trial and execution of Judith Defour. The trial took place in March 1734. Defour was a single mother, aged about thirty, and was charged with strangling her own child, a two-year-old toddler. Judith's background was that she was born into a sober, hard-working family who worked in the weaving trade. As a young girl, she had started to work as a silk winder but, in the words of the Newgate Ordinary, in her mid-twenties 'she fell into bad Company, and had a Bastard-Child, which died; and then she had another, the unfortunate Child lately murder'd by her'.

She lost her job (quite possibly because she had a child out of wedlock) and drifted in and out of the gin shops. On several occasions, she dropped off her child, called Mary, at the local work-house. She did this in January 1734 but at the end of that month, she returned to collect Mary, who by then had been clothed by the Parish. She was accompanied by her friend Sukey, who was described as 'one of the most vilest of Creatures in or about the Town'. In order to get Mary released from the control of the parish Judith first had to forge a letter of release from the Church. Judith and Sukey then hit upon the idea that they could make a few bob if they sold the baby's clothing. The Old Bailey Proceedings recounted that the court heard how Defour 'took the Child into the Fields, and stripp'd it, and ty'd a Linen Handkerchief hard about its Neck to keep it from crying, and then laid it in a Ditch'. They then presumably went off to flog the clothes so that they could go off boozing for the rest of the week.

Later, in court, Judith admitted that she throttled the child in order to sell 'the Coat and Stay for a Shilling, and the Petticoat and Stockings for a Groat'. That makes it sixteen pence for the life of a child. Worse, she was motivated to do this so that she could afford to go out and purchase 'a Quartern of Gin' with her mate Sukey, who was with her at the time and was egging her on.

She was caught and sent for trial within a matter of days. The jury found her guilty of murder; her punishment was death. The sentence was carried out immediately despite the fact that she 'pleaded her belly', i.e. claimed that she was pregnant at the time. The execution was duly carried out at

Tyburn on 8 March 1734, after which her body was anatomised – in other words, handed over to the medical profession for dissection.

At her trial, Judith Defour confessed her crimes and according to the records contained in the Ordinary of Newgate she said that 'she was very sorry for what was done, that she never was at Peace since it happened, that she scarce desired to live; and therefore she made a voluntary Confession she had been always of a very surly Disposition, and untractable Creature, a Despiser of Religion, negligent in her Duty to God and Man, and would take no good Advice of her Friends, nor of any good or sober People. She drank and swore much, and was averse to Virtue and Sobriety, delighting in the vilest Companies, and ready to Practice the worst of Actions. She acknowledged the Justice of her Sentence, and died in Peace with all Mankind'.

Hers was a truly shocking case and one which helped ensure that Parliament had no choice but to intervene once more to try and curb the worst excesses of the gin trade.

Chapter 6

From half a Dozen Whiffs to Black Cats ... up to 1735

Some of the other objections to gin drinking may seem surprising. In 1736, Adam Holden wrote in a book called *The Trial of the Spirits* that the Revenue was suffering because gin, unlike beer, led to a reduction in 'consumption of tobacco, no inconsiderable a branch of his Majesty's revenue, and to which the populace do not a little contribute. An honest man may smoak a pipe or two of tobacco, with a pint or two of good beer, a whole evening, but is so suddenly demolish'd by the force of tyrant gin, that he has scarcely time to puff out half a dozen whiffs'. Somewhat bizarrely, the same book also suggested that drunkenness was bad for the woollen

Gin, the devil's brew…

trade ('People given to this Liquor choose rather Nakedness for themselves and Family than abstinence from this comfortable cordial ...').

The drift of the population from the rural areas into cities, particularly into London, led to a large pool of unskilled labour, unable to secure well-paid employment, living in crowded and unsanitary conditions. Unable to secure a decent standard of living and with no prospect of improvement, the wretched poor turned to gin as a way out from their predicament. Poverty led to overcrowded living conditions and to ill-health, and early death. Nationally, the mortality rate remained extremely high and in London, perhaps one in five children died before their second birthday. In poor areas such as St Giles, outbreaks of disease could result in the infant mortality rate reaching three-quarters of all births. It was not only cholera, smallpox and typhus which were endemic, but diseases such as measles and outbreaks of diarrhoea could be equally fatal in children. For many years in the eighteenth century deaths in London exceeded baptisms and the only reason why the population was not declining as a consequence of this imbalance was that the shortfall was more than made up by the drift into the City of London of the rural poor. Without this immigration, the population of the capital would have dropped dramatically. Of course, gin was not the cause of the spread of all these illnesses and deaths, but it was part and parcel of the whole problem.

Commentators drew a clear distinction between intoxication among the gentry and drunkenness among the working classes. If a rich or better-educated man got drunk, it was labelled as amusing, convivial, harmless. Hogarth might show the scene of happy, drunken, behaviour in *Midnight Modern Conversation*, shown in Plate 12 but it contrasted strongly with the way the labouring classes were shown, as in his *Gin Lane* (see Plate 13). The latter was drawn by Hogarth as a straight piece of propaganda in support of the brewing trade and shows a contrasting scene to his *Beer Street* (Plate 14) in which the populace are happy, hard-working and prosperous. Beer was the 'happy produce of our Isle' as opposed to gin, which was foreign and therefore intrinsically dangerous and unnatural. *Gin Lane* shows a picture of indolence, disease and death, linked to an abandonment of moral standards, and is mentioned in more detail in the next chapter.

One factor was undoubtedly the effect of inflation on food prices throughout the middle years of the eighteenth century. Poorer families were accustomed to spending well over half of their income on the basic necessities of life, with bread being a central feature of the daily diet. As more and more grain was being diverted to the gin distillers, prices for wheat needed by the bakers went up, and a loaf of bread cost more as a result. In years where there was a bad harvest, there simply was not enough grain to go round, and the poor faced starvation. This in turn led to the threat of civil unrest – politicians were always worried about 'the mob' and the risk of rioting – and to increased criminality.

The Grand Jury in its submission was also concerned about national security, writing: 'The Nation (if obliged to enter into a war) will want strong and lusty soldiers, the Merchant sailors, and the Husbandman Labourers'. Their concern was that without a sober labouring class England would lack the manpower to win a war. This worry was passed on to those right at the top of the government with the publication in 1736 of an address called 'The trial of the spirits: Or, Some considerations upon the pernicious consequences of the gin-trade to Great-Britain; (as it is destructive of the health and lives of His Majesty's subjects; and as it affects the trade, manufactures and landed interest of this island) humbly offer'd to the Right Honourable Sir Robert Walpole, and to the Right Honourable Sir Joseph Jekyll. By a lover of mankind.' Going by the name of 'Philanthropos', the author denounced gin for contributing to 'idleness' and crime, and for weakening the country's collective manpower. Gin was undermining the ability of the Nation to defend itself.

Observers also noted the devastating link between gin consumption in women and a rise in prostitution. Perhaps that was not surprising given that females made up a majority of the economic migrants drifting into the city, only to find employment opportunities for women were extremely limited and poorly paid. Disillusionment would give an understandable impetus to frequent visits to the gin shop. Gin was particularly popular with women, hence its female nick-names of 'the Ladies Delight', 'Cuckolds Comfort', 'Mother's Ruin', 'Mother Gin' and 'Madam Geneva' and caricaturists loved to show the once well-dressed lady reduced to common harlotry because of her fondness for gin. Central to the image of *Gin Lane*, Hogarth shows a young woman oblivious to the fact that her baby is falling out of her grasp, headlong towards the cellar and sets out the oft-quoted slogan containing the words:

> Drunk for a penny
> Dead drunk for two pence
> Clean straw for nothing

There is no other evidence to show that this was a universal street cry of the time and it is believed that Hogarth may have been inspired by one particular gin shop which he saw in Southwark. The Press were always keen to stress the link between gin and fallen women, with the *Universal Spectator* of 1737 reporting that 'when I behold the woman ... degraded into the most infamous habit of drinking ... when I see deadness in her features, folly in her behaviour, her tongue faltering, her breath tainted ... my concern, like her debasement, is inexpressible.'

The other thing we would find noteworthy was how the effects of intoxication were so visible on the streets. It is important to remember how little privacy there was in Georgian London. People defecated in the streets, had sex in shop doorways (the colloquial 'threepenny stand-up') and if they died in the streets their corpses might remain, visible, for a considerable time. People had no qualms about getting drunk in the street, any more than the users of skunk and so-called zombie drugs do in our present times when they are found lurching around town centres or collapsed on park benches. In the eighteenth century, as now, homelessness brought life in all its aspects out onto the street.

Thomas Wilson, son of a bishop, was active in the Society for Promoting Christian Knowledge (the SPCK) as well as in various other Societies for the Reformation of Manners. His tract *Distilled Spirituous Liquors, the Bane of the Nation* was regularly reprinted and blamed the ills of society on the existence of too many luxuries, which corrupted the poor. Instead of contenting themselves with wholesome, simple, bread and beer, they wanted luxuries and, being unable to afford them, turned to spirituous liquors. The drinkers were a 'drunken ungovernable set of people'. The farmers were to blame, for giving a bad example. In fact, everyone was to blame – the distillers, the consumers and above all the gin shops for reducing the drinker to little better than beasts of burden: 'I am informed in one place not far from East Smithfield ... a Trader has a large empty Room backward, where as his wretched Guests get intoxicated, they are laid together in Heaps, promiscuously, Men, Women and Children, until they recover their Senses'. At that point 'they either proceed to drink on, or having spent all the time they have, go out to find wherewithal to return to the same dreadful pursuit'. The result was, Wilson maintained, an unreliable workforce. Worse, it led to almost certain death: 'Thousands bring upon themselves by this cursed Practice, various Diseases that carry them off, if not suddenly, yet in the End, as certainly, as if they had been stabb'd through the Heart'.

At the same time, others were writing in support of the distillers. Some maintained that it was not the spirit which was at fault, but the people who consumed it, and claimed that the problem was that the labouring classes did not know how to behave and that raising the price of the drink was the answer. Others said that it was better to have English gin than French brandy ...

The author of *A Proper Reply to a Scandalous Libel Intitled the Trial of the Spirits* stressed the value of the spirits trade to the economy because it boosted manufacture, agriculture and revenue and gave valuable employment opportunities. There was 'no Necessity of destroying the Whole to prevent an Abuse of a Part' merely because some people drank more than was good for them. It was also argued that any increase in taxation levels would result in the appropriation of revenues to the Civil List and lead to further corruption in government. This was a favourite charge against the Walpole administration.

The newspapers stoked the fires against gin, by stressing the damage it was causing to women – 'the mothers of our future generations'. In 1735, *Read's Weekly Journal* published a story about a wife who 'came home so much intoxicated with Geneva, that she fell on the Fire, and was burnt in so miserable a Manner, that she immediately died, and her Bowels came out'.

The late 1730s saw a constant battle in the streets over gin, with the 'mob' targeting informers, fighting off the constables, and, if possible, grabbing as much free booze as they could. In 1735, one small riot seems to have involved the simple storming of a gin shop, leading to the newspapers carrying a story that on Tuesday 8 April 'At Seven Dials occurred a Riot at the closing of a Gin Shop owned by Captain Speke. When the Mob became outrageous in their attempts to force the stoutly defended Building, Justice of the Peace Mr Maitland read the Riot Act but the Mob refused to disperse peaceably as required, the Guard of the Tower was called to enforce the Peace with Ball, Butt and Bayonet, after which all was quiet. The Shop was wrecked by Intruders and all the Genever Spirits lost.'

An explanation of what had happened was given in a satirical piece, purportedly written by someone calling themselves 'Cholmondeley-Fitzroy, Lord Foppingham'. He wrote:

> Here I must add, the remarkable facts that the honest builder Jack Church had obtained in regard of the gin shop of Captain Speke. This novel innovation of trade has no entrance, doors, nor any visible shop-man. In their stead, one pays custom by introducing coin into a slot, whereupon gin issues forth from a spout below. The expense is of the common sort for such trade – perhaps one shilling for a pint bottle. Their trade was brisk. Church struck up an acquaintance with two Tipstaffs, there to serve a summons ... They had, he heard, been unable to serve it, their diligence baffled by the extraordinary nature

of the place. None had been observed to enter or leave. Boldly, that night, Church effected an entry to the premises, in search of incriminating evidence. He reports that the place is so shuttered as to be wholly dark within. The gin is stacked up, crammed into every space.

The idea of a slot-machine-operated gin-delivery system was certainly new and it was designed to get around the law by concealing the identity of the person selling the liquor. Being a blank wall with no visible door meant that the Excise Officers did not know who to go against, whereas the legislation stated that they had no power of entry unless the identity of the retailer was known to them. It was actually the idea of Dudley Bradstreet, an Irishman born in Tipperary in 1711 and who subsequently went on to publish his story in a book published in 1755 under the modest title of *The Life and Uncommon Adventures of Captain Dudley Bradstreet Being the Most Genuine and Extraordinary, perhaps, ever written.*

The enterprising Captain Bradstreet had an interesting career, including being a government spy, criminal, entrepreneur, brewer, playwright and serial seducer. Some reports suggest that the good Captain already had a murky background linked to the trade in gin – that he himself had traded gin illegally and also that he had acted as an informer, securing the conviction of others. He certainly was well-versed in the new law and its limitations and apparently used his last £13 to buy a consignment of gin from Langdales Distillery in Holborn. He then nailed a wooden figure of a cat's head to the wall of a building rented in the name of a lawyer-friend in a quiet area behind the Barbican in Islington. In doing so he established what was soon known as a 'Puss and Mew shop' – 'Puss' because a buyer would address the cat with the words "Puss, do you have two penn'orth of gin?" to which Bradstreet, hidden from view, would answer in the affirmative by replying "Miaouw".

In the book, Bradstreet explained his scheme:

> The Mob being very noisy and clamourous for want of their beloved Liquor, which few or none at last dared to sell, it soon occurred to me to venture upon that Trade. I bought the Act, and read it over several times, and found no Authority by it to break open Doors, and that the Informer must know the Name of the Person who rented the House it was sold in.
>
> To evade this, I got an Acquaintance to take a House in Blue Anchor Alley, in St Luke's Parish, who privately

convey'd his bargain to me. I then got it well secured… and purchased in Moorfields the Sign of a Cat, and had it nailed to a Street Window; I then caused a Leaden pipe, the small End out about an Inch, to be placed under the Paw of the Cat; the End that was within had a funnel in it. When my House was ready for Business… I got a Person to inform a few of the mob, that Gin would be sold by the Cat at my Window next day, provided they put the Money in its Mouth, from whence there was a Hole that conveyed it to me… I heard the chink of Money, and a comfortable Voice say, "Puss, give me two Pennyworth of Gin."

I instantly put my Mouth to the tube, and bid them receive it from the Pipe under the paw, and then measured and poured it into the Funnel, from which they soon received it. Before Night I took six Shillings, the next Day above Thirty shillings, and afterwards three or four Pound a Day…

The ruse soon caught on and in the space of one month, Bradstreet cleared £22 – equivalent nowadays to a net profit of perhaps £1,700. No one could see who was sitting inside behind the sign of the cat and therefore no one could act as informer and pass details to the Excise men. All that the authorities could establish was that the premises were rented by a lawyer who declined to name the occupier, claiming it was in breach of his client confidentiality.

Sadly, nothing remains of the premises used by Bradstreet and the entire Blue Anchor Alley disappeared from maps when the site was redeveloped with a modern, concrete, block of flats in the 1960s. As for the sign, this has long disappeared although a replica can be seen at the Beefeater Gin Distillery premises at Kennington in London.

Before long the sign of the Black Cat was everywhere, an indication that both retailers and purchasers were determined to flout the law. Soon, Captain Bradstreet was able to emerge from the dark room in which he would barricade himself, and retire from this particular venture in order to concentrate on his main interests, namely wine, women and song. He was a chancer, a flamboyant extrovert, going on stage, writing a play and bragging about his numerous affairs. He died in 1761, long after the 'copycats' had been caught, prosecuted or driven out of business.

The association between cats and the selling of gin remained for many years and may have contributed to the reason why a popular brand of gin was known as 'Old Tom' in the Victorian era, forever associated with the gin palaces of the mid-nineteenth century. 'Old Tom' gin was a sort of distant cousin of the old genever popular in Holland, considerably sweeter than the London Dry gin which later replaced it in popularity. The bitter flavours were masked by the addition of lemon or aniseed, or sweetened by the addition of liquorice and even sugar. Old Tom and the depiction of a cat on bottles of gin is described in more detail in the description of gin palaces in Chapter 12. Nowadays it is enjoying a resurgence of popularity as enthusiasts seek out different tastes and a number of distillers, including Hayman's Distillery, have brought out limited editions of Old Tom as a nod to their heritage.

Chapter 7

The third Gin Act – 1736

The upshot of all the pressure on Parliament was the passing of the Spirit Duties Act 1735 (commonly known as the Gin Act of 1736). The main promoter of the legislation was Sir Joseph Jekyll, who had been appointed Master of the Rolls in 1717. He was well into his eighties, not particularly effective, but was well-liked in Parliament and had always been an advocate of reform of the Poor Laws. His was an especially anti-gin stance and in his capacity as President of the Westminster Infirmary, he had introduced a rule banning gin drinkers from being admitted. His lobbying for stricter laws put Sir Robert Walpole, the Prime Minister, on the spot; on the one hand, he wanted to curb the risk of civil unrest caused by an inebriated labouring class and on the other, he did not want to see controls introduced which might lead to the Revenue taking a hit. Walpole did take part in the debate in

the House of Commons and would have been aware of the intense pressure from those with commercial interests in the West Indies not to do anything which would prejudice the trade in sugar, molasses and rum. In the event, Walpole insisted that if the annual amount produced by the taxation of gin went down (in other words if gin consumption dropped as a result of tighter controls and higher levels of duty) the deficit was to be made good by other taxation. His critics argued that all that he was interested in was maintaining the size of the Civil List – the money which he, Walpole, could control and use to dish out favours and award patronage to his followers. Walpole's opponents bitterly railed against the idea that the Civil List should be made up to the tune of £70,000 per annum, by way of compensation, arguing that if receipts from the tax of gin went down, the sales of beer, and hence the tax receipts from brewing, were bound to go up in equal measure.

The debates in the Commons reflected a range of views, especially as to how hitting gin drinkers might also affect people who preferred beer, with one MP saying:

> I am persuaded that nothing will tend more to the rendering our People sober, frugal, and industrious, than the removing out of their Way the many Temptations they are now exposed to, by the great Number of Gin-Shops, and other Places for the Retail of Spirituous Liquors; for before a Man becomes flustered with Beer or Ale, he has Time to reflect, and to consider the many Misfortunes to which he exposes himself and his Family, by idling away his Time at an Alehouse; whereas any Spirituous Liquor in a Moment deprives him of all Reflection, so that he either gets quite drunk at the Gin-Shop, or runs to the Alehouse, and there finishes his Debauch. From hence, Sir, I think it most natural to conclude, that the Bill now under our Consideration, if passed into a Law, will diminish the Consumption of Beer and Ale; and consequently the Produce of the Excise on those Liquors, as well as the Consumption of Spirituous Liquors, and the Produce of the Duty on them...

Another MP drew a comparison with the effect which the 1729 Act had upon Excise Duties, commenting:

> In the Year 1729, the late famous Act against Geneva, and other Compound Spirits, was passed; and tho' that Act was evaded by the Sale of a new Sort of Spirit call'd *Parliament-*

Brandy, yet, ineffectual as it was, it diminished a little the Consumption of Spirituous Liquors, and consequently the Produce of the Duties on such Liquors; so that in the Year ending at Midsummer 1732, they produced but £100,025 which was £4348 less than they produced in 1729. But as to the Excise upon Beer and Ale, what was the Consequence? As soon as that Act passed, that Excise began to increase, so that in the Year ended at Midsummer 1732, it produced £1,071,240 which is £107,477 more than it produced in 1729.

There were rough attempts to compute how many gin drinkers there were and what effect it would have on Excise receipts if they were persuaded to switch to wine or beer, with one Member of Parliament maintaining:

I may modestly compute there are 20,000 Houses and Shops within the Bills of Mortality, where Geneva and other Spirituous Liquors are sold by Retail; and tho' the People within the Bills of Mortality are computed to be but a fifth, or a sixth Part of the People of England, yet I shall reckon but 20,000 Houses and Shops in all the other Parts of England, where Spirituous Liquors are sold by Retail, the Whole being 40,000. Now to each of these Houses I shall allow but ten Customers, who are excessive Drinkers of Gin, such I call those who may drink about half a Pint a Day, one Day with another; and ten Customers who are moderate Drinkers of that Liquor, such I call those who do not drink above half a Quartern a Day, one Day with another. This makes in England 400,000 excessive Drinkers, and 400,000 moderate Drinkers of Spirituous Liquors; and considering how universally the Custom of drinking such Liquors has got in among the common People, Men, Women and Children, I believe this Number will not be reckon'd too large.

But the question to be answered was whether you could simply transfer a heavy gin drinker to beer? As one person pondered:

It is well known, that those who once get into the Way of committing Debauches in Gin, can have no Relish even for the strongest Malt Liquors; and I am convinced there are very few Instances, if any, that ever a Club of excessive Gin-drinkers went from a Gin-shop, to finish their Debauch at an Ale-house; because even to quench their Thirst they generally take small Beer or Water, and mix it up with Gin; and many of them continue at the Gin-shop till they cannot find the Way to an Ale-house, or even to their own Beds, if they have any, but content themselves with the clean Straw, which at some of those Places they have for nothing: So that even from the Nature of the Thing we must conclude, that those who have once taken to the excessive drinking of Gin, give over almost entirely drinking of Beer or Ale; and if we can lay those People under a Necessity of returning to the drinking of strong Beer or Ale, we must necessarily very much increase the Consumption.

You can see where the hearts of the MP's really lay when you see the parliamentary reports. They seemed to focus more than anything else on how to ensure that punch, that great favourite of the better-off, should not be hit by the proposed law. It was one thing to punish the great unwashed for being poor and for liking gin, but it was another for MP's to penalise people of their own class by making punch more expensive. There was much debate on the subject:

April 6. The House resumed the Consideration of the Report from the Committee on the Bill for preventing the Retail of Spirituous Liquors, when the following Clause was offer'd for excepting Punch; *viz.* 'Provided always, that nothing in this Act contained shall extend, or be construed to extend, to charge with any of the Duties directed to be paid, levied, or collected, by this Act, on any Spirits or Strong Waters, to be made into the Liquor commonly called Punch, to be retailed and consumed in the House, or Houses, of any Person, or Persons, keeping a publick Inn, Coffee-house, Victualling-house, or Ale-house, who shall have been first licensed to sell Wine, Beer, Ale, or other Liquors, or to subject the Makers, or Retailers of the said Liquor called Punch, to take out Licences from the Commissioners of Excise, as herein before directed for Retailers of Spirituous Liquors, or Strong Waters.

MP's had a mixed view as to whether the evil lay in gin or in drinking alcohol *per se*. One went on to say:

I shall readily agree, Sir, that the present Number of our Punch Houses is too great; but there is a great Difference between too great a Number, and none at all: By the Proposition now made, the Retailing of Punch will be confined to Houses where other strong Liquors are by Licence to be sold, which will of Course very much diminish the Number of our Punch-Houses; and where Men are allowed to drink any other Sort of strong Liquor, I can see no Reason why they may not be allowed to drink Punch, for I am persuaded it is as wholesome a Liquor as can be found at such Houses. ... Though the publick Good certainly requires an immediate Restraint upon the excessive Use of Spirituous Liquors, yet I cannot think that a Prohibition of selling any such Liquors by Retail, especially when they are rectified by Water, or made into Punch, can be absolutely necessary.

Another MP was worried about the far-reach of the Bill – and feared that restricting punch consumption as well as gin would be a step too far:

The Bill now before us may indeed, Sir, very properly be called an Experiment: It is, I believe, one of the boldest Experiments in Politicks that was ever made in a free Country; and seems as if intended to try the Submission and Obedience of our People.

It was recognised that Parliament was walking a tightrope – balancing the need to protect the sugar trade with the need to protect society from civil unrest. The Parliamentary Reports show that:

the Clause offer'd for excepting Punch out of the Bill relating to Spirituous Liquors is rejected. The Question was then put, Whether the above Clause be added to the Bill; which pass'd in the Negative, by 203 to 98. And then the Bill was ordered to be engross'd.

April 20 1736. The Bill relating to Spirituous Liquors was read a third Time, and pass'd without a Division; and Sir Charles Turner was ordered to carry it up to the Lords.

Walpole appears to have suspected that the legislation would go down like a lead balloon with 'the drinking classes' and wanted to distance himself from authorship of the Bill. It is said that he made sure that the finger would always be pointed at the Master of the Rolls, who he hated whole-heartedly, by posting a guard of thirty men to be set around the Master's house, under the pretence and show of protecting it from the attacks of the mob. It was just as effective as a sign outside the door saying 'Here is the man who stole your gin'.

Slightly surprisingly, no one in the course of the negotiations over the passage of the Bill through Parliament thought to consult the Excise Board, whose job it would be to enforce any new rules. In contrast, they had been involved six years earlier, when Parliament had last considered the topic, but this time their views went unheard. This may well explain why the law, as enacted, swiftly became hard to enforce. Much lobbying of Members of Parliament was carried out by a curious alliance of disparate groups – moral reformers and the Middlesex Jurors in one camp, the brewers and the West Indian Plantation owners in another, and the Distillers Company in yet another. In July 1735, the Distillers Company set up a committee to lobby anyone they thought would promote their cause – MP's, the officers of the City of London and the Treasury. The Distillers argued in favour of self-regulation and wanted greater powers of control given to them and them alone. Rumours spread that the Distillers Company even contributed to a pot of money so that MP's could be bribed up to £5,000 to kibosh the Bill. They paid for pamphlets to be printed and circulated and worked tirelessly to promote the interests of the company and its members.

In the summer of 1736, *The Craftsman* published articles critical of the legislation. *The Craftsman* had been a constant thorn in the side of Walpole's government, to the extent that Walpole even resorted to ordering raids on the offices of the paper's printer, Richard Franklin, every six months, often on flimsy pretexts. He arranged the ransacking of Franklin's print shop and even blocked the Post Office from circulating the journal through the post. When Franklin was charged with libel, Walpole saw to it that the jury was nobbled, by packing it with his own followers. As a result, Franklin spent much of his time trying to avoid jail and dodge heavy fines.

In September 1736, *The Fall of Bob, or the Oracle of Gin* appeared, ostensibly written by Thomas Scrub. Written in verse and in the form of a mock play, it bemoaned the attack on gin drinking, as in this passage:

> Is then inspiring Gin at length deny'd
> And must this Spring of Wit and Mirth be dry'd?
> The Rash, with Gin, were cautious, Cowards stout;
> Hunger was dampt, and piercing cold shut out.

Inspir'd by Gin I patiently have born,
The Stings of Poverty, and rich fools scorn...

The Act introduced the idea of annual licenses for gin sellers, costing a massive fifty pounds each as well as imposing a retail tax of one pound on gin sold in small quantities There would be a fine of £10 for anyone selling gin 'about the streets, highways or fields, in baskets, wheelbarrows etc or in boats on the river or in stalls, bulks or in any shed'. Failure to pay the fine could result in two months' hard labour.

As far as the annual licences were concerned, apparently only two were ever purchased. Instead, gin production moved out of the public eye and into back-street factories.

Anti-prohibition ballads were immediately brought out and sold by street hawkers' while plays and pamphlets ridiculed the government's attack on 'Madame Geneva'.

Rumours started to spread that the smell of rebellion was in the air, and that mass opposition to the government would be launched on the day the Act was to come into force. This was 29 September (Michaelmas Day). Letters seized by Excise Officers indicated that someone had written to a number of gin sellers and tavern owners, alerting them to the plans for an uprising and exhorting them to give away gin to the crowds to encourage them in their fight. The codeword for the uprising was to be 'Sir Robert and Sir Joseph' (a reference to the Prime Minister and to Joseph Jekyll, Master of the Rolls). The letter called upon 'dealers in distill'd liquors to keep open shop on Tuesday next, being the eve of the day on which the Act is to take place and give gratis what quantities of Gin, or other liquors, shall be call'd for by the populace... then christen the streets with the remainder, & conclude with bonfires ... All retailers whose circumstances will not permit them to contribute to the festival shall have quantities of liquor sent before the time ... Invite as many neighbours as you can conveniently, & be under no apprehension of the Riot Act, but whenever you hear the words 'Sir Robert and Sir Joseph' joyne in the huzza.' There were even rumours that the army would support the uprising and this really worried the government. Stories spread like wildfire about guns being landed on beaches in Kent. Extra troops were called into the capital and guards were doubled at key installations such as Kensington Palace, Horseguards and Whitehall. There was much marching around of soldiers in an attempt to overawe the populace. Meanwhile, the Prime Minister slipped out of London until things quietened down ...

In the event, there was minor sporadic rioting and acts of civil disorder, but nothing amounting to a serious full-blown riot. There were scuffles:

> When Discontents express'd the bitterness in their Hearts by committing Violences, the Horse and Foot-Guards and Train'd Bands were order'd to be properly station'd to repel the Populace where it might gather. Some Shots were necessitated to be fired when, after the reading of the Riot Act, those inflamed by the Spirit of Madame Genever, failed to lawfully disperse while seeking to petition his Majesty at St James' Palace at Midnight. Disturbances occurr'd through the night, in divers Locations, with some damaging of Property and House breaking, but the Mob dispersed at the merest Hint of Authority and few firm Encounters are reported, though many spent an unquiet Night in pursuit.

Some people took to the street to protest and to carry on drinking, and a few arrests were made mainly for selling gin. On 1 October a mock funeral and wake for 'Madame Geneva' was apparently held in the vicinity of Piccadilly. A few gin distillers marched to the Excise Office to protest the legislation, but apart from this, it was left to a newspaper to report that 'Mother Gin had died very quietly'.

The idea of a funeral for 'Madame Geneva' proved popular with caricaturists, as in the etching shown in Plate 11. In the days and months there was a widespread discussion about whether the new law was fair and whether it could be enforced effectively – or indeed whether there should be an outright ban, and if so whether this should be restricted to gin or extended to rum and other spirits.

An article, purportedly in the form of a tongue-in-cheek letter from the public, was published in the March 1736 edition of *The London Magazine, or, Gentleman's Monthly Intelligencer*. It contained the following words:

> As for Mother Gin it must be own'd that she hath been a great offender and that some course ought to be taken with her, but I am not for having her knocked on the head without any trial, or so much as being heard in her own defence. The charge against her is, that being an evil spirit and dealing with the Devil, she hath such a power over the minds and bodies of the common people that she can command them at pleasure and put them upon the most desperate attempts; that she hath

almost destroyed the present race altogether, by her pernicious influence, and if she is further suffered to go on in these practices much longer there will hardly be a labouring man or a breeding woman left in the whole Kingdom.

The writer wanted to avoid a total ban and felt that if five hundred wise men put their heads together they should be able to come up with a compromise. The letter also pointed out, perhaps in a somewhat scurrilous manner, that banning gin would be a severe problem for the army, describing gin as a 'constant follower of the camp and was always received there with marks of the highest esteem'. The letter urged army leaders to acknowledge that 'the glorious victories in the last war were in great measure owing to the assistance of gin' and asked whether army officers thought that they could go into another war without it. The letter went on: 'supposing Mother Gin to be as vile a creature as her worst enemies have represented her, why should other innocent people suffer on her account? Why must our good friend and ally, Monsieur Nantz, our countryman Mr Rum, and that moderate lady Mrs Punch, with all the collateral branches of that numerous family be charged with her enormities and included in the same sentence?' (Nantz was a colloquial name for spirits distilled in Nancy, which was at that stage a town belonging to the Polish king and only became part of France in 1766).

In the writer's opinion 'Mr Rum' and 'Madam Punch' were in a special category because 'our sugar colonies and several other branches of our trade depended very much upon them'. Against that 'neither our trade nor our colonies did the nation half so much good as that damned bitch Mother gin did it mischief'. The letter continued with the comment that closing down gin shops might help the farmers because it would boost the sale of beer – but equally, would encourage a revival of brandy and port drinking ('Mr French' and 'Mr Port') – saying that they 'have already gained too much footing amongst us'.

A letter later in 1736 to the *London Magazine* pointed out the damage which would be caused by outright prohibition: 'Let us consider how difficult it is for a man who has been bred up and has long exercised one sort of business to turn himself all at once to another, by which he may support his family'. The letter pointed out the loss a distiller would make if a distiller had to sell all his equipment and utensils in a market that no longer existed. 'The difficulty on all occasions be great, the loss must be considerable, but by turning such multitudes adrift at once we shall make the difficulty insurmountable and the loss irreparable'. There would be huge unemployment and he hoped that any increase in duty would not be put on all at once. He called for a small duty upon all sorts of spirits sold by retail, to be increased at yearly intervals. 'By this method people will have time to look about them and will get out of the trade by degrees'.

The *London Magazine* of 1736 contained an anthology of articles, one of which was ostensibly dated in May 1736 and which asserted that since the 1736 Gin Act came into force no fewer than 3,487 gin shops in London alone had closed down. Either those figures were wrong, or the dates were confused because although the Act passed through Parliament in 1735 it did not receive the Royal Assent and come into force until September 1736. The closures must have come about after that date, not before, or alternatively were an example of the exaggerated claims put forward by both sides of the argument. It was claimed that by the summer of 1738 some 7,000 retailers had been convicted along with another 5,000 being hit with penalties by the Excise Board. These figures were far from accurate and in fact just 1,300 retailers were fined in the four years up to 1740.

The threat of civil unrest was more of a worry to the government than the public scandal of drunks passed out in the street. The king, in his speech at the close of the 1736-7 session of parliament, attacked the disturbances as a 'defiance of all authority'. He issued a proclamation calling on Justices of the Peace to make sure that the law was enforced in all respects and to take all necessary steps to put down any related disorder. As mentioned, there was initially a sharp increase in the number of prosecutions, but once the threat of civil disorder had been brought under control, the JP's soon went back to their usual lethargy and further prosecutions diminished for the next few years.

It was the use of informers which infuriated the public. It was felt that there was something rather foreign, intrinsically 'not British', about paying money to neighbours to tell tales. The magistrates were unhappy accepting the (possibly tainted) evidence of informers, the person betrayed was incensed, and the public was horrified. There were cases of the public contributing to the fines imposed as a result of evidence from informers. Equally, when informers were identified they faced being beaten up or, as in one case in Bristol, being tarred and feathered.

What is clear is that defiance became more open and it quickly became apparent that there were insufficient resources to enforce the full provisions of the Act. Many of the distillers and retailers were what we might now term 'pop-ups' – small outlets which were very much 'here today, gone tomorrow'. For instance, in the 1730s there were believed to have been 1,500 distillers in London alone, of whom 1,200 had stills costing less than

£100. Not only that, but much of the selling of gin was in the hands of street hawkers – one-man, or, more often, one-woman operatives who were hard to police. As an operation, it was totally different to beer-brewing, which tended to be in the hands of just a few major brewers. For instance, there were only a hundred stills in the whole of London costing more than £1,000, and the legislation was aimed at the wrong people.

During the Bill's passage through Parliament, the Press kept up a barrage of news linked to the gin trade. Rival papers stoked the flames of a furious debate about the effects of spirituous liquors, some featuring letters from those opposed to prohibition, while others such as the *Daily Gazetteer* were keen to present the public with horrific tales about the tragic effects of inebriation. Take the case of the child-minder Mary Estwick, who, according to the *Daily Gazetteer* of 19 February 1736, was 'quite intoxicated with gin' when she sat down in front of the fire, the baby in her lap. The unfortunate child 'fell out of it on the hearth and the fire catched hold of the child's cloathes and burnt it to death. People heard the child cry and ran into Erstwick's room and found the child in the hearth burnt to death, and the fire catching hold of the old woman'. Once revived, the woman was still so intoxicated that she knew nothing of what had occurred. The courts were strangely forgiving of her lapse in concentration, declaring that she was a good woman and that it was all 'owing to that pernicious liquor'. Well, at least it wasn't deliberate, unlike one story of the nursemaid who mistakenly threw the baby she was looking after onto the fire, thinking it was a piece of wood. One would have to be fairly far gone with gin not to sense the difference between child and log …

The roll-call of deaths was relentless. *The Gentleman's Magazine* in March 1736 did not go into detail but informed its readers that 'Four persons drinking Geneva together in an alley near Holbourn Bridge dy'd next day and about ten more were mentioned in the News Papers this month to have kill'd themselves in the same manner'. The following month the same magazine devoted a whole section to the provisions of the new Act, clause by clause – an indication perhaps, of how important it was regarded.

The newspapers were full of salacious tales, none more so than the *London Daily Post and General Advertiser* of 29 March 1736 when it told its readers about Jane Andrews, a 'servant maid to Mr William Bird, a brewer at Kensington Gore'. Apparently, Mr Bird set off on a journey and on the basis that when the cat's away the mice will play, Jane Andrews headed off to the nearest gin-shop where she quickly befriended a motley crew; a drummer in the guards, an off-duty chimney sweep and a woman traveller. After a few drinks, she invited her new friends back to the house where six hours of solid drinking took them to mid-afternoon. At this point in time, Jane hit upon the idea of them having a frolicking foursome and proposed to the company that 'they and she should all go to bed together; and thereupon they shut up the doors and windows, and tho' 'twas but about four o'clock in the afternoon, they stript, and all four went into one bed together (as the maid called it, *to ring the changes*) and lay there till a mob, hearing of this affair, surrounded the door and disturbed the happy pairs.' One supposes that Mr Bird returned to be immensely relieved that the chimney sweep had removed his clothes before slipping between his sheets. Quite what happened to the very modern-sounding Miss Andrews is not recorded, but somehow one hopes she found new employment and prospered ...

Chapter 8

The Gin Acts 4, 5, 6 and 7 – and bodies bursting into flames!

The original legislation had passed through Parliament in something of a rush, going through the House of Commons in a mere three weeks. As already mentioned, its passage was opposed by the distillers and also by the rum and molasses importers, who feared getting caught up in the anti-gin furore. Further tinkering with the provisions, intended to correct matters which had been overlooked, were passed in 1737 in what has been called the fourth Gin Act. In fact, it never amounted to a piece of legislation in its own right and was done by adding a few clauses to what was termed the Sweets Act, ensuring that informers would be rewarded even if the person informed against was operating on a very small scale.

Ladies in a gin-shop ('Refreshment at St Giles's')

The 1736 Gin Act had not been effective in curing the ills it was intended to address and within two years was replaced with another piece of legislation, the 1738 Gin Act. That has been classed as the fifth such Act. Commenting on the failures of the 1736 Act, it was noted in the contemporary *Pamphleteer*, volume 29, that 'the great increase of the duties and penalties seems to have engendered much illicit traffic and all kinds of artifice to escape detection'. The preamble to the Gin Act of 1738 'lamented the inefficiency of former Acts and notes ... that the persons selling without licences are not seen but are behind some wainscot partition, curtain or are otherwise concealed'. It, therefore, raised the penalty for illegally selling gin to £100. Attacking an informer was made a felony, and the restrictions on gin distilling amounted to a virtually complete ban. As a result, distilling disappeared from view – it didn't stop, it merely went into hiding.

Parliament was being pulled in different directions and for every person lobbying for stricter measures, there was another calling for restraint. In 1738, Reay Sabourn brought out a text entitled *A Perfect View of the Gin Act, with its Unhappy Consequences.* His main concern was that the existing law was turning the country into a nation of informers. Sabourn felt that the legislation had the opposite effect to the one intended – it enabled 'unfair, loose and uncreditable Persons' to sell gin illegally while bringing ruin to 'the fair and creditable Dealer'. By driving the production underground, Sabourn warned that control and regulation would become unworkable. He felt that a profitable trade would help the economy, whereas the legislation only helped the informers to line their pockets. He was not the only person to despise the growth of the paid informer, with one of the Middlesex Justices (Colonel Thomas de Veil) complaining that the law had 'set loose a crew of desperate and wicked people who turned informer merely for bread'. The informers became highly organised, operating in gangs and resorting to all sorts of tricks to entrap traders.

Some opponents to the controls on gin resorted to satire, as in '*An Elegy on the Much Lamented Death of the Most Excellent, the Most Truly-Beloved and Universally Admired Lady, Madam Gineva*'. The mock-lament bemoaned the fact that banning gin would make abortion more difficult, with the words:

> pregnant Dames gin cou'd Abortion cause,
> And supersede prolific Nature's Laws:
> Mothers cou'd make the genial Womb a Grave,
> And anxious Charge of Education save.'

Meanwhile, it is undeniable that respectable distillers were finding it hard to cope with the repeated legislative changes. *The Gentleman's Magazine* of 1739 mentions the 'Death of Mr Simpson, an eminent Distiller, who, at the passing of the Gin Act, went distracted; he has left a wife and 8 children'.

Another sad tale, possibly not true, relates to an event in 1741 at Newington Green, on the outskirts of London. A young farm labourer, up from the country and unused to gin and spirituous liquors but fully accustomed to drinking from a pint glass, was offered a shilling for each pint of gin he could drink. The people egging him on later stated that they saw it as 'a frolick'. He reportedly managed three – and then dropped down dead. In a way, it is amazing if he had got that far, given the double strength of eighteenth-century gins.

By 1743 the country was caught up in the war which swept much of Europe and is generally known as the War of Austrian Succession. The British were allies of the Dutch in opposing France, Prussia and Bavaria in a dispute as to who should accede to the Hapsburg throne following the death in 1740 of Emperor Charles VI. By and large, Britain had kept its troops out of the land conflict and bided its time until it became a straight conflict with France as to which country would be the major naval power across the world. Wars cost money and that meant higher taxes.

A fierce debate in Parliament took place as to whether it was appropriate to free-up gin distilling, and encourage gin drinkers by reducing the excise duty, in the hope that this would encourage drinking and lead to extra revenue. It was not always a popular argument, A letter to the editor of *The Gentleman's Magazine* dated March 1743, ostensibly from a Simon Freeman, is interesting because it puts forward so many of the concerns which affected the decision to frame the new law, enacted later in that same year. It starts:

> Your late strenuous opposition to the Gin Bill demands our publick thanks whether we consider it as proceeding from your distinguished zeal to promote religion and virtue or from a laudable resolution to discourage profaneness and immorality, or from your tender regard for your fellow subjects and their posterity; or from a previous concern for the peace of the Kingdom in general and the security of the most excellent constitution. However trifling and inconsiderable the passing of this Bill may seem in the eyes of some short-sighted gentlemen the consequences of it appear to us to be dreadful, shocking and of the utmost importance. And

whether the grievance it is designed to redress is in any way equivalent to the mischief it will produce deserves our most serious consideration. The intention of this Bill, (as we ... are informed) is to raise a large sum of money, part of which is to be applied to the carrying on of the war upon the continent; a scheme allowed by all parties to be expensive, impracticable and fundamentally wrong. The method by which the savagery must be advanced is to encourage villainy, to licence debauchery and to propagate iniquity.

Describing the war as 'impolitic, dangerous and altogether anti-Christian', the letter writer asked the law-makers to balance:

the miseries of our own people, unrestrained from drinking spirituous liquors, enervating themselves, enfeebling their children and impoverishing their families with the innate pride, inflexible disposition and unavoidable sufferings of a foreign queen and you must make many grains of allowance from common prudence, brotherly love and Christian charity to make the scales equal, for though the fury of a distant enemy may fall heavy upon many particulars, yet the dismal consequences of an intestine depravity are more epidemical and more permanent.

In other words, it's all very well going to war to help Maria Theresa inherit her father's empire, but that is too high a price if it leaves all of our workforce poisoned by drink.

The letter continues:

It is a melancholy prospect ... to look forward and reflect upon the great mischief which may one day possibly befall this nation from a number of its inhabitants being intoxicated and inflamed with this *Liquid Fire*, and thereby made capable of perpetrating the most enormous wickedness, if they should at any time hereafter (which heaven avert) pour forth unexpectedly from their gloomy cells, as from the body of the Trojan horse, with design to lay the City in flames, that they might share in the plunder ... and to strike at the very foundations of Church and State. And altho' we should be very much concerned, we should not be so much surprised to hear that the chief promoter of this pernicious Bill was himself arrested by the desperate hands of some of his own licentiates. Such and so terrible are the effects of profligacy, madness and misery when they are blended together.

This particular concern, of the mob rioting and destroying parts of London, was a prescient comment in the light of the Gordon Riots which occurred in 1780 and which, as will be seen, ended up with the burning down and looting of a distillery. The mob have always liked a good riot, and there is none so good as one where free booze is to be had …

Are these, my lord, the only mischiefs which may be apprehended from the late indulgence, with regard to posterity there are still greater for in the less time than half a century Britons will probably be distinguishable from other nations by name and language only; their form, strength and courage which were the glory of their ancestors and the terror of their enemies will be lost, their size will dwindle, their vigour will decay, and their spirits will be broken by the drunkenness and debauchery of their parents. Our successors will, by these means, be rendered incapable of defending themselves, or even of guarding their own coasts and must inevitably forfeit their freedoms, quit their hereditary possessions, and be made a sacrifice to some foreign invader.

Good patriotic jingoism, followed up by the ominous warning that 'we should forbear any longer to think Mahomet an imposter and must receive the Koran for gospel' unless we opened our eyes to the dangers inherent in relaxing the drinking laws.

By 1743 it was estimated that consumption was equivalent to each and every adult consuming ten litres of gin per year and Parliament decided to try a different tack. The 1743 Gin Act (the 'sixth Gin Act') lowered the cost of a licence from £50 to £1. The retailer no longer had to pay a duty of twenty shillings per gallon and in its place the distiller was asked to pay a levy of three pence a gallon, Selling without a licence would lead to a maximum fine of £10, instead of £100.

It was like flinging fuel on a fire and it triggered a storm of comment. By this time gin was known by a multitude of names: to 'Madame Geneva' and 'Knock me down' add 'Blue Lightning' and 'Dorothy Addle-Brain' – the list seemed endless. These, and many other synonyms, are set out in the first Appendix. The one thing all these gins had in common was that they were very strong – as high as 80% alcohol (nearly double the strength we are used to today).

The scale of drinking was unbelievable – the equivalent nowadays would be if every fifth shop in the High Street was selling crack cocaine. Gin was not unlike drugs such as these, which do not necessarily give the user a high like cocaine – the whole point is that they offer oblivion, an escape from a life that offers no hope. Two hundred and fifty years ago, neat gin was the oblivion-maker of choice. It offered total shut-down and yes, it really was readily available throughout the City. For the poor, they could afford to buy a means of escaping from the poverty, the hardship and the unrelenting misery of life for the have-nots in eighteenth-century London.

The High Constable of Holborn reported that there were 7,066 gin shops in his district alone, meaning that roughly one house in every five was competing to sell rough spirits to the local inhabitants. However, we cannot be certain that this was true for all of London because Holborn was known to be the gin-making centre of the whole capital. Even so, the figures suggest a labouring population spiralling into poverty and wretchedness, to the extent that by 1743 more than 15,000 of the 96,000 houses in the capital sold alcohol. Of these around 9,000 were gin-shops. In St Giles, one of the poorest and most overcrowded wards in the City, there were apparently 506 gin shops against 2,000 residential premises. This did not take into account some 'eighty-two two-penny houses of the greatest infamy where gin was the principal liquor drank'. There was even some evidence to support the claim that drink was damaging the interests of millers and bakers, with two bakers reporting that 'the consumption of bread amongst the poor was greatly diminished since the excessive drinking of gin … The poor laid out their earnings in gin, which ought to purchase them bread for themselves and families and that in many of the out-parts, the bakers were obliged to cut their loaves into halfpenny-worths, a practice unknown to the trade till gin was so universally drank by the poor.'

Gin-related deaths soared, as did hospital admissions, together with the number of children born deformed by foetal alcohol syndrome. The truth was that the 1743 Act with its near free-for-all was leading to a real risk that the fabric of society would completely break down. There was one further attempt to tinker with the legislation, with what can be termed the seventh Gin Act, a law passed in 1747. This raised the licence fee for distillers to a massive £50 but allowed the distillers to sell directly to the public. This law was really only concerned with raising money to pay for the war, which was by now in its final stages and ended in 1748. It meant that this money-raising 'tweak' to the legislation was not in any way concerned with the social consequences of uncontrolled gin consumption – it was a problem that wasn't going to go away.

There was one slightly surprising claim made against gin in 1745: it was causing spontaneous combustion in its imbibers! Onlookers were always banging on about the dangers of alcohol abuse and claimed that there was a spate of cases where consumers had caught fire spontaneously and had been reduced to a pile of gin-smelling ashes. News had reached England of the remarkable circumstances surrounding the death of an Italian noblewoman some years previously. In a translation of an Italian text made by a man called Paul Rolli, it was reported that on 15 March 1731, Countess Cornelia Zangari de Bandi of Cesena, a woman aged sixty-six and a known alcoholic, had been found burned to death in her bedroom. Mr Rolli's account explained:

> Four Feet Distance from the Bed there was a Heap of Ashes, two Legs untouched, from the Foot to the Knee, with their Stockings on; between them was the Lady's head; whose Brains, Half of the Backpart of the Scull, and the whole Chin, were burnt to Ashes; amongst which were found three Fingers blacken'd. All the rest was Ashes, which had this particular Quality, that they left in the Hand, when taken up, a greasy and stinking Moisture. The air in the Room also observed cumbered with Soot floating in it: A small Oil-Lamp on the Floor was cover'd with Ashes, but no oil in it. Two Candles in Candlesticks upon a table stood Upright; the-Cotton was left in both, but the Tallow was gone and vanished. Somewhat of Moisture was about the Feet of the Candlesticks. The Bed receiv'd no Damage; the Blankets and Sheets were only raised on one Side, as when a Person rises up from it, or goes in: The whole Furniture, as well as the Bed, was spread over with moist and ash colour Soot, which had penetrated into the Chest-of-drawers, even to foul the Linnens: Nay the Soot was also gone into a neighbouring Kitchen, and hung on the Walls, Movables, aid Utensils of it. From the Pantry a Piece of Bread cover'd with that Soot, and brown black, was given to several Dogs, all which refuse to eat it. In the Room above it was moreover taken notice, that from the lower Part of the Windows trickled down a greasy, loathsome, yellowish Liquor and thereabout they smelled like a Stink, without knowing of what.

This gruesome explanation is set out in detail because it appears to have captured the imagination, to the extent that when Charles Dickens was writing his preface to *Bleak House* nearly a century later, he speaks of the Countess (wrongly named as being Countess Cornelia de Baudi Cesanate) and of 'the possibility of what is called spontaneous combustion'. He uses the preface to try and ward off criticism by scientists, who were increasingly sceptical of spontaneous combustion, and to justify why, later in the book, Dickens bumps off the character of Mr Krook when he catches fire spontaneously. The same fate befalls an alcoholic sailor called Miguel Saveda in Herman Melville's novel *Redburn*. Doctors had examined a number of unexplained cases of death by burning and in 1832 a book had appeared entitled *Medical Jurisprudence* stating that there were half a dozen features common to all such cases:

> the victims are chronic alcoholics;
> they are usually elderly females;
> the body has not burned spontaneously, but some lighted substance has come into contact with it;
> the hands and feet usually fall off;
> the fire has caused very little damage to combustible things in contact with the body;
> the combustion of the body has left a residue of greasy and fetid ashes, very offensive in odour.

No one was pointing the finger directly at drinking gin, as opposed to any other spirit, but the feeling seems to have been that if a woman of noble birth could catch fire without any logical explanation, it must follow that the poor, the labouring classes, were even more likely to succumb to a similar fate.

There were some who were slightly more benevolent towards the drunken masses. Ever pragmatic, Samuel Johnson was asked the reason why it was worth giving a ha'penny to beggars, when they would 'only lay it out in gin or tobacco'. He replied with the question: 'Why should they be denied such sweeteners of their existence? … It is surely very savage to refuse them every possible avenue to pleasure, reckoned too coarse for our own acceptance. Life is a pill which none of us can bear to swallow without gilding; yet for the poor we delight in stripping it still barer.' It was perhaps a first step in recognising that the Poor did not ask to be poor and were entitled to get their hands on whatever little pleasure was available – just as much as their social superiors!

An eighteenth century tub thumper… (note the bottle in the coat pocket of the man standing next to the orator).

Chapter 9

The final Gin Act of 1751 – and on to frost fairs and fuddling tents

By 1750 an appetite for change was evident. The magistrate Sir Henry Fielding had reflected on the rising levels of criminality which he could see before him in his Court and wrote a paper entitled '*Enquiry into the Causes of the Late Increase of Robbers*'. It started with the warning: 'The great increase of robberies within these few years is an evil which to me appears to deserve some attention'. He feared that although the evil was flagrant it was bound only to get worse if action was not taken. He wrote of the appearance on the London scene of criminal gangs ('a great gang of rogues whose number falls little short of a hundred, who are incorporated in one body, have officers and a treasury; and have reduced theft and robbery into a regular system. There are of this society of men who appear in all disguises and mix in most companies. Nor are they better versed in every art of cheating, thieving and robbing than they are armed with every method of evading the law').

Fielding laid the blame on the fact that luxuries had become too cheap. He felt that the poor were becoming lazy and indolent – they were at fault for wanting luxuries in their lives without being prepared to work hard. That envy, coupled with drunkenness in the lower orders, was the root problem of crime. He took a swipe at the masquerades and ridottos which had gone so down-market that they now appealed to the common classes and above all he took aim at gin-drinking, writing:

> The drunkenness … is acquired by the strongest intoxicating liquors and particularly by that poison called gin; which I have reason to think is the principal sustenance (if it may be so called) of more than an hundred thousand people in the Metropolis. Many of these wretches there are, who swallow pints of this poison within the twenty-four hours; the dreadful effects of which I have the misfortune every day to see, and to smell too.

Vil you give us a Glafs
OF GIN.

I'll see you
D--N'D FIRST.

Fielding was convinced that we were breeding a generation fit only for the almshouses, with men and women 'infecting the streets with stench and diseases' and unable to provide labour needed by society, or for providing soldiers for our armies and sailors for our navies. He concluded by suggesting that the disease and mortality rates were so alarming that we faced extinction:

> For though the increase of thieves and the destruction of morality; though the loss of our labourers, our sailors, and our

soldiers, should not be sufficient reasons, there is one which seems to me unanswerable, and that is this, the loss of our gin drinkers. Should the drinking of this poison be continued in its present height during the next twenty years there will be, by that time, very few of the common people left to drink it.

Fielding's broadside was well-timed because, with the war over, Parliament was concerned at the increase in criminality. In 1751, it set up a committee, known as the Felony Committee, to look into the cause of increased crime levels. The conclusions were unequivocal: the increase in robberies and murders could be attributed directly to the prevalence of cheap gin. Law and Order were breaking down, not just in London but in the other major centres of population such as Bristol, Manchester and Norwich. All three cities submitted petitions calling for restrictions on distillers and retailers alike.

Many were shocked at the public display of drunkenness by females, to the extent that in 1750 the writer Eliza Haywood published a book addressed to her sisterhood under the title of *A Present for Women Addicted to Drinking*. In it, she took aim at 'the pernicious custom of drinking, which prevails amongst women at present, [holding it] to be the great source of that corruption and degeneracy which all the world must allow to be the subject of a just and general censure'. She went on to observe that the 'practices of drinking enervates the body and destroys the faculties of the mind' and further announced that if a doctor sat down to devise a way of destroying health and life, then drinking, especially the drinking of spirituous liquors, was the method he would choose. She contrasted the 'present condition of the English people and that in which they were fifty years ago. In those days, it is certain, that our women were sober, religious and good Housewives; and it is as certain that our men were generous, upright, loyal, industrious and full of public spirit. We had then no balls, masquerades or evening assemblies to corrupt our women and we had not debts, taxes or a declining trade to oppress and deject the men.' The writer then went through all the different categories of women – young and single, rich and poor, old and widowed, to explain how that second glass of wine, or the first taste of strong liquor, would be a sure and certain prelude to degradation and death.

A letter to *The Gentleman's Magazine* in April 1751 identified two great evils which afflicted the nation; gambling and gin drinking. 'Palliatives are vain: inveterate diseases cannot be extirpated but by active and powerful remedies. I cannot therefore conclude without suggesting what I think to be such – gaming for money or gain of any kind, either in publick or private, by great or small, ought to be prohibited under the severest penalties … as to gin drinking the whole distillery should be suppressed. Making gin a penny a pint dearer is doing nothing an it would be better for this kingdom if no sorts of spirits was ever hereafter to be tasted in it.'

That year's edition of the same magazine had started with a resumé setting out the points put forward by Henry Fielding in his attack on gin drinking (mentioned above) and month by month gave prominence to the evils of gin. In March there was a pause while the magazine told readers of the curious reaction of a dealer from Banbury finding his wife in bed with a neighbour ('on which he got assistance and took them out of bed and tying their arms together set them before a large fire and had tea, coffee and punch provided and he sent to invite the neighbours to whom he exposed his wife and the gallant for some hours …') before moving on to tell readers that 'upwards of 4000 persons who sell spirituous liquors without licence have been convicted of the penalty of ten shillings each from January 1749 to January 1750'. It then moved on to give a detailed explanation of the provisions of the new Bill before Parliament. 'It is said that the bill for preventing the consumption of cheap compound liquors proposes an additional duty of £8 per ton on all malt spirits, that no compounder shall make or sell any spirituous liquors unless he has a still of 100 gallons in his dwelling house, and served a legal apprenticeship, and that no distiller shall have more than one apprentice at a time'.

The appalling conditions on the streets of London inspired William Hogarth to publish his two prints, *Gin Lane* and *Beer Street*, already mentioned. Beneath the etching of *Gin Lane* is the verse:

> Gin, cursed Fiend, with Fury fraught,
> Makes human Race a Prey.
> It enters by a deadly Draught
> And steals our Life away.
> Virtue and Truth, driv'n to Despair
> Its Rage compells to fly,
> But cherishes with hellish Care
> Theft, Murder, Perjury.
> Damned Cup! that on the Vitals preys
> That liquid Fire contains,
> Which Madness to the heart conveys,
> And rolls it thro' the Veins.

It is worth having a close look at the imagery in the etching of *Gin Lane*. It is dominated by the scene of the neglectful mother, showing obvious symptoms of syphilis, dropping her baby to its almost certain death, but a close inspection shows many other signs of depravity and squalor. In the background a lunatic beats himself over the head with a set of bellows while holding a baby skewered on a spike; a barber has committed suicide in the attic above his empty shop, his trade ruined; in the cellar area beneath the central figure, a pamphlet-seller has either died or collapsed, while still holding a pamphlet entitled *The Downfall of Mrs Gin*. Next to him is a black dog, still a common expression for depression and despair. People have pawned much of their clothing and a blind man is being beaten about the head by his companion, who wields his crutch as a weapon. An unclothed baby bawls its head off as its mother is carted off in a coffin and a young boy fights with a dog over a bone. A mother pacifies her baby with a drink of gin and the three balls of the pawn-brokers shop form a cross in front of the church. Some have argued that the etching shows St George's Church, Bloomsbury while others point to St Giles-in-the-Fields. The pawn shop has taken the place of the church in people's lives, and the air of poverty and squalor pervades the atmosphere. It is a scene without hope and was intended to be a total contrast to the happy healthy scene portrayed in *Beer Street*.

Some resorted to poetry with the *Ladies Magazine* of March 1751 containing a poem with the arresting title of 'Strip me Naked'.

> I must, I will have gin! - that skillet take,
> Pawn it. - No more I'll roast, or boil or bake.
> This juice immortal will each want supply;
> Starve on, ye brats! so I but bung my eye.
> Starve? No! This gin ev'n mother's milk excels,
> Paints the pale cheeks and hunger's darts repels.
> The skillet's pawned already? Take this cap;
> Round my bare head I'll yon brown paper wrap.
> Ha! half my petticoat was torn away
> By dogs (I fancy) as I maudlin lay.
> How the wind whistles through each broken pane!
> Through the wide-yawning roof how pours the rain!
> My bedstead's cracked; the table goes hip-hop –
> But see! the gin! Come, come thou cordial drop!
> Thou sovereign balsam to my longing heart!
> Thou husband, children, all, We must not part!

> Drinks Delicious! 0! Down the red lane it goes;
> Now I'm a queen and trample all my woes.
> Inspired by gin I'm ready for the road
> Could shoot my man, or fire the King's abode.
> Ha! my brain's cracked. - The room turns round and round;
> down drop the platters, pans: I'm on the ground.
> My tattered gown slips from me. - what care I?
> I was born naked and I'll naked die.

Meanwhile, the *London Magazine, or, Gentleman's Monthly Intelligencer* for 1751 contained the couplet:

> To banish Gin, let each man conspire
> As he'd rebellion quench, or spreading fire

Before going on to describe gin as a 'subtle poison which glides pleasantly thro' the veins; that liquid fire which parches the entrails; and debauching and ... unhumanising the understanding; rouses the mad quaffer to theft, murder and the most enormous crimes'. The writer emphasised that the ill-effects of gin-drinking went far further than destroying the lives of those doing the drinking: it also ruined the economy because that drinker was eating less bread, putting bakers out of business, was not furnishing his home properly, was not providing clothing for his children – in other words, was not acting as a responsible consumer. A few pages later, there was a long 'Remonstrance against spirituous liquors' – largely along the lines of 'how can the respectable property-owning classes be protected from these frightful common people who drink too much and then steal our goods?' Those were not the actual words, but they were the sentiments. It was followed by a demand for action: 'I would call upon every person in the kingdom from the merchants and inhabitants of London and Westminster to those of the smallest corporation in the country to join us in a petition to parliament and to his most gracious majesty, the father of his people'.

What these complainants were not doing was asking the question: why? Why were the common people so devoid of hope, so lacking in decent accommodation, so deprived of affordable food that they were prepared to imbibe such a gut-rotting head-splitting corrosive liquid? Why was it acceptable for the punch-sodden land-owning rake to drink and gamble away his family fortune when it wasn't okay for a member of the labouring class to do the same in gin shops? The law was made by people who owned property, to protect people who owned property. It was for this reason that offences against property ranked as far more evil than offences against the person, because such crimes threatened the patently unjust system whereby the 'haves' continued to hold and the 'have-nots' continued to go without. The ruling class was not about to vote for measures that would improve the lot of the labouring poor. After all, that would be tantamount to turkeys voting for Christmas …

In February 1751, the *London Magazine, or, Gentleman's Monthly Intelligencer* contained a four-line poem holding itself out to be an honest label for a bottle of gin:

> When fam'd Pandora to the cloud withdrew,
> From her dire box unnumber'd evils flew,
> No less a curse this vehicle contains:-
> Fire to the mind, and poison to the vein.

For the poet, the gin-bottle was the equivalent of Pandora's box; once opened, it was sure to curse the mind and body with its all-consuming evils. In the same year (1751) in *The Ladies Magazine; or, The Universal Entertainer* another small verse appeared, under the title of 'Chalk'd on the Shutters of an Infernal Gin-Shop'. The four-line poem sets out the dangers which would undoubtedly ensue for any person entering such a shop:

> Briton! If thou would'st sure Destruction shun,
> From these curs'd walls, as from Serpent run:
> For there a Thousand Deaths in Ambush lie,
> Fatal to all, who dare approach too nigh.

Writing about the effects of gin drinking on Society in 1754, the writer Stephen Hales stated in his book *A Friendly Admonition to the Drinkers of Gin, Brandy, etc.* that gin 'makes its Way into the World as a Friend to Mankind, and insinuates itself under the Disguise of grateful Flavours' and that while gin was a gift from God, mankind had corrupted a liquor 'which his bountiful Creator intended for his Comfort'. In contrast to earlier claims made regarding the benefit of gin drinking, Hale spoke of gin creating 'Obstructions and Stoppages in the Liver' giving rise to 'jaundice, Dropsy, and many other fatal Diseases'. Gin had the power to 'destroy and burn up the Lungs' and 'weaken and wear out the Substance and Coats of the Stomach'. The only way of stopping this was to rescue the poor wretch 'from his own inordinate Desires; he must be dealt like a Madman, and be bound down to keep him from destroying himself'.

Why the accusations? Partly because Hale was a member of the Society for Promoting Christian Knowledge, vigorously opposed to drunkenness and immorality. And partly because the consequences of excessive drinking had been all too evident on the streets of London. The SPCK had been formed towards the end of the seventeenth century and was becoming influential in disseminating Christian literature. The society had appeared at much the same time as the first of the Societies for the Reformation of Manners – a crusading group aimed at raising moral standards and driving out prostitution and drunkenness throughout London. But the tentacles of the Societies for the Reformation of Manners, with their reliance upon paid informers, were beginning to lose their grip by the mid-1730s, whereas the SPCK was growing stronger and more influential. One of the most prominent supporters of both societies was Sir John Gonson, who sat for forty years as a magistrate and was chairman of the Quarter Sessions for the City of Westminster. He, like the magistrate Sir Henry Fielding, was a strong, booming voice for reform. He was also a governor of the Foundling Hospital, a role he shared with his friend William Hogarth. The Foundling Hospital offered accommodation to homeless children, many of them born to prostitutes – the very people who Gonson so vociferously campaigned against. Hogarth had included Gonson (twice) in his series *A Harlot's Progress* and it may well have been his friendship with Gonson which prompted Hogarth to produce his Gin Lane/Beer Street images. Equally, it has been suggested that the prints were commissioned by Sir Henry Fielding as a blatant piece of propaganda.

The government, now led by Henry Pelham, listened to the concerns and consulted with the various groups with an interest in the matter. This involved not just the distillers but also those with a responsibility for enforcing any new law, from the Excise Officers to the magistrates. A new law was then framed aimed at imposing controls at all stages, from production to retail in shops to consumption in public houses. It became the 1751 Gin Act – regarded as being the eighth in the series. More properly known as The Sale of Spirits Act 1750, the new law proved to be remarkably effective. Known sometimes as the Tippling Act, it resulted in a decline in gin consumption which quickly became self-evident.

Under the legislation, the cost of licenses permitting the sale of gin was adjusted to £2 per annum and these licences were only to be issued to places such as taverns, inns and ale-houses. There was a prohibition on the sale of spirits except in outlets belonging to respectable rent and rate-paying shopkeepers – more specifically, to shops with a rental value of at least £10 per year. There was also a modest increase in the duty on spirits.

The changes meant that distillers were free to sell their products through legitimate trade outlets whereas the fly-by-night street sellers disappeared, and this came about as much as anything else because the law stated that spirits could only be distilled in stills holding 1,800 litres. Gin production could no longer be a 'cottage industry.'

The new law happened to coincide with events in the agricultural world which assisted the law-makers. There were a number of poor harvests leading to higher prices for farmers, who no longer needed to offload surplus grain supplies onto the distillers. At the same time, beer prices were beginning to fall. The result was dramatic: consumption of spirits fell by a third, from 8.5 million gallons in 1751 to 5.9 million in 1752, falling to 2.1 million by 1760. The gin craze was over. Gin's popularity would return in waves over the centuries which followed, but never again would it be such a public, obvious, threat to the fabric of society.

Although the Gin Act of 1751 effectively marked the end of the gin craze there were two more legislative changes worth noting. In 1757, Britain was hit by a particularly bad harvest, meaning that there was a risk of food prices going so high that starvation was probable. To ensure that such grain as had been harvested found its way to the bakers rather than to the distillers, the government outlawed distilling. The ban lasted two years but an especially good harvest meant that the restrictions were lifted altogether in 1760, but with the excise duty payable on spirits doubled. In a sense it was a compromise: the farmers and distillers wanted to be able to use grain for the distilleries, but moral reformers were keen to curb excessive drinking. The increase in duty meant that beer was now cheaper than gin, encouraging the move towards the consumption of beer, but that in itself provided an incentive to distillers to improve their product in order to justify their prices. The result was a plethora of new distillers emerging, many of which are still with us today. These will be looked at in the next chapter.

The growth of popularity of gin was one curious side effect of the Frost Fair, held on the Thames whenever the river froze over. This tended to happen once in every generation – there were Frost Fairs in 1684, in 1716, in 1744, in 1789 and in 1814. Before the Rennie Bridge with its five arches replaced the old London Bridge in 1831, the nineteen irregularly spaced arches carrying the old medieval bridge tended to restrict the flow of water. Also, before the days of the Embankment, constructed in 1866, the river was wider and more sluggish and therefore more prone to freezing. In addition, the country was going through a mini Ice-Age with temperatures often dropping below zero for months on end during the winter. When this resulted in the River Thames freezing over it prompted an extraordinary pop-up City of Fun on the ice. In the days before there was a police force to control public gatherings, it was the prerogative of the watermen to control 'their' water, by charging a fee for people to go on to the ice. With the city streets virtually closed by heavy snow, the people took to the ice in their tens of thousands, intent on eating and drinking to excess, spending money on gewgaws and souvenirs, playing skittles and football and generally enjoying the Georgian equivalent of a rave party. There would be ox-roasts and there would be slices of mutton served up as 'reindeer meat'. Gin consumption was central to the fun, with structures erected from sails and oars, given the delightful name of 'fuddling tents'. Here, hot gin was served to a delirious crowd, along with chunks of gingerbread, traditionally laced with gin.

Purl was a drink popular with the watermen. Based on hot gin and containing spices and wormwood wine, it was highly alcoholic and was in effect an early variant of absinthe. Some of the Frost Fairs lasted only a few days, while others lasted for several weeks, but it was a time of carnival, a chance to make the most of the disruption to normality and a chance to get hopelessly drunk.

The Gentleman's Magazine liked telling stories of disasters befalling people under gin's influence, as in the gruesome tale of the woman who fell through the ice as it cracked apart, only for the gap to close up and decapitate her, leaving her head rolling on the icy surface. It sounds apocryphal if not downright untrue, rather like the sad story retold in 1739 of the old woman 'who had accustomed herself to drink three gallons [of gin] a day, but it soon put an end to her miserable life'. The following year *The Gentleman's Magazine* reported:

> January 31: This month the frost, which began the sixteenth of last [month] grew more severe than has been known since the memorable winter of 1715-16, so that many who had lived years at Hudson's Bay declared they never felt it colder in those parts. The Thames floated with Rocks and shoals of ice and when they fixed, represented a snowy field, rising everywhere in hillocks and huge rocks of ice and snow, of which scene several painters took sketches. Booths, stalls and printing presses were erected and a Frost Fair held on it. Multitudes walked over it and some were lost by their rashness.

Sometimes, the weather conditions changed suddenly and the carnival atmosphere was brought to an abrupt end. In January 1789, tragedy struck when a 'sudden breaking up of the ice' led to five people being crushed to death. On another occasion, the owner of a pub standing on the river bank thought it would be a good idea to place the anchor of a delivery ship in his beer cellar. The high tide receded, the ice melted and the ship was dragged along by the tide, pulling the pub down around its ears and killing a number of people caught up in the disaster.

It has to be said, the revellers had fun with or without gin. When describing the Frost Fair of 1683-84 the diarist John Evelyn had explained that even His Majesty (Charles II) was entertained on the ice:

> Coaches plied from Westminster to the Temple, and from several other stairs too and fro, as in the streets; sleds, sliding with skeetes, a bull-baiting, horse and coach races, puppet plays and interludes, cooks, tipling and other lewd places, so that it seemed to be a bacchanalian triumph, or carnival on the water.

There was a certain continuity in the festivities even if they were totally spontaneous and unpredictable. The watermen from one generation passed on the money-making scams and attractions to the next generation and the fuddling tents were a sure-fire way of attracting custom. The final Frost

The Frost Fair of 1814, showing drinkers in their 'fuddling tents', knocking back spirits. 'Gin and Gingerbread' was a firm favourite with the ice revellers.

Distillation apparatus for aqua-vitae, from 1512. See page 14.

Distilling Oven, circa 1500.

Frontispiece to Pierre Morel's *The expert doctor's dispensatory: apothecary's shop* 1657. See chapter 2.

DISTILLATIO.

In igne ſuccus omnium, arte, corporum
Vigens fit vnda, limpida et potiſſima.

Sixteenth century Distillery. See chapter 2.

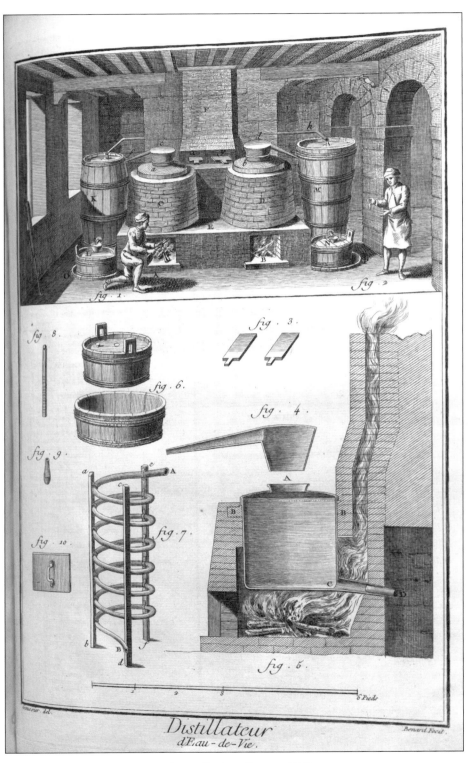

Extract from Diderot's Encyclopaedia *Distillateur*, 1751.

THE
Englifh Phyfitian:
OR

An Aftrologo-Phyfical Difcourfe of the Vulgar
Herbs of this Nation.

*Being a Compleat Method of Phyfick, whereby a man
may preferve his Body in Health; or cure himfelf, being
fick, for three pence charge, with fuch things only
as grow in England, they being moft fit
for Englifh Bodies.*

Herein is alfo fhewed,

1. The way of making Plaifters, Oyntments, Oyls, Pultif-
fes, Syrups, Decoctions, Julips, or Waters, of all forts of
Phyfical Herbs, That you may have them readie for your
ufe at all times of the yeer.
2. What Planet governeth every Herb or Tree (ufed in
Phyfick) that groweth in *England.*
3. The Time of gathering all Herbs, both Vulgarly, and
Aftrologically.
4. The Way of drying and keeping the Herbs all the yeer.
5. The Way of keeping their Juyces ready for ufe at all
times.
6. The Way of making and keeping all kind of ufeful
Compounds made of Herbs.
7. The way of mixing Medicines according to *Caufe* and
and *Mixture* of the *Difeafe,* and *Part* of the Body *Afflicted.*

By *Nich. Culpeper,* Gent. Student in *Phyfick*
and *Aftrologie.*

LONDON:
Printed by *Peter Cole,* at the fign of the Printing-Prefs in
Cornhil, near the Royal Exchange. 1652.

The English Physitian dated 1652, by Nicholas Culpeper.

Distillery of an Apothecary by Johannes Jelgerhuis.

The Alchemist in his laboratory.

Plague doctor outfit.

The Funeral Procession of Madam Geneva, 1751. See chapter 9.

Hogarth's *A midnight modern conversation*.

Hogarth's *Gin Lane* 1751.

Beer, happy Produce of our Isle
Can sinewy Strength impart,
And wearied with Fatigue and Toil
Can chear each manly Heart.

Labour and Art upheld by Thee
Successfully advance,
We quaff Thy balmy Juice with Glee
And Water leave to France.

Genius of Health, thy grateful Taste
Rivals the Cup of Jove,
And warms each English generous Breast
With Liberty and Love.

Hogarth's *Beer Lane* 1751.

One man sits soundly sleeping as his drunken companion offers him another drink from 1773.

Thomas Rowlandson's *Rum Characters in a shrubbery drinking Gin.*

Doctor Drainbarrel conveyed home in order to take his trial for neglect of family duty by Thomas Rowlandson, 1806.

The gin shop displayed by Carington Bowles.

The Battle of A-GIN-COURT by T McLean.

Gin Juggarnath by George Cruikshank, 1835.

I want a small glass of Gin. Etching, 1830.

The Gin Shop by George Cruikshank, 1829.

THE DRUNKARD'S CHILDREN.

PLATE III.—FROM THE GIN SHOP TO THE DANCING ROOMS, FROM THE DANCING ROOMS TO THE GIN SHOP, THE POOR GIRL IS DRIVEN ON IN THAT COURSE WHICH ENDS IN MISERY.

Above and below: Two versions of *The Drunkard's Children* by George Cruikshank, dating from 1846 and 1848.

THE DRUNKARD'S CHILDREN.

PLATE I.—NEGLECTED BY THEIR PARENTS, EDUCATED ONLY IN THE STREETS AND FALLING INTO THE HANDS OF WRETCHES WHO LIVE UPON THE VICES OF OTHERS, THEY ARE LED TO THE GIN SHOP, TO DRINK AT THAT FOUNTAIN WHICH NOURISHES EVERY SPECIES OF CRIME.

Fair began in February 1814 and lasted for four days. It stretched from Blackfriars to Three Crane Stairs, to the east of Southwark bridge. *The Gentleman's Magazine* described the scene:

> At every glance, there was a novelty of some kind or other. Gaming was carried on in all its branches. ... Skittles was played by several parties, and the drinking tents were filled by females and their companions, dancing reels to the sound of fiddles, while others sat round large fires, drinking rum, grog, and other spirits. ... Several tradesmen, who at other times were deemed respectable, attended with their wares, and sold books, toys, and trinkets of almost every description.

The frozen river was given the temporary name of City Road, and was lined with tents and booths. A highlight was when an elephant was brought onto the ice, but the thaw was swift and all evidence of the fair disappeared in the space of an afternoon.

Chapter 10

From the Gordon Riots to Gordon's Gin

In the aftermath of the Gin Acts things changed: the duty paid by distillers, combined with the comparatively low cost of beer, meant that the spirits producers had to re-think their strategy. Before, it was a case of 'how cheap and how strong can we make it?' whereas the distillers now had the opportunity to go slightly more upmarket and to make gin drinking aspirational, with a quality product. The distillers recognised that if gin was going to cost more to produce than beer they had to improve the quality

The Gordon Riots, 1780.

to justify the price. However, it would be wrong to think that every single distiller 'went legit'. A limited amount of unlicensed distilling went on for a few years, as evidenced by an entry in 1765 in the *London Gazette* where it reported on a distillery in a house on Clerkenwell Green. It had gone unnoticed until a carpenter went to repair a well and found that it was being used by the unlicensed distiller to get rid of waste water and gin by-products, via a drain running from the house. This was however an exception and records suggest that the 1751 Act cleaned up the distillery trade almost overnight.

One of the first respectable distilling companies to emerge was the Langdale Distillery, situated originally at 81 Holborn. In 1779, the business was moved to 26 Holborn on the corner of Holborn Hill and Fetter Lane by the sign of the Black Swan. Consisting of two sets of buildings, it was run by Thomas Langdale, who at that stage lived next to the distillery where 120,000 gallons of gin were made and stored. Langdale was a Roman Catholic, and was rumoured to have his own private chapel inside his home, at a time when anti-Catholic sentiments were high. Nevertheless, he prospered and because his gin was of a higher quality than the 'bootleg spirits' his gins were often bought by unscrupulous traders who would then water it down prior to re-sale, often adding unpalatable additives to bulk it out and give the spirit more 'bite'. It is hard to see why else sulphuric acid would feature in the list of ingredients ...

It is noteworthy that the gin obtained for Captain Bradstreet in the Black Cat episode, mentioned earlier, came from Langdales. His distillery was famous, and something of a landmark, so when in 1780 anti-Catholic feelings spilt out onto the streets in what became known as the Gordon Riots, it soon became clear that the distillery would be a prime target. In part, this was because Langdale was a Catholic, and in part, because rioters always fancied free booze if they could get their hands on it, and 120,000 gallons was a tempting prize.

The Gordon Riots were named after Lord George Gordon, the man blamed for being responsible for the rioting. It lasted seven days, with mayhem being caused in a shuddering explosion of violence and hatred. The prison at Newgate was ransacked and all the prisoners let out. A number of other prisons were destroyed including the Clink in the Borough of Southwark. In total, some 1,600 prisoners unexpectedly gained their freedom and gladly joined in the riot. Both the library and home of Lord Mansfield were burned to the ground and large swathes of Covent Garden and Bloomsbury were set ablaze. The Bank of England and Blackfriars Bridge were regarded by the authorities as being vulnerable to attack so the armed forces guarding the distillery were moved to offer protection at those places, leaving the distillery unguarded. On the evening of 7 June at 6.00 p.m. the mob descended on Langdales, broke in, and simply helped themselves, even though much of the liquor was still unrectified and was full of impurities. In vain Thomas Langdale tried to save his property, offering the mob cash and gin if they would leave him alone. However, there was no way that the mob could be fobbed off by simple bribery when such a treasure lay at their mercy. Barrels were rolled out onto the streets and smashed open, the gin pouring down the channels running down the centre of the cobbled roads. This was then ladled up by the joyful mob until hundreds were utterly drunk. A pig trough was used to bring the gin out of the building and into the open. Some decided to torch the distillery and before long this set fire to the flowing spirits in the kennels, burning the people in the vicinity. Some were so drunk that they walked towards the blazing building and perished in the flames. The conflagration was compounded when the fire brigade arrived and pumped what they thought was fresh water onto the flames. In fact, it was pure gin, highly inflammable, and it served to spread the flames far and wide so that they were visible from thirty miles away. All the vats of raw spirits exploded in what was described by one onlooker as a fiery volcano. Allegedly, one of the fire hand-pumps was commandeered by an old cobbler who used it to draw the gin up from the cellars, selling it on to the thirsty rioters at a penny a mug.

One person who described the events that night was Ignatius Sancho, who ran a tobacconist's shop near the Houses of Parliament. Writing to his friend Jon Spink the day after the conflagration, he wrote:

> ' Happily for us, the tumult begins to subside—last night much was threatened, but nothing done—except in the early part of the evening, when about fourscore or an hundred of the reformers got decently knocked on the head;—they were half killed by Mr. Langdale's spirits—so fell an easy conquest to the bayonet and but-end.—There is about fifty taken prisoners … the streets once more wear the face of peace—and men seem once more to resume their accustomed employments;—the greatest losses have fallen upon the great distiller near Holborn-bridge, and Lord M[ansfield]; the former, alas! has lost his whole fortune;—the latter, the greatest and best collection of manuscript writings, with one of the finest libraries in the kingdom.—Shall we call it a judgement?—or what shall we call it? The thunder of their vengeance has fallen upon gin and law—the two most inflammatory things in the Christian world.

The sight of dozens of men and women being burned in the inferno seared itself into the consciousness of Londoners. It was still fresh in the mind of Charles Dickens when, sixty years after the event, he wrote *Barnaby Rudge*. He describes the events of the Gordon Riots – but not the actual destruction of the distillery – substituting it with the burning down of the Magpie Public House. It was Dickens's fifth novel, published as usual in serial form, and was his first historical story (the other being *A Tale of Two Cities*). Dickens defined the mob as 'a creature of very mysterious existence, particularly in a large city. Where it comes from or whither it goes, few men can tell. Assembling and dispersing with equal suddenness, it is as difficult to follow to its various sources as the sea itself; nor does the parallel stop there, for the ocean is not more fickle and uncertain, more terrible when roused, more unreasonable, or more cruel.' Describing the looting and burning of the tavern Dickens wrote:

> …some had no time for escape and were seen, with drooping hands and blackened faces, hanging senseless on the window-sills to which they had crawled, until they were sucked and drawn into the burning gulf. The more the fire cracked and raged, the wilder and more cruel the men grew; as though moving in that element they became fiends and changed their earthly nature for the qualities that give delight in hell.

By the time the actual fire had been extinguished the distillery had been totally destroyed along with twenty-one local houses and the mob evaporated as quickly as it had appeared. In the rioting, hundreds of people lost their lives, either by the militia, or in the blazing inferno at the sign of the Black Swan. Writing shortly after the event, Horace Walpole wrote that 'As yet there are more persons killed by drinking than by ball or bayonet.' In a later letter to the Earl of Strafford, he wrote:

> Religion has often been the cloak of injustice, outrage, and villainy: in our late tumults, it scarce kept on its mask a moment; its persecution was downright robbery; and it was so drunk, that it killed its banditti faster than they could plunder.

The memory of the original distillery lives on, with the Edward Langdale cinnamon distillery still in operation nearly three hundred years after it was first established. As for Thomas Langdale, his company received compensation from the government in 1782 in the sum of £18,974, enough to rebuild his business by 1784/5. When asked before a Select Parliamentary Committee in 1783 to explain how that figure was arrived at, Marmaduke Langdale (believed to be the eldest son of Thomas Langdale) replied that it was calculated by averaging out the stock so that it was all regarded as being of export quality and strength. The company then claimed compensation at the rate of £40/10/0 per ton, based upon the prevailing Excise Duty for export spirits. The Excise Board challenged the figure, offering £33 or £34 per ton, but a meeting was held between the parties and a compromise of £37 per ton was accepted.

Thomas Langdale became Master of the Worshipful Company of Distillers in 1795, and was succeeded to that office by Marmaduke Langdale the following year. Marmaduke was the eldest of fifteen children and went on to join his father in running the family company, for a short while appearing in trade directories such as *Kent's Directory for the year 1794* as 'Marmaduke and Thomas Langdale, Distillers of 26 Holborn'. In 1795, Marmaduke became sole proprietor, before taking John Anderson into partnership in 1823. Three years later the company changed its name to John Anderson & Co, and the company finally ceased trading in 1954 having been owned by James Buchanan since 1890.

Another long-lasting distiller with roots in the first half of the eighteenth century was Booths, established in around 1740 by John Booth. As such, it was one of the first major distilleries operating in what became the centre of gin production – Clerkenwell. Derived from 'Clerks well', a name in use since the Middle Ages, Clerkenwell enjoyed a plentiful supply of fresh water from a local spring. Operating under the sign of the Red Lion from its Turnmill Street premises, the Booth's company became famous for its hexagonal-sided bottles. John Booth had four children and the eldest son Philip joined his father in the business in 1760, before passing it on to his three sons William, John and Felix. It was to Felix that credit must go for moving the business on to a much higher level, opening additional distilling premises at Brentford and then acquiring the rival distilling company of Hazard & Co, re-naming it the Red Lion Brewery. Felix also developed a new distillery in Edinburgh, making Booths the major player of the age. He was a remarkable man, with a contribution that fell way beyond the boundaries of distilling gin, and is mentioned in more detail later (see Chapter 14). As for the Booth's distillery, a new building was erected in 1903, featuring a five-panel frieze carved in Portland stone, illustrating the distilling process. The panels were salvaged when the building was demolished in 1976, and were moved to Britton Street, where they can still be seen. UK production of Booth's gin has ceased; the trademark and name were originally owned by Diageo but were sold on to an American purchaser called the Sazerac Company in 2018.

Another distillery based in Clerkenwell and in operation since 1740 was the Finsbury gin company founded by Joseph Bishop. Unlike the other main gin distillers, the product was based on a neutral base derived from molasses (as opposed to grain). The company was also responsible for making Stone's Green Ginger Wine, named after a Mr Joseph Stone who ran a grocery shop in Holborn. Under the 1751 Gin Act, distillers could only sell their spirits through a retail shop, not direct to the public. In recognition of Stone's importance as a major retailer, the wine, made from a fermented blend of raisins and root ginger, was named after him. The Stone and Bishop families were close friends and the drink enjoyed a huge spike in popularity in the 1830s when it was believed that ginger helped ward off cholera. It is still going strong but nowadays is manufactured by Constellation Europe, part of Constellation Brands Inc, the largest wine company in the world. As for Finsbury Gin, the name now belongs to the German company of Borco International and is still being made, using a molasses base and following the 1740 recipe.

The firm of J & W Nicholson & Co claims to have its origins in the formation of a partnership between two families, the Nicholsons and the Bowmans, in 1736. They operated as distillers and spirit merchants, but records of those early years are lacking. By 1806 the Nicholsons had established a distillery in Woodbridge Street in Clerkenwell. They outgrew these premises and moved to a larger site in Clerkenwell, at St John's Street. The company claim that when the Duke of Wellington was alive he liked a glass or two of Nicholson Gin, so when the Iron Duke died, it was a team of horses provided by the Nicholson Distillery which drew the eighteen-ton funeral car.

It was not the only time gin had been linked to the life and achievements of the Duke of Wellington. It was rumoured that the British army facing the forces of Napoleon in 1815 did so on a breakfast of gin, bread, hard biscuits, something called 'mystery porridge' and perhaps a piece of meat. Gin also features in the story of Field Marshal Leberecht von Blücher. On 16 June 1815, his Prussian forces sustained a severe defeat at the hands of Napoleon's army at Ligny. During the battle, Blücher was unsaddled, and fell under his dying horse, lying there trapped for several hours as the battle raged around him. Eventually, he was rescued by his aide-de-camp but was unable to resume command for some hours. He was reportedly revived with gin (it isn't clear whether this was applied externally to clean his wounds, or internally to raise his spirits) and promptly marched his forces to Waterloo, arriving late in the afternoon of 18 June 1815, just in time to turn the tide decisively in favour of the Allies.

Not all the major distillers chose to be based in London. In 1761, a twenty-five-year-old by the name of Thomas Dakin, bought premises at Bridge Street in Warrington and began distilling gin, something which the firm (now known as G & J Greenall) has been doing ever since. Dakin was never going to be happy churning out Mother's Ruin full of impurities and with an inconsistent taste. Instead, he used the finest ingredients and built his reputation on quality. The business he founded is the oldest firm of distillers in continuous operation and while it is perhaps best known for having produced Vladivar vodka (later sold to Whyte and Mackay and now produced in Scotland) it still produces gins of the highest quality, with its London Dry Gin still made to the original family recipe, with its eight botanicals including cassia bark and ground almonds, and with strong citrus notes. After Thomas Dakin died in 1790 the business passed to his son Edward, who continued distilling gin to the same recipe. After Edward died his family eventually sold the business in 1870 and the premises at Bridge Street were leased to a friend of the family called Edward Greenall. The Dakin Warrington Gin was renamed Greenall's Gin (same recipe, new name). When Edward Greenall decided to incorporate the business he named his company after the initials of his two younger brothers, Gilbert and John, and so it was that G & J Greenall Ltd was formed in 1894. More recently, the company has brought out a gin named after the founder, Thomas Dakin, as a reminder of their heritage. It apparently contains eleven botanicals including what is termed 'red cole' – that's horseradish to you and me. The company have expanded greatly by producing gins for other businesses – from Tesco's Finest Gin to Bulldog Gin, producing over 11 million litres of gin each year and thereby meaning that the company makes roughly a fifth of all gin produced worldwide. Part of the Quintessential Brands Group, the company won the title of 'The World's Best Gin Producer' in 2019 for the fourth time in five years.

Dakin was not the only gin distiller to rise from the collapse of the gin craze – another was Gordon's, started in 1769 and nowadays the manufacturer of more grain-based gin than any other company in the world. Alexander Gordon had his roots in Scotland but came down to London and opened premises at Southwark, where the water supply was considered to be relatively clean and less polluted than other streams flowing into the River Thames. His unique selling point was quality – in complete contrast to the emphasis on quantity and strength which had applied so disastrously in earlier decades. Earlier, less proficient, distillers were unfazed by allowing impurities to flavour the spirits – they kept the 'heads' and 'tails' as well as the 'heart' of the distillate and were not too worried about the quality of the flavourants being used. In contrast, Alexander Gordon used only the finest ingredients. He was particularly keen on juniper berries and produced a Dry Gin (i.e. unsweetened after the distillation process) which is regarded as one of the 'ginniest' tastes around.

Alexander Gordon may have expanded operations to include premises in the Grange Road area of Bermondsey between 1773 and 1783. This was in the vicinity of Bermondsey Spa, which had been discovered in 1770, but by 1786 a decision was made to relocate his factory to Clerkenwell, near to where Joseph Bishop was making gin. The original still, known as 'Old Tom' has been in continuous use ever since, even though it has been moved to Scotland where today's distilling takes place.

The company developed a strong link to the British Navy (more about that in chapter 13). Alexander married and had ten children, with his son George Osborne Gordon following him into the business. George Osborne Gordon married particularly well, into the Onions family (pronounced 'innions'). They were pioneers of the Industrial Revolution, major ironmasters operating in Shropshire. In time Alexander's grandson, Osborne Gordon, succeeded to the business and the company remained in family ownership until Charles Gordon died in 1899. Nowadays it is part of the Diageo Group.

By 1830 gin had become much cleaner and purer. Unlike the spirit known as Old Tom gin, Gordon's gin did not have flavours that needed to be hidden with sugar: London Dry Gin emerged as a drink in its own right. It used, and still uses, a variety of botanicals including coriander seeds, angelica roots, liquorice, orange and lemon peel, ginger, cassia oil and nutmeg. What emerged were gins manufactured to suit the market in particular areas. The poorer the area, the greater the number of working-class residents, the sweeter the gin. Conversely, London Dry was the gin of choice in more affluent areas.

According to Gordon's they sample up to 3,000 botanicals every year in an attempt to produce the consistently perfect spirit. Its juniper berries are stored for two years before being used, allowing the flavours to mature and intensify. In the UK it is sold in a green bottle, at 37.5% ABV whereas for export a stronger gin of 47.5% ABV is used, sold in clear glass bottles. This distinction has existed since 1907, (before that, green was always used). At much the same time Gordons started to market a Sloe Gin and a new batch is brought out every year. Sloes are traditionally harvested after the first frost of the year, and grow on blackthorn bushes.

Back in 1770, just one year after Gordon's was established, another distillery started up in Southwark, this one under the Burnett banner. The Burnett family were grain dealers on Horsleydown Road, a few doors away from a distillery owned by Mr Faffet. Going into partnership was a sound idea, since distilling could use up poor quality grain which was otherwise unsaleable and the London Directory for 1780 makes reference to the business of 'Faffet and Burnitt, distillers, Vauxhall'. Another directory of 1781 uses the same spelling of Faffet and Burnitt but describes them as 'vinegar makers and distillers'. Later, the Burnett part of the partnership dominated and by 1787 the Faffet link had disappeared. According to a popular urban myth, Robert Burnett then progressed to being Sir Robert Burnett, Lord Mayor of London. It is claimed that he launched White Satin gin, using a name based on the lining colour of the Lord Mayor's robes of office. In practice that is somewhat fanciful: there is no record to show that he was ever Lord Mayor, although Sir Robert Burnett did serve as Sheriff of London, jointly with Sir John Eamer, in 1794, some twenty-four years after the name was allegedly first used. Nowadays part of the Seagram Group, Burnett's White Satin gin is made at Heaven Hill Distilleries in Kentucky and bottled at 40% ABV. Burnett's Gin claims to be made to the same recipe as the one originally used in 1770, but now aims at the lower-price end of the market.

The new distilleries were not confined to London and one curious anomaly occurred in the town of Maidstone, some thirty miles to the east of the capital. Here, the mayor by the name of George Bishop was keen to see new industry brought to his town and he personally lobbied Parliament for a special concession. He argued that the best way of deterring smugglers from bringing in brandy from France was to produce a quality home-grown gin in a controlled and regulated manner. Parliament accepted Bishop's argument and for years the Maidstone Distillery produced fine gin, renowned for its quality, taking advantage of a concession made by the government in the form of lower Excise Duties, unique to Maidstone gin. In its heyday, the Maidstone Distillery was producing some five thousand gallons of gin every week, and the tax exemption was protected in all of the various Gin Acts. Nowadays, the Maiden Distillery produce their version of Maidstone Gin, using cardamom, cassia bark, coriander seed, meadowsweet, fresh orange zest, and the roots of angelica, liquorice, marshmallow, and orris to enhance the juniper flavour.

Other cities had slightly different traditions in terms of how the gin was produced. Bristol gin was recognised as being different because of the way the botanicals were treated. In London and elsewhere the botanicals were used after they had been dried. They would then all be combined to go through a maceration process, before distillation took place. This contrasted with Bristol where only fresh ingredients were used, so that each different herb, peel or seed was distilled separately as it came into season. These separate distillates would then be blended together according to the taste of the person in charge of the distillery, apparently resulting in a fresher, cleaner taste on the palate. It is a method recently recreated in Smeaton's Bristol Method Dry Gin, which is stated to be made with freshly picked Valencian oranges and newly harvested juniper berries from Tuscany, distilled in separate copper stills and using a recipe kept in the Bristol city archives and dating from the nineteenth century.

Hot on the heels of Gordon's came Plymouth Gin, with its claim to be the oldest working gin distillery in England, using the same recipe since 1793. Nowadays the description of 'Plymouth' no longer means that the spirit is produced in Plymouth. Like the word 'London Dry' it is used to describe a type of gin, in this case one where flavourings and colour are added after the distillation has taken place. This contrasts with London Gin, where no additives or colours can be used. It follows that London Dry is always colourless, whereas a Plymouth Gin can be pink.

The original Plymouth firm was called Fox & Williamson and they operated out of the Black Friars premises at Southside Street in Plymouth. The business was taken over by Coates & Co but eventually was transferred to Allied Domecq before being acquired by Pernod Ricard. Today's Plymouth gin still features a 'navy strength' variety which is 57% ABV (100° English proof). This was the traditional strength demanded by the British Royal Navy and sailors developed a way of establishing the 'proof' that it had not been adulterated by seeing whether a small trickle of the alcohol could catch fire and therefore set off a small amount of gunpowder placed alongside. For the sailor, setting off the gunpowder was a way of ensuring that the spirit had not been watered down.

One of the remarkable things about the new gin entrepreneurs was their age. Many of them were in their early twenties when they started. Not for them a business with a seven-year apprenticeship. Men such as James Lys Seager and William Evans were only just out of their teens when they went into partnership, forming a company in 1805 known as Seager Evans. They went on to build a distillery on leased premises at Millbank in Westminster and by 1832 they were sufficiently well-established in their chosen industry to be invited to join the Rectifiers Club. This had been formed in the late 1780s and met at the City of London Tavern to discuss matters relating to the trade of distilling. All branches of spirit production were represented, apart from whisky manufacture. The members of the Club included many prominent London distillers including men representing companies such as Booth's and Gordon's.

After nearly a century of catastrophic gin consumption, by 1800 the problem had largely disappeared. It paved the way for a change of image for gin – it was no longer just the drink of the labouring classes, a social evil to be railed against and punished. Instead, gin became more respectable, moving slowly towards gentrification.

She ain't heavy...

Chapter 11

G & T (Gin and Temperance) – an unfortunate mixture

In a book published in 1764 with a short title of *Low-life, or, One half of the world, knows not how the other half lives*, the unnamed author described a typical Sunday in London, seen through the lives of a whole host of different citizens – apprentices, merchants, whores, newly-weds – starting at midnight on one particular Saturday. It described the prostitutes walking the streets in the early hours of the morning, bribing the watchmen with a bottle of Geneva to 'look the other way', and explains how midnight was the middle of the working day for many publicans, gin-shop owners and bawdy-house keepers – a reminder how even in the eighteenth century London was a city which never slept, on-the-go around the clock. At two in the morning, the Geneva shops were said to be full of whores, thieves and beggars. Within a few hours of these shops closing, the book describes them opening their doors at six in the morning to welcome back their unchanging clientele. By noon, 'poor Devils of Women with empty bellies, naked backs,

Miseries of London.

and heads intoxicated with Geneva' were standing and gossiping with each other in the street.

And so it continues until early evening when, eighteen hours into the day, 'people who have drunk too freely in the afternoon are inclinable to sleep an hour, before they give a fresh attack to the liquor'. The description paints a fascinating picture of the contrast between the rich and the poor, describing the boiled sheep's tongues, stinking butter, rotten cheese, muddy beer and Geneva punch' which were swallowed down by the 'visitants at low christenings'. Then you had the 'Rakes of quality employed in privately visiting their kept ladies, and giving nature a fill-up with wine, jellies, oysters and other provocatives'. Setting to one side these provocatives, or aphrodisiacs, the book describes the genteel poor attending social gatherings, where they were 'pretty far advanced in liquor by too plentiful a drinking of common beer, hot pots and gin punch'.

In short, the whole twenty-four hour period is awash with spirits. Always, the drinking of genever is portrayed with its association with low morals of women, with criminality and with vice. However, the main gripe of the author was that drink, especially drinking gin, promoted idleness. It was bad for the economy not just because it led to absenteeism and poor timekeeping but because it made the drinker into a bad consumer. By eating less, by not bothering to buy new clothes, or keep his house in good repair and by squandering money on alcohol, the drinker was less valuable to the economy. In the preface, the author of the piece refers to the fact that people 'have left no hour unemployed, either in the different scenes of debauchery, luxury, or yawning stupidity … London, indeed, and its adjacencies, are at present so utterly absorbed by places of entertainment, and inventions, as before hinted, to destroy that inestimable jewel, time'. In that sense, although the book was dedicated to William Hogarth, and in particular mentioned Hogarth's series of prints 'The Four Times of Day' (Morning, Noon, Evening and Night), the book is far more in line with Hogarth's 'The Idle Prentice' or his 'A Midnight Modern Conversation', shown in Plate 3.

The catalogue of characters revealed in *Low Life* also reveals two other sides opposed to drunkenness, neither of which had anything to do with economic malaise: the work of the Society for the Reformation of Manners and the growth of Methodism. The book states that at two in the morning there were 'Justices of the Peace and members of the Society for the Reformation of Manners in full search after bawdy houses and whores'. In practice, although the Society had something of a re-launch in 1757 it had largely fizzled out within six years. During that time it consisted of a general assortment of campaigners, including Methodists, social reformers, churchmen and dissenters such as Quakers, backed by Justice John Fielding and the Middlesex and Westminster Sessions. While active, the Society was responsible for bringing some 9,500 prosecutions for a range of activities, mostly linked to lewd behaviour, breach of the Sabbath rules and keeping a disorderly house. In other words, it was not anti-alcohol *per se*. But as with previous guises, the Society relied heavily on paid informers, many of whom were corrupt, or guilty of both entrapment and perjury. It reached the stage when magistrates were loath to convict if informers were in any way involved.

In 1787, King George III was persuaded by anti-vice protesters to issue a proclamation against drunkenness, gaming, profane swearing and cursing, lewdness, profanation of the Sabbath, 'or other dissolute, immoral or disorderly practices'. It led to the formation of a Proclamation Society, otherwise known as William Wilberforce's Society for the Suppression of Vice. In time, this broadened its base to evolve into the Society for Bettering the Condition of the Poor.

The book *Low Life* describes how, in the afternoon, 'Great numbers of people of all nations, opinions, circumstances and sizes of understanding, [were] going to the Bantering Booth on Windmill Hill, Upper Moorfields, to hear their beloved apostle Mr Wesley'. Later still, there was 'an abundance of scriptural speeches made use of by the followers of Whitfield and Wesley in their evening visits to each other'.

This reflects the growing concern about the moral danger in drinking, as opposed to worries about the economic consequences. For the first time, there was a coherent argument that the poor would be happier if they led God-fearing lives and abstained from alcohol. It was an argument that found favour with the poor themselves: it was preferable to having abstinence forced upon them by social superiors who claimed to know what was best for them. Methodism in particular became a strong focal point for self-control, if not total abstinence. That is not to say that the founder of the Methodist movement, John Wesley, was against all forms of alcohol consumption. Indeed, his stand on alcohol was often contradictory: he was known to drink wine in moderation and referred to it as 'one of the noblest cordials in nature'. He seemed to be mostly opposed to the sale of spirituous liquors and in one of his sermons entitled *The Use of Money*, he gave two reasons to abstain from profiting from alcohol: 'We may not gain by hurting our neighbour in his body. Therefore, we may not sell anything which tends to impair health. Such is, eminently, all that liquid fire, commonly called drams, or spirituous liquors. We may not gain by hurting our neighbour in his soul, by ministering, either directly or indirectly, to his chastity or intemperance … it concerns all those who have anything to do with taverns.' Wesley was more concerned with the need for self-control and with the responsibility every person holds for each other in relation to the use of alcohol. So, when Rules were drawn up for the United Societies in 1743, members were instructed to avoid 'drunkenness and selling spirituous liquors or drinking them'.

John Wesley pioneered the idea of travelling the country, giving sermons in the open air to huge crowds. His cause was greatly advanced by his friend George Whitfield, who was perhaps one of the greatest orators of the time. It was said that Garrick, the great Shakespearian actor of the eighteenth century, remarked that Whitfield could pronounce the word 'Mesopotamia' and move an audience to tears. Given that their audiences were mostly uneducated, poverty-stricken men and women living in poor accommodation, frequently hungry and without any prospect of improving their lot in life, it was an extraordinary achievement to make so many of those followers into God-fearing and sober people. Over a fifty-year period, Methodism attracted some 500 itinerant preachers to their cause. By 1791 membership of the various British Methodist societies stood at 50,000. Within forty-five years this had mushroomed to a third of a million followers and by the time the national census was held in 1851, nearly one and a half million people were proud to call themselves Methodists.

By then, there had been a move away from an emphasis on personal choice to abstain, towards full-scale temperance and legislative control. It was a move that led to the creation of the first temperance society, in Glasgow, in 1829, and ultimately to the formation of the United Kingdom Alliance in 1853 (see chapter 15). In the meantime, several significant campaigners dedicated their time to promoting self-control, if not total abstinence. One writer, Thomas Turner, was a self-confessed alcoholic and in his diaries written in the period between 1754 and 1765 he defined gin as 'that baneful liquor, a liquor more surer to kill than even a cannon ball'. He admitted that drinking spirits 'sets the best friends at variance, and even incapacitates a man from acting in any respect like an human being because it totally deprives him of reason'.

The resurgence of a moral crusade against drunkenness was strengthened by the expansion of the work of the Society for Promoting Christian Knowledge, a mouthpiece for Christian evangelists. It had been founded in 1698 and the first three King Georges all supported the SPCK in one way or another. Society members opened church schools throughout the century, open to both boys and girls. The Society provided religious texts to the navy, with Horatio Nelson writing in January 1801 requesting more reading material for his sailors, with the words 'I am again a Solicitor for the goodness of the Society ... to hope that the Society will again make a present of Books ...' Later, Queen Victoria became patron of the SPCK two years after her accession and throughout the eighteenth and nineteenth centuries, the Society published hundreds of Christian titles, covering all denominations, as well as translating the Bible into various languages.

The Quakers were vociferous in their opposition to the excessive use of alcohol. Back in 1751, the Minutes of the Yearly Meeting in London recorded:

> As temperance and moderation are virtues proceeding from true religion...we beseech all to be careful of their conduct and behaviour, abstaining from every appearance of evil; and excess in drinking has been too prevalent among many of the inhabitants of these nations, we commend to all Friends a watchful care over themselves, attended with a religious and prudent zeal against a practice so dishonourable and pernicious.

Quakers were not actually prohibited from knocking back a glass of gin, although the actual Meeting Houses were and still are alcohol-free, with many Quakers being supporters of full temperance. In the eighteenth century, Quakers promoted cocoa and chocolate as ethical alternatives to alcoholic drinks. Fry's of Bristol, Cadbury's of Birmingham and Rowntree's of York were all Quaker-owned companies.

Towards the end of the century, the educationalist and moral reformer Hannah More entered the fray in support of abstinence. In 1795 she wrote a pamphlet entitled *A plan for establishing a repository of cheap publications* in which she promoted:

> religious and useful knowledge, as an antidote to the poison continually flowing thro' the channel of vulgar and licentious publications. These, by their cheapness, as well as by their being, unhappily, congenial to a depraved taste, obtain a mischievous popularity among the lower ranks.

She attracted enough wealthy backers to enable her to publish her own moralising tracts for sale at well below cost price. Their targets were drunkenness, idleness and gambling, contrasting the evil of such activities with the virtues of honesty, hard work and thrift. We may see the tracts as simplistic – and even at the time, they were subjected to ridicule. But they worked, enjoying phenomenal success. One of Hannah's early tracts was her 1795 poem *The Gin-Shop; or, A Peep into a Prison* in which she announced that:

> The State compels no man to drink,
> Compels no man to game;
> 'Tis GIN and gambling sink him down
> To rags, and want, and shame.
> The kindest husband, chang'd by Gin,
> Is for a tyrant known;
> The tenderest heart that nature made
> Becomes a heart of stone.

It became part of a series of one-penny tracts aimed at the ill-educated urban poor. Hannah More wrote three such 'Cheap repository Tracts' every month from 1795 to 1798 and enlisted other authors to contribute. The tracts were published simultaneously in Bath, London and Dublin and booksellers, news outlets and street hawkers were selling 300,000 copies a month in that first year, rising to a staggering two million copies in July 1796. Eventually, publication was taken over by a firm acting under the auspices of the SPCK. This continued until 1817 and thereafter various collected editions came out, until 1831.

Some would argue that whereas the tracts may have had a limited effect on the literate poor, they had a huge effect on the upper classes who acted as philanthropists, buying the tracts in bulk to be issued free of charge to the poor in their neighbourhood. It established a pattern of 'do-gooding' which meant that the inebriated poor were never again going to be allowed to fend for themselves. Their social superiors were on-hand to make sure that in future they were kept to the straight and narrow. The newly arrived middle classes were to be the moral arbiters of the Victorian Age.

Hannah More was not of course alone: the baton was picked up by George Cruikshank, caricaturist, who in 1829 brought out the first of a series of prints entitled *The Gin Shop*, shown at Plate 22. At one stage a heavy drinker, Cruikshank emerged as a satirist committed to supporting the Temperance Movement. The detail in *The Gin Shop* is worth looking at carefully – Cruikshank shows the visual pun of the family at the bar of the public house caught in a 'gin-trap'. The wife is forcing her baby to drink gin rather than mother's milk; the pretty barmaid is in fact a skeleton, holding up a painted mask; the Old Tom gin cask is shown as a coffin;

the figure of Death enters the room with a lantern and death rattle and is uttering the words 'I shall have them all dead drunk presently! They have nearly had their last glass.' The picture has four supports: the work-house, the mad-house, the gibbet and the gaol. The couple's children are drunk and the signs on the walls all refer to the perils of drink, with one marked 'The Spirit Vaults' on the extreme right showing the evil spirit emerging from the image of the alembic still.

Another George Cruikshank print entitled *The Gin Juggernath* is shown at Plate 20. The Juggernath (nowadays spelt juggernaut) depicts the worship of 'the great spirit of the age' i.e. gin. The huge wheeled statue is a representation of the Hindu deity Jaganath, whose followers would hurl themselves beneath the deity by way of self-sacrifice. By analogy, drinkers of gin are killing themselves by their devotion to the barrels of gin upon which the spirit rolls. Cruikshank went on to produce some ten thousand prints during a career that also included illustrating several of the novels by Charles Dickens, including *Sketches by Boz* and *Oliver Twist*. Increasingly, his works reflected his opposition to the drinking of spirits, and his illustrations were used by both the National Temperance Society and the Total Abstinence Society. In 1856, he was made vice president of the newly-formed National Temperance League.

These various temperance groups resulted in greater lobbying power and in 1835 when Parliament considered the whole question of drunkenness in society it interviewed dozens of individual proponents of teetotalism. The result of those interviews was the *Digest of Evidence before the Committee of Parliament on the extent, causes and consequences of Drunkenness*. The Committee took evidence from representatives of various Temperance Societies and made reference to the 1833 Convention held in Philadelphia and attended by 400 delegates, calling for prohibition. In the Convention's own words: 'It is the opinion of the Convention that the traffic in ardent spirits as a drink, and the use of it as such, are morally wrong and ought to be abandoned throughout the world'.

The committee reviewed the current level of gin consumption and availability. It also contained an analysis of the history of legislative measures taken in the previous century, commenting: 'Coxe, in his *Life of Walpole* .... says "The 1743 Act led to the usual proceedings of riot and violence, the clandestine sale of gin was continued in defiance of every restriction, the demand for penalties which the offenders were unable to pay, filled the prisons and by removing every restraint plunged them into courses more audaciously criminal." The committee also were told that after the 1743 Act, some 12000 people had been convicted within less than two years, of whom 500 had been fined £100 and 3000 had been fined £10 as an alternative to being sent to the Bridewell. They also heard that in 1733 the quantity of distilled low wines and spirits was 10,500000 gallons in England and Wales, increasing to 15,250,000 gallons in 1740 and 19,000,000 three years later, 'yet the population was but half the present number.'

There was an interesting exchange of words with a Mr Herapath:

> Questioner: 'During your residence in your present situation, has drunkenness increased much?' Answer; 'Yes, particularly among the lower classes.'

> Questioner: 'Are women as frequently in a state of intoxication as men? Answer: 'I really believe more.'

> Questioner: 'Are children occasionally seen in that condition too?' Answer: 'I have frequently seen them in that state by accompanying their parents to the gin-shop.'

> Questioner: 'The spirits are given them by their parents?' Answer: 'Yes, as if it were part of their food.'

The committee considered reports from temperance groups in Scotland and Ireland – countries where gin was not the main spirit of choice. It also considered the effect of prohibition on members of the armed forces. The Honourable Colonel Leicester Stanhope gave evidence that during his service he observed intemperance prevail among the British troops, it being 'very universal and leading to great crimes'. There were particular problems with members of the army serving in India. Perhaps unfamiliar with spirits when they enlisted, they were given daily drams during the long journey around the Cape to India, and when they arrived they received double dram rations. He said that 'the practice of compelling men to receive their drams is highly objectionable. To avoid being ridiculed by their more hardened comrades they gradually conquer their aversion ... and by degrees become professed dram-drinkers'.

The committee was told that perhaps three-quarters of all floggings carried out by the British army resulted directly from the actions of men who were intoxicated. Captain Brenton of the Royal Navy was asked 'Has the subject of intemperance of seamen attracted your attention?' To which he replied 'Certainly, for the last 46 years.' In his opinion drinking in hot climates was always fatal, and in cold climates, the men were totally debilitated 'and never worth half what a temperate man usually is'.

He referred to seeing men falling from the masthead and from the top-sail yards and mentioned a number of cases he had seen where boats had been upset and lives lost. It was his experience that there would be fifteen or sixteen men incapacitated through drink on the days that the grog allowance was distributed, leading to floggings the following day. In the end, he found the experience so harrowing, and the floggings so unproductive, that he discontinued the grog allowance, paid the men money in lieu, and watched the floggings diminish dramatically.

He also stated that he knew of many instances where fires on board had either started or spread as a result of drunkenness or had been caused by carelessness in holding a match near a barrel of spirits from which the bung had been removed, allowing inflammable vapours to escape. In fact, he held that spirituous liquors were more dangerous than gunpowder in terms of being a fire hazard and quoted a number of cases where ships such as the *St George* of eighty-four guns had been burned to the water in 1756, or the *Edgar* of seventy guns which had caught fire off Spithead or the *Ajax* of seventy-four guns which caught fire off the Dardanelles in 1806.

The Committee took evidence from a number of doctors, one of who asserted that 65% of his patients were suffering in one way or another from

'A Sketch from Nature.'

alcohol-related diseases, including in particular heart and liver disease. Asked whether the habit of drinking ardent spirits was more difficult to cure or to reclaim than the habit of drinking wine, he replied: 'I believe, speaking as a medical man, and as having paid some attention to the subject, that a man may confine himself to a moderate portion of beer, and a moderate allowance of wine ... but I believe it is utterly impossible for a man to confine himself to a moderate quantity of spirits.' Immoderate consumption of ardent spirits went hand-in-hand with illness and disease, leading the drinker into a lifestyle of sin and iniquity. And, just in case the link between drink and immorality was lost, the Committee was reminded of a toast recently given at a public dinner by an influential distiller: 'To the distillers' best friend – the poor whores of London'.

And so it went on for 138 pages, a catalogue of propaganda directed against drink in general and spirituous liquors in particular. It even ended with a 'plug' for anyone wanting to form their own temperance society – all that was needed was for an unspecified number of individuals to sign a pledge that they would 'Resolve to refrain from Distilled Spirit and Promote Temperance'. It is far from clear whether the parliamentary committee then commissioned representations from drinking clubs, distillers and gin palaces, in order to ensure a fair balance of views ...

Chapter 12

The Victorian Gin Palaces

It would not be long before gin would start to appear in print alongside a completely new word to the English language – cocktail. The first appearance of 'cock tail' (in an English newspaper) was in March 1798. That was in the *Morning Post and Gazetteer*, containing an imaginary inventory of money owed by politicians to a publican running the Axe and Gate tavern at the end of Downing Street. Among the tongue-in-cheek list of debtors was Mr Pitt, who owed him for 'two petit vers of L'huile de Venus, one ditto of perfeit amour, and one ditto 'cock tail' (vulgarly called 'ginger'). The article is not especially helpful – the writer uses the word 'vers' when he means 'verres' i.e. glasses. And to define 'cock tail' as 'ginger' makes little sense unless it referred to a drink made from fermented ginger, or possibly references the way that 'ginger' was used as a noun to denote a cock with red plumage and

THESE are the *Drinks* that are sold, night and day,
At the bar of the Gin-shop, so glittering and gay.

THESE are the *Customers*, youthful and old,
That drink the strong drinks which are sold night and day
At the bar of the Gin-shop, so glittering and gay.

Above left and above right: The Gin shop.

109

hence, by extension, any combination of spirits and mixers resulting in a red coloured liquid.

Another early use of the word was in a New Hampshire newspaper article published in *The Farmer's Cabinet* of 28 April 1803, where someone described the cure for his morning-after hangover as being when he 'Drank a glass of cocktail – excellent for the head; all sauntered away to see the girls; Miss – not up … Girls not so bright after dancing'.

In 1806, 'cocktail' went on to be defined in a New York publication called *The Balance and Columbian Repository* as being 'a stimulating liquor composed of any kind of sugar, water and bitters, vulgarly called a bittered sling'. But why 'cock tail'? There seem to be almost as many theories as there are actual cocktails. Try the fictitious Betsy Flanagan, bar-keeper, who adorned her mixed drinks with a feather. The story places her running a bar in Yorktown in 1779 after her husband had died in the American War of Independence. She supposedly served up portions of bracer, a popular spirit-based drink, with a tail feather taken from a cockerel belonging to a much-hated British neighbour. Having a cocktail thus became an act of patriotism. One problem with this version is that it first appeared in a work of fiction called *The Spy* written by James Fenimore Cooper in 1821, but has since been embroidered and re-issued as a factual account of a real event.

Instead, how about the bar in New Orleans which served its drinks in an egg cup, called in French a 'coquetier', shortened to 'cockatay'. Or, try the idea that a horse's tail was said to be 'cocked' if it was perky and raised up – a sign of spirit. Because this feature was much sought-after by horse buyers, unscrupulous vendors resorted to using a form of suppository made of pepper and ginger to ensure that their horse would be properly displayed. Pepper and ginger were universally used in punch, and in individual drinks made of mixed ingredients, and hence by extension, these perked up the drinker in the same way as a horse. A bit far-fetched? Try the suggestion that when a publican got down to the dregs in a cask he would put the cask to one side until he had several barrels containing what were termed 'tailings'. These would be decanted into one barrel, using a spigot called a cock. Poor people, who could never afford the drink in its premium form, would instead ask if they could buy the cocked tailings – in other words, a mixture. It is also possible that 'cock-tail' was a variant of 'cocked ale', in turn derived from 'cock ale' which Grose's *Dictionary of the Vulgar Tongue* defined as 'a provocative drink'. One version suggests that this 'provocative drink' was a mixture of spirits fed to fighting cocks in order to inflame them – with any leftovers being knocked back by the owner of the winning bird. Yet another possibility was that a 'cocked tail' was simply an expression meaning a mixture, something not entirely pure. We can perhaps disregard the idea that the word 'cocktail' derived from the Aztec Princess Xochitl, who apparently went around serving mixed drinks, or that it derived from 'kaketal', a West African word for a scorpion i.e. something with a sting in its tail. Perhaps it is best to forget the etymology and, as the Oxford English Dictionary suggests, simply accept that the origins of the word are lost in the mists of time.

By 1820 things had moved on from the dire scenes of seventy years earlier. The cities had not suddenly become sober, but they no longer resembled the description by Smollett, the eighteenth-century Scottish novelist, when he wrote that 'In these dismal caverns ('strong water shops') they (the poor) lay until they recovered some of their faculties and then they had recourse to this same mischievous potion'. Similarly, Lord Hervey had declared: 'Drunkenness of the common people was universal, the whole town of London swarmed with drunken people from morning till night'. The poverty and despair were still there, but it was less obvious, less 'out in the open' and more behind closed doors. Besides, there was a positive drive towards encouraging beer drinking, culminating in the Beerhouse Act of 1830. Ironically, it was so successful in promoting beer sales that it forced the gin distillers to open new outlets, to make their drink far more attractive than beer and to change how the nation knocked back its favourite tipple.

The Beerhouse Act of 1830 followed on from an Act of Parliament five years earlier which reduced the levy on spirits – originally at 11s 8¼d a gallon – by 40% in an effort to kill off smuggling. It was hoped that by cutting the rate of duty, illegal imports would dry up and the Exchequer would benefit from the revenue on increased quantities of legitimate spirits. The tax was lowered to seven shillings per gallon, making the spirit much more affordable to the urban poor. It worked fairly spectacularly, with the consumption of declared spirits going up from between 3.7 and 4.7 million gallons in the early 1820s to more than 7.4 million gallons by the end of the decade. In other words, it almost doubled in less than ten years. Beer consumption was static and things looked as if they might get out of hand, with a second gin craze on the horizon. Parliament's cure was surprising: the Beerhouse Act embraced the ideal of free trade by de-regulating the licensing of beer shops to an astonishing degree. Any rate-payer could apply for a licence to brew and sell beer on payment of an annual licence fee of two guineas. They did not need to own a pub, they merely had to be a rate-payer. At the same time, the rate of duty on beers and ciders was lowered. The result was that the price of a pint of beer dropped by 20% overnight. Within six months 24,000 new beer shops had sprung up and within eight years this figure had doubled.

Full-scale public houses also benefitted with numbers swelling from 51,000 in 1830 to 56,000 eight years later. In total, the number of licensed premises, pubs and beerhouses combined, had doubled in the decade.

Gin producers were not going to take this tide of ale lying down. The very mushrooming of 'home beerhouses' gave them a chance to differentiate themselves. They would not sell gin in places resembling homes, they would sell it in places resembling palaces. It coincided with a coming-together of numerous trends – in architecture, in building materials, in retail habits. The first department store had appeared in 1796 when Harding and Howell & Co opened in Pall Mall. In the first half of the nineteenth century, many more retailers followed suit, a fine example being the firm of Swan & Edgar who opened premises at the corner of Piccadilly Circus in 1848. All around, new-style retail shops were starting up, with large windows displaying the luxuries inside. Above all, changes in the production of glass meant that shop designers were no longer limited to small diamond-shaped window panes, separated by lead strips, or dozens of small rectangular glass panes within a sash frame, divided up by glazing bars. Instead, larger pieces of plate-glass were being rolled out, letting light into the interiors of modern retail outlets. The invention of polished plate-glass dated back two centuries but had reached England from France in 1773 when Ravenhead Glass started production. It involved casting the glass onto a flat iron table where it was allowed to cool before cutting, polishing and grinding took place. It was a process involving a high capital outlay, making the glass expensive, but the introduction of steam-powered machinery helped speed up the polishing and grinding process and it quickly caught on with the new trend in retail shops, pioneered by men such as Josiah Wedgwood.

The same improvements in the manufacture of larger glass panels led to a vogue for larger mirrors. Mirror glass had always been a luxury item and although the idea of coating glass with a tin and mercury amalgam to produce a mirrored, reflective surface had been known for several centuries it was an extremely skilled and dangerous process. However, in 1835, a German chemist called Justus von Liebig developed a way of coating the glass with a thin layer of metallic silver, by means of the chemical reduction of silver nitrate. Suddenly, larger mirrors could be produced at an affordable cost. They still looked expensive, especially when engraved or etched, but stuck behind a shelf full of bottles, or lining the back of the bar, they could be mightily effective. All they needed was a source of light to be reflected, and that is where the new-fangled gas lighting came in. No more flickering candles and dark, badly-lit corners; no more half-light with outsiders unable to look in. In its place, the gentle hiss of gas supplied courtesy of the discovery of an effective method of using gas derived from coal, by William Murdoch. Back in 1797 Murdoch had installed gas lighting in his home in Redruth, and subsequently installed lighting in factory premises in Preston, enabling the factory owner to operate on a shift system. Murdoch was a partner of James Watt and Matthew Boulton but try as he might, he was unable to persuade his partners that there was a commercial dimension to his discovery. It was left to the German engineer Friedrich Albrecht Winzer – known in Britain as Frederick Albert Windsor – to see its commercial possibilities. In 1807, he demonstrated the effectiveness of gas lighting by installing lamps down one side of Pall Mall. It caused a public sensation. Soon his company, the Westminster Gas Light and Coke Company, was constructing gas works and digging up streets to lay miles and miles of gas piping all around London. By 1819 there were 290 miles of pipework, serving over 50,000 burners. And many of those burners ended up … in the new emporiums selling gin. Throw in big windows, acres of polished mahogany bars, huge richly embellished mirrors and suddenly you had a building that was unmissable and glamorous – a veritable gilded palace. The interiors were lavishly decorated, and instead of a grumpy pot-man, the drinks were dispensed by attractive young women, drawing off the spirits in measured quantities from the gin barrels lining the bar.

The first gin palace was built in 1830 for a firm of wine merchants known as Messrs Thompson and Fearon. It was located at 94 Holborn Hill using premises adapted from a wine shop. The ostentatious design was prepared by J. B. Papworth between 1829 and 1832. Papworth was one of the founder members of the Royal Institute of British Architects (RIBA) and among his more famous commissions were whole areas of Regency Cheltenham, including the Lansdown Crescent and the Montpelier Pump-Room. In practice, the Holborn Hill premises only lasted until 1860, when they were pulled down to make way for the Holborn Viaduct, but when the premises first opened they created a real stir. As the Victorian writer Henry Viztelly wrote in his 1893 work entitled *Glances back through Seventy Years:*

> It was near Field Lane that the first London gin palace was built. The polished mahogany counters, the garish bar fittings, the smartly painted vats, inscribed 'Old Tom' and 'Cream of the Valley', the rows of showy bottles of noyau and other cordials, and above all the immense blaze of gas light within and without these buildings as soon as dusk set in, were all so many novelties and came as a vision of splendour to the besotted denizens of the neighbouring slums.

The place was run by Henry Bradshaw Fearon. Born in Ireland, he was a dissenter who was to become one of the founders of London University and who, some twelve years earlier, had published a book entitled *Sketches of America. A Narrative of a Journey of Five Thousand Miles through the Eastern and Western States of America*. Evidently, Mr Fearon was selling spirits for consumption both on and off the premises, as indicated by the fact that he features in an Old Bailey court case in 1835 involving the twenty-four-year-old Andrew Waters and a forged order for spirits. Waters was a porter who turned up at the Holborn Hill premises of Mr Fearon, wielding an order for two gallons of gin, two gallons of brandy and two gallons of rum to be delivered to the proprietor of the Union Pottery in Vauxhall. Well, it was a hot day, and pottery-making was obviously thirsty work. However, it later transpired that the order had been forged by Waters, who ended up transported to New South Wales, but the order is interesting because the case shows that it was perfectly normal trading practice for gin outlets to supply spirits in considerable quantities around the metropolis.

The early success of Thompson & Fearon's is demonstrated by an article in a publication called *The Gin Shop* which came out on Saturday 12 November 1836 and stated:

> Indeed, to such a height was the fame of Thompson's carried that it was almost looked upon as an omission of duty for a person journeying from Paddington to Bow, or from Highgate to Newington Butts, ... not to turn into that celebrated gin-shop, to taste one of the famed cordials, served from the fair hand of one of four handsome, sprightly and neatly-dressed young females, but of modest deportment. For retaining such was that establishment particularly noted. To receive it from such fair hands appeared to enhance the value of the dram, led to an after-conversation among friends and a recommendation to go and do likewise.

While the men went in order to chat up the barmaids, women wanted to go in to see what all the fuss was about and in order to see what the barmaids were wearing. The instant success of the gin palaces apparently led to a rush to convert existing public houses. *The Gin Shop* continued:

> Public houses began to be ransacked and turned into Gin-shops. The mania spread like a contagion; each one seemed to infect a dozen more; they became regularly trained into a system ...

a system which soon became a most prolific monster planting its deformed and insatiate brood at every turn.

But *The Gin Shop* also warned of the death and degradation associated with these new outlets, writing:

> Instances are not wanting where the dram-drinking propensity has been allowed, and indeed, fatally encouraged. In the early part of the current year [1836] a victim fell lifeless in a Palace near Golden Square, and vast numbers linger out a miserable existence in degradation and poverty, from the effects of the poisonous liquor…

It was not the only fatality: at the Rose & Crown in Gilbert Street in the 1840s, the premises were destroyed when an error meant that gin was pumped into the rubber piping linked to the gas lights, instead of the pipework leading to the barrels displayed by the bar. The result: a huge explosion which meant the end of the Rose & Crown gin palace, and the death of a handful of unfortunate locals.

A second London gin palace had been opened, known as Weller's, in Old Street and this was followed by dozens more soon afterwards, so that by 1852 there were estimated to be over five thousand such premises in London alone. Even at the time of the 1835 *Parliamentary Report on Drunkenness* there were stated to be more premises selling gin than there were bakers, butchers and fishmongers put together. There was a particular reference to 'public houses in the East End of London which had long rooms attached to them capable of containing from 100 to 300 persons, and were frequented by the worst characters, some of them being open at all hours of the night, crowded with sailors, crimps and prostitutes, who frequently rob the unsuspecting sailor while intoxicated'. Other testimony presented to the committee included a statement from a Mr Twells, who recalled visiting the White Conduit House at Islington where, he stated, 'I once made it an object of curiosity to go: I am not now clear, but I think there were between 4,000 and 5,000 persons on a Sunday evening.' The scale of operations revealed to the Committee were alarming, with a Mr White commenting that he owned a shop where there were no fewer than nine gin palaces within a radius of 150 yards of his premises. His estimate was that each and every one of those gin palaces took more than £20,000 per year, for spirits consumed on the premises.

One of the men giving evidence to the parliamentary committee was a Mr Benjamin Braidley who had monitored the comings and goings at one particular spirits emporium, over eight separate occasions during the evening. He noted that people were entering at the rate of 412 people an hour, with only a third of them being male. He also noted that there appeared to be no shame attached to entering the gin palaces and that 'latterly, the blaze of light from the window of the dram-shop has been much greater, and it is pursued much more openly as a trade and calling than before'.

These edifices designed for the sale of gin cost many thousands of pounds to fit out and there was considerable obfuscation as to who was putting up the money. It is safe to assume that the distillers themselves were investing heavily in the new buildings, but the proprietors kept their involvement hidden from public view, rarely appearing except perhaps to collect their takings. In 1838, the *Morning Chronicle* ran an article complaining about 'the gin-seller, who drives up to his establishment in his four-wheel chaise, and who leaves the spinning of his gin and the gathering of his large profits to his bar-maids'. It was echoing the comment in *The Gin Shop,* published in 1836, which refers to 'the four-wheel double-seated phaeton, with the Hundred-Guinea horse, kept for the recreation and pleasure of the Old Tom family'.

Converting an existing public house into a minor gin emporium might cost £2,000, but a fine new building could cost five times as much – a vast capital outlay. If the money was underwritten by the distillers themselves it had its parallel in the brewing trade, where more and more public houses were tied to the major breweries. However, the only way that the distillers could make money twice over – by manufacturing the spirits for sale to the gin shops and then selling them from those same shops to the general public – was to water down the spirits to a considerable degree. The dilution of the neat spirits was masked by the addition of fruit cordials and it has been estimated that 50% of the liquor was actually … water.

Sadly, none of the early gin palaces exist in London in their original form, although some have been lovingly recreated and restored with elaborately carved wooden fittings and glittering tiles and mirrors, as in The Princess Louise on High Holborn. It was actually built in 1872 and even the urinals are protected by being listed as being of architectural importance. The premises retain the style of an original gin palace, as does the Princess Victoria in Uxbridge Road which dates from 1829. The Salisbury in St Martin's Lane was not built until after the gin palaces had passed into history, but the quality and opulence of the etched and polished glass and the carved woodwork is certainly reminiscent of the earlier palaces.

Outside London, restored premises originally built as gin palaces include the Philharmonic Dining Rooms in Liverpool and Baker's Vaults in Stockport, where the underground vaults still retain the brick stalls designed to hold the barrels of gin. In Northern Ireland, there is the newly-restored Crown Liquor Saloon, also known as the Crown Bar, in Belfast's Great Victoria Street. Dating from 1826, it claims to be an outstanding example of a Victorian gin palace, is owned by the National Trust and is leased to Mitchells & Butlers who run it as a Nicholson's pub.

An idea of what the interiors of these palaces were like is shown in *Sketches by Boz*, published by Charles Dickens in 1836 but first appearing in a newspaper article in the Evening Chronicle of 19 February 1835:

> The primary symptoms were an inordinate love of plate-glass and a passion for gas-lights and gilding ... The extensive scale on which these places are established, and the ostentatious manner in which the business of even the smallest among them is divided into branches, is amusing. ... Then, ingenuity is exhausted in devising attractive titles for the different descriptions of gin; and the dram-drinking portion of the community as they gaze upon the gigantic black and white announcements, which are only to be equalled in size by the figures beneath them, are left in a state of pleasing hesitation between 'The Cream of the Valley,' 'The Out and Out,' 'The No Mistake,' 'The Good for Mixing,' 'The real Knock-me-down,' 'The celebrated Butter Gin,' 'The regular Flare-up,' and a dozen other, equally inviting and wholesome LIQUEURS.
>
> Although places of this description are to be met with in every second street, they are invariably numerous and splendid in precise proportion to the dirt and poverty of the surrounding neighbourhood. The gin-shops in and near Drury-Lane, Holborn, St. Giles's, Covent-garden, and Clare-market, are the handsomest in London. There is more of filth and squalid misery near those great thorough-fares than in any part of this mighty city. We will endeavour to sketch the bar of a large gin-shop, and its ordinary customers, for the edification of such of our readers as may not have had opportunities of observing such scenes; and on the chance of finding one well suited to our purpose, we will make for Drury-Lane, through the narrow streets and dirty courts which divide it from Oxford-street, and that classical spot adjoining the brewery at the bottom of Tottenham-court-road, best known to the initiated as the 'Rookery.'

Dickens noticed that the more brilliantly-lit buildings were constructed nearest the poorest, most densely populated and dilapidated areas of town:

> ... All is light and brilliancy. The hum of many voices issues from that splendid gin-shop which forms the commencement of the two streets opposite; and the gay building with the fantastically ornamented parapet, the illuminated clock, the plate-glass windows surrounded by stucco rosettes, and its profusion of gas-lights in richly-gilt burners, is perfectly dazzling when contrasted with the darkness and dirt we have just left. The interior is even gayer than the exterior. A bar of French-polished mahogany, elegantly carved, extends the whole width of the place; and there are two side-aisles of great casks, painted green and gold, enclosed within a light brass rail, and bearing such inscriptions as 'Old Tom, 549;' 'Young Tom, 360;' 'Samson, 1421' - the figures agreeing, we presume, with 'gallons,' understood. Beyond the bar is a lofty and spacious saloon, full of the same enticing vessels, with a gallery running round it, equally well furnished. On the counter, in addition to the usual spirit apparatus, are two or three little baskets of cakes and biscuits, which are carefully secured at top with wicker-work, to prevent their contents being unlawfully abstracted. Behind it, are two showily-dressed damsels with large necklaces, dispensing the spirits and 'compounds.' They are assisted by the ostensible proprietor of the concern, a stout, coarse fellow in a fur cap, put on very much on one side to give him a knowing air, and to display his sandy whiskers to the best advantage.

It is worth remembering that this description of gin parlours was written by a man who was a keen gin-drinker, a devoted mixer of cocktails and someone who kept a well-stocked cellar. A list, hand-written by Dickens, of the contents of his cellar in 1865 included one fifty-gallon cask of ale, one eighteen-gallon cask of gin, a nine-gallon cask of brandy and a nine-gallon cask of rum. This was in addition to copious quantities of fine wine and champagne. Writing to his editor William Henry Wills, Dickens asked 'I am impatient to know how the Gin Punch succeeded with you, it is the most wonderful beverage in the world'. On another occasion he left written instructions to his butler, insisting that pre-dinner drinks were kept to a minimum ('At supper, let there be a good supply of champagne all over the table. No champagne before supper, and as little wine as possible, of any sort, before supper') but adding that his servants were 'to keep gin punch in ice under the table, all evening, and to give it only to myself or Mr Lemon'. Mr Lemon was the editor of *Punch* magazine, and as such was his employer. In his 1980 book *Drinking with Dickens*, the writer's great-grandson Cedric Dickens set out the family gin punch recipe. It involved simmering for half an hour over a medium heat the following ingredients:

> Two cups of gin,
> Two cups of sweet Madeira wine,
> One tablespoon of dark brown sugar,
> The peel and juice of one lemon and one orange,
> A whole peeled, cored and sliced pineapple,
> Three whole cloves,
> Three cinnamon sticks and a pinch of ground nutmeg.

Other writers refer to the panoply of names by which different types and flavours of gin were sold, as in Max Schlesinger's *Saunterings in and about London*, written in 1853:

> But the gin-palaces are the lions of Drury-lane ; they stand in conspicuous positions, at the corners and crossings of the various intersecting streets. They may be seen from afar, and are lighthouses which guide the thirsty "sweater" on the road to ruin.
>
> For they are resplendent with plate-glass and gilt cornices, and a variety of many-coloured inscriptions. One of the windows displays the portrait of the "NORFOLK GIANT," who acts as barman to this particular house; the walls of another establishment inform you, in green letters, that here they sell "THE ONLY REAL BRANDY IN LONDON," and a set of scarlet letters announces to the world, that in this house they sell "THE FAMOUS CORDIAL MEDICATED GIN, WHICH IS SO STRONGLY RECOMMENDED BY THE FACULTY." Cream Gin, Honey Gin, Sparkling Ale, Genuine Porter; and other words calculated utterly to confound a tee-totaller, are painted up in conspicuous characters, even so that they cover the door-posts.

Schlesinger continues with a description of the sad and depressing scene inside the gin palaces, contrasting with the bright lighting illuminating the scene:

> It is a remarkable fact, that the houses which are most splendid from without, appear most dismal and comfortless from within. The landlord is locked up behind his "bar," a snug place enough, with painted casks and a fire and an arm-chair; but the guests stand in front of the bar in a narrow dirty place, exposed to the draught of the door, which is continually opening and shutting. Now and then an old barrel, flung in a corner, serves as a seat. But nevertheless the "palace" is always crowded with guests, who, standing, staggering, crouching, or lying down, groaning, and cursing, drink and forget…. To provide against the Sunday, he takes a supply of fire-water on Saturday evening when he has received his week's wages, for with the stroke of twelve the sabbath shuts the door of all public-houses, and on Sunday-morning the beer or brandy paradise must not open before one o'clock in the afternoon, to be closed again from three to five. Hence that unsacred stillness which weighs down upon Drury-lane on Sunday-mornings. The majority of the inhabitants sleep away their intoxication or *ennui*. Old time-worn maudlin-ness reigns supreme in the few faces which peer from the half-opened street-doors; maudlin-ness pervades the half-sleepy groups which surround the public-house at noon to be ready for its opening; chronic maudlin-ness. pervades the atmosphere. And if a stray ray of light break through the clouds, it falls upon the frowsy loungers and the dim window-panes in a strange manner, as though it had no business there.

Somehow you might expect the interior to be a convivial meeting place but what actually comes across is a conveyor belt of lonely individuals moving in single file, pennies in hand, barely conversing except to ask for their favourite tipple by name, knocking it back in one and then leaving by a door at the end of the bar. In *Low-Life Deeps – A Night with Old Tom'* written by James Greenwood in 1875, there is this description:

> It is curious to watch the accomplished dram drinker's peculiar method of procedure. Urgent as is his want, of all drinkers who approach the metal counter he is least demonstrative. He will flit in, usually behind some other customer who has pushed

open the door, and his quick eyes detecting the thinnest part of the crowd, there he edges his way. He has the money all ready in his hand, and catching the barmaid's eye he ejaculates as hurriedly as though he had not a moment to spare, "Glass of Old Tom." In seven seconds the liquor is drawn, the vessel raised to his pale lean jaws, and with a sudden gulp, such as ordinarily attends the swallowing of a pill, it is gone. Three pence disposed of as rapidly as a conjurer could twitch a halfpenny from his hand up into his sleeve, and with what profit to the investor? Mighty little to judge from his appearance. There is so little to feel grateful for that he does not even lick his dry lips, nor does the merest twinkle in his leaden eyes denote that he has obtained what he bargained for. He feels no thrilling of his nerves, no gush of warmth in his veins, - he is as horribly sober as ever, and mean, miserable, despairing wretch that he is, with one quick glance of malignant envy on the mirthful beer-drinking crew about him, he vanishes stealthily as he came, to make a "call" at the next of Old Tom's renowned abiding places, and the next, and still the next; as long as he has threepence left or the "houses" remain open. Then, his aim still unattained, he will slink home to that terrible bed, and troubled and dream-haunted, and filled with heat which yields no warmth to his shaking limbs, lay and quake until morning.

Various suggestions have been put forward for the origin of the name 'Old Tom'. Simon Difford, who writes the informative online *Difford's Guide*, identifies two men called Thomas who worked in the gin trade with Hodges, distillers in Church Street, Lambeth. The younger one was Thomas Norris, called 'Young Tom' to distinguish him from his mentor Thomas Chamberlain, aka 'Old Tom'. When Young Tom left to run a gin palace at Great Russell Street in London's Covent Garden he would buy in barrels of gin from Hodges, and took to marking one particular, sweetened, gin with the name of Old Tom as a tribute to the man to whom he was originally apprenticed, and to distinguish that particular gin from other flavoured spirits supplied by Hodges. It all sounds rather more plausible than other suggestions – that this gin got its name from the time a cat fell into the distilling tank, or that it was in some way named after the coin-in-the-slot cat used by Captain Bradstreet nearly a century earlier. Whatever the origin, the name 'Old Tom' was widely used and generally features in eighteenth-century caricatures and drawings featuring gin palaces.

The soul-less, soul-destroying and often solitary aspect of the way the gin palaces operated amazed many onlookers. Henry Bradshaw Fearon, the proprietor of that very first gin palace, commented that eight out of ten of his customers would drink a penny's worth of gin 'in less than a minute' – and then leave. As another observer put it in 1831: 'Every minute the door opens, and some slide in, and some slide out, without saying a word to each other'. No chairs were provided and no attempt was made to encourage conviviality. If you wanted to play shove ha'penny or read a newspaper, you went to a public house and ordered a pint of beer; if you wanted company, to smoke a pipe and have a chat, you avoided the gin palaces. They were for people who did not know each other, did not belong to the local community, and did not want the experience of having a shot of spirits to take up either time or effort. They wanted an intoxicant that could blind them to the miseries of life at work and at home, the quicker the better.

The growth in the number of gin palaces was not a phenomenon confined to London. J. Ewing Ritchie, in *Studies at the Bar in 1880* writes:

> But what is to be done? The publican, whether he keeps a gin-palace or a refreshment bar, must push his trade. The total number of public-houses, beershops, and wine-houses in the Metropolitan Parliamentary boroughs is 8,973, or one to each 333 persons. This is bad; but Newcastle-on-Tyne is worse, having one public-house to 160 inhabitants, and Manchester has one to every 164 inhabitants. The amount paid in license-fees by publicans in the Metropolitan district last year amounted to £108,316; the total for the kingdom being £1,133,212. But great as is the number of these places, the trade flourishes. A licensed house in one of the finest parts of London (Bethnal Green), lately sold for upwards of £22,000. Another, a third or fourth rate house in North London, sold for £18,000; other licensed houses sell for £30,000, £40,000, £50,000, and even more. As to the refreshment bars, it lately came out in evidence that a partner in one of the firms most connected with them stated his income to be £40,000 a year. It is said one firm, whose business is chiefly devoted to refreshment bars, pays its wine merchants as much as £1,000 a week.

What is clear is that the gin palaces appeared as beacons of welcoming light across the land, particularly in the towns enjoying rapid growth such as Liverpool, Manchester, Leeds and Hull. But it was in London that the palaces proliferated, with the largest fourteen of them serving half a million customers each and every week. However, various factors meant that the future lay not with the gin palaces but with the public houses. In part, the profit margins on the sale of gin were too small to justify the overheads. In part, there were simply too many palaces, more than could be supported by the local population. In part, it was because the general public houses, selling a mixture of beers, wines and spirits, raised their game and offered surroundings that matched the palaces. Elaborate bar fittings and opulent mirrors – indeed the whole package which might be described as 'the bright lights' – were now installed in a conventional public house setting. Partly it was because the standard of living increased throughout the century until men and women could afford to do more than simply line up for their dose of instant intoxication. Instead, they could afford to experience something infinitely more satisfying: pub culture. The chance to meet others, to chat, to relax, to sit down and play games such as dominoes, or darts, or skittles was far more alluring than simply imbibing alcohol.

The Gin Shop.

Chapter 13

Distillers, Developments – and the Dirty Martini

It is easy to think that gin production in the Victorian era was entirely based in England. It wasn't, it was a worldwide industry. In Belgium, there had been a ban on distilling, which lasted for 112 years but which ended in 1713. Belgian distillers soon looked to make up for lost time, while their neighbours in Holland increased the production of gin by 400% between 1733 and 1792. English exports of sweetened gin (Old Tom) to the former colonies in America gradually increased in the early 1800s especially after 1850 with the abolition of duty on exported gin. The first time that a London-style (unsweetened) gin was produced in the United States was still a long way off, with the Fleischmann Brothers Distillery not opening – in Ohio – until 1870.

Meanwhile, on the other side of the world, in the Philippines, two gentlemen thought that there might be a market for a distilled juniper-flavoured spirit amongst the European settlers, particularly the Dutch merchants trading in the area from their stronghold in Batavia (modern-day Jakarta). They were Antonio Ayala and Domingo Roxas and in 1834 they started distilling gin, using a base spirit derived not from grain but from sugar cane. Once the Coffey still reached the Philippines, production soared. It may taste like fire-water to modern British and American tastes, but the Filipino gin, known as Ginebre San Miguel de Ayala, was no flash in the pan. It became synonymous with Filipino culture, deeply embedded in the national psyche. How else do you explain how the company formed by Messrs Ayala and Roxas developed into Ayala y Cia, and then eventually into Ginebra San Miguel Inc., the largest gin producer in the world? With its logo of Saint Michael (San Miguel) slaying the dragon, it is the main product of the company which also manufactures rum, vodka and brandy. Not heard of it? Well, you should: Filipinos drink more gin per capita than anyone else in the world, and their favourite tipple is GSM. In fact, the company accounts for around 43% of all gin sales worldwide. Perhaps you thought that the

A nineteenth-century still house from the gallery.

title of 'World's best-selling gin' was held by Gordons, but it is a midget compared with GSM, who in 2019 sold 30 million nine-litre packs, more than four times the total for Gordons.

No doubt, sales in the Philippines are helped by the fact that their gin costs the same price per litre as beer. It is identified with Filipino success, a symbol of national pride. It is also promoted to an astonishing degree with a significant percentage of the profits swallowed up in advertising, in sponsorship and in merchandising. Filipinos regard drinking GSM as being macho, healthy and giving physical strength, no doubt partly due to the qualities associated with the game of basketball. This is one of the most popular sports in the country and one of their top teams goes by the name of Barangay Ginebra San Miguel. They are by far the most popular team in the Philippine Basketball Association Premier League, and are thirteen-times championship winners. No matter that one set of tasting notes for the drink describes it as 'rough and thin' and sums it up as having an 'acrid, chemical, after-taste reminiscent of inexpensive vodka'. The average Filipino will not be put off by such disparagement: they like their drink, and if you don't, that's your problem! Another taste report concluded that it was 'best drunk with a mixer' and even Filipinos tend to prefer it when knocked back with pomelo juice (a type of citrus fruit, similar to a small grapefruit). Perhaps 'ginpo', as it is known, can disguise the fact that to Western taste buds, we are talking about a fairly unsophisticated form of moonshine.

While the distillation of spirits from sugar cane was taking place in the Philippines in the 1830s, great changes were becoming apparent in the UK market, linked to the invention of what became known as the Coffey still. Named after a French-born Irishman called Aeneas Coffey it revolutionised the production of spirits. Away went the old batch method of production and in its place came a continuous production process giving a cleaner, purer, spirit than ever before. It had the added advantage that condensed liquids could be drawn off separately at different stages in the production, meaning that a skilful distiller had much more control over the end-flavours. It also meant a much larger-scale production of spirits was possible and these spirits can be of a much higher ABV – in fact, up to 95% ABV. The Coffey still, also known as a column still, is used in most bigger distilleries, whether for the production of gin, rum or whisky, although some distillers make a point of retaining their old pot stills for particular special-edition spirits.

When using the Coffey still, steam is brought into the lower part of the still as a heat source. The steam then rises up through the numerous chambers inside the still. The wash is introduced near the top of the column and runs down through the chambers as a liquid, but as it gets hotter because of the steam, the ethanol is heated, evaporates and rises back up, condensing and evaporating at each stage. This multiple evaporation and condensing results in a purer spirit. Nearly all the water and many of the congeners (chemical components which give a distinctive character to the spirit) are drawn off and the resulting pure spirit is led through a condensing chamber and into a collection vessel.

In fairness to various other distillers, particularly a Scotsman called Robert Stein, Coffey did not invent the column still 'out of the blue' as it was the culmination of a series of improvements made by distillers of different nationalities in the first twenty-five years of the century. The German Heinrich Pistorius had come up with a method of distilling alcohol from potato mash in a continuous operation patented in 1817, while in Ireland a whisky distillery was adapted by Sir Anthony Perrier to use a series of partitions allowing the wash to move gradually and continuously over the heat. The method was patented in 1822. In the following year, the Frenchman Jean-Jacques St. Marc came to England to obtain finance for his 'Patent Distillery Company' aiming to distil potato brandy. The venture failed but St. Marc developed a continuous distillation apparatus which he patented and took back to France. It was left to Robert Stein to take things a stage further, with the development of a continuous process whereby the wash was fed through a series of inter-connecting pots. Steam was used to power pistons which forced the vapours produced by evaporation into a horizontal cylinder. It was a big step forward but could only be used to produce an ABV of around 60%. It used less fuel than other systems and was therefore cheaper to run, but it needed to be stopped regularly to allow for cleaning. Nevertheless, it was adopted by several major distillers of whisky in Scotland after Stein took out a patent in 1827.

When Coffey submitted his patent application in 1830 he set out what he saw as the three improvements attributable to his invention. Firstly, it forced the wash to pass rapidly through a series of pipes of small diameter, during which time it acquires heat. Secondly, it caused the wash, after it had come in contact with the vapours, to flow into a continued and uninterrupted stream over numerous metallic plates, furnished with valves. Thirdly, it introduced a means of ascertaining whether or not all of the alcohol had been drawn off from the wash 'whereby the vapour to be tried undergoes a process of analyzation or rectification, and is deprived of much of its aqueous part before it is submitted to trial'.

It caught on gradually, especially once further improvements came along such as a steam regulator (1852). By then Coffey had been able to give up distilling in his own right and concentrate entirely on building and selling distillery equipment to others. From then on, major distilleries throughout the world have installed stills based on the Coffey design, although ironically in his home country of Ireland, whisky producers preferred the older, less efficient, pot stills.

However pure the spirit may have been when it left the distillery, it was unlikely to be in the same state when it reached the public. In the days when gin was sold in casks, not bottles, it was not just easy for the publican to 'doctor' the spirits, it was positively encouraged so that the gin reflected the tastes of the local population. It has been estimated that only one in four gin drinkers in the first part of the century wanted 'dry' gin. The vast majority wanted their gin sweetened. It is worth remembering that there were no rules as to the strength at which gin could be sold, and as the writer W. R. Loftus said in his 1869 book on mixing and reducing spirits:

> the character of the compounded liquors … is changed. The gin and the 'ratafia' of our forefathers are unknown to us except by name. The taste of the public demands an article

very dissimilar in flavour and composition to that which once
pleased it … The nauseous and hurtful drugs that used to be
added to the contents of the still would not be now tolerated.

Loftus defined proof as 'any spirit which weighs twelve thirteenths of the
weight of an equal bulk of water at the same temperature' and went on to
say that 'every spirit weaker than the standard is said to be so many degrees
per cent Under Proof, or U.P'. He explained that 100 gallons of spirit at
20% **over** proof are equivalent to 120 gallons of proof spirit, whereas
100 gallons at 20% **under** proof are equivalent to only 80 gallons of proof
spirit – a comparison which showed the importance of the retailer relying
on his hydrometer to assess exactly what he was buying. There was no legal
maximum or minimum and having bought the spirit the retailer was then
free to reduce it or modify it however he wished.

Loftus then set out guidance as to amounts to be used. Spirit was
generally supplied to the retailer at 17 or 22% 'Under Proof' but would
then be watered down to 30 or 40% Under Proof. Loftus quoted from an
article in *The Lancet* which tested the proof of gin on sale in thirty-eight
different trade outlets in London. One was selling gin at a massive 60%
Under Proof – hardly stronger than a good ale, and Loftus was convinced
that the only way for that particular publican to disguise the weakness of
the brew was by adulterating it with something to give it an artificial kick.

Adding sugar – usually in the form of sugar syrup known as capillaire,
meant two things: firstly it meant that it was then impossible for the proof
of the spirit to be measured by a hydrometer, because the instrument would
always be fooled by the sugar; and secondly the syrup itself diluted the gin.
Typically, four gallons of capillaire (each gallon containing eight pounds
of dissolved loaf sugar) would be added to every one hundred gallon cask,
thereby increasing the volume of gin available to be sold by 4%. The same
sample of gin suppliers analysed in *The Lancet* showed that some were
retailing gin with over eight ounces of sugar per gallon – in other words,
adding fifty pounds of sugar to every 100 gallons. If you really liked your
gin sweet, you needed to head for one of the poorer parishes in town, such
as St Giles, and visit the premises of R Sinclair in the High Street. He ladled
in more than thirteen ounces of sugar to every gallon. More sugar meant not
just a greater quantity of gin – but also bigger profit margins, since sugar
was comparatively cheap. The problem was that the gin then lacked 'bite'.
This was a shortcoming easily remedied by the addition of caustic soda or
a few slices of horseradish (which Loftus favoured) or by cayenne pepper,
which he did not.

RESULTS OF THE EXAMINATION OF 38 SAMPLES OF LONDON GIN OBTAINED FROM RECTIFIERS, SPIRIT DEALERS, AND RETAILERS.			
NAME.	Place of Business.	Strength under Proof.	Quantity of Sugar per Gal.
1 Bowerbank & Sons	77½, Sun-st., Bishopsgate-st.	29	Unswet.
2 J. & J. Vickers & Co.	Stoney-st., Borough	14	do.
3 Hodges & Co.	Church-st. Lambeth	15	5½ oz.
4 J. Bell	25, Cable-st., Whitechapel	54	4½ „
5 Rose & Matthews	4, Wells-st., Whitechapel	28	5½ „
6 R. Skipper	Cable-st.	37	5 „
7 W. Coates & Co.	25, High-st., Whitechapel	28	7½ „
8 D. Morton	2, Whitechapel-road	30	6½ „
9 F. Gunge	66, Cable-st.	40	5½ „
10 J. Hancock	11, Somerset Place, Aldgate	31	4½ „
11 J. Brown	30, High-st., Whitechapel	31	5½ „
12 W. Freshwater	Back church-lane, Whitchpl.	39	4½ „
13 J. Williams	45. High-st. Whitechapel	37	5½ „
14 J. Brand	77, Leman-st., Whitechapel	39	6½ „
15 J. Colliss	King-st, Smithfield	40	6½ „
16 M. Chance	66, Long Lane, Smithfield	37	8½ „
17 J. Champion	33½, Gray's Inn Lane	42	5½ „
18 G. Stockdell	78, Gray's Inn Road	55	5½ „
19 J. Young	72, High Holborn	41	6 „
20 J. Denyer	15, High-st., St. Giles	37	4 „
21 W. Latimer	47, Broad-st., St. Giles	39	4½ „
22 R. Sinclair	36, High.st., St Giles	28	13½ „
23 H. Cusack	6, Tottenham-court-road	31	5½ „
24 W. Cripps	1, Newport Market	39	5½ „
25 W. Tillyard	19, Moor-st., Soho	43	4½ „
26 W. Moss	Seven Dials	27	5½ „
27 G. A. Compton	84, Edgware-road	32	6½ „
28 Walker & Co.	63, Westminster-bridge-road	30	9½ „
29 C. Watchorn	1, Marsh Gate, Lambeth	26	6½ „
30 J. Empson	107, Lambeth Marsh	39	5 „
31 T. Grammar	Waterloo-road	28	7½ „
32 W. Jorden	52, Tothill-st., Westminster	58	3½ „
33 W. Carpenter	11, King-st., Westminster	35	7½ „
34 W. Vickress	11, Bridge-st., Westminster	28	8 „
35 H. Bennell	High-road, Knightsbridge	61	6 „
36 W. Weatherbey	Knightsbridge	44	4 „
37 I. Upton	Hemmings-row, Charing-crs.	44	5½ „
38 T. West	9, Bear-st., Leicester square	37	5½ „

Extract from the findings in *The Lancet* referred to in Loftus's New Mixing and Reducing Book.

Adding sugar and water often made the mixture cloudy. Loftus recommended fining with alum (i.e. aluminium sulphate) and either potassium carbonate or carbonate of soda. He does however warn against the use of 'sugar of lead' – in other words, lead acetate. He knew it to be highly poisonous but the fact that Loftus mentions it suggests that in the previous century it was often used. And it is worth remembering that many experts believe that the composer Ludwig van Beethoven may have died from lead poisoning caused by drinking wine sweetened with sugar of lead. One side effect of this type of long-term exposure to lead is slowly progressive hearing loss – something which Beethoven suffered from after the age of twenty-eight. He died in 1827 when he was fifty-six years old. Technically illegal, sugar of lead had been used to sweeten wine since

Roman times but as Loftus said: 'nothing can justify the employment of even small quantities of so fearful a poison as sugar of lead'.

If the gin was discoloured, Loftus suggested that it should be mixed with pounded chalk, vinegar and isinglass (obtained by drying swim bladders from fish). Really bad discolouration could be cured by filtering through charcoal, although it might be necessary to add back some flavour by adding a few drops of essential oils such as oil of juniper, coriander and carraway. You want your gin to taste creamy? Add garlic, Strasburg turpentine or Canadian balsam. Your gin is so watered down that it no longer has a 'bead' or meniscus ring at the top of the gin where it touches the side of the glass? Fool your customers by adding oil of vitriol. Nowadays it is known as sulphuric acid ...

Another refining agent recommended by Loftus was nitric acid. For every 100 gallons of spirit, he recommended adding two ounces of nitric acid, plus oil of almonds but with the advice that 'it is necessary to be careful not to use more than the assigned quantity of this oil which in the least excess is apt to produce unpleasant if not poisonous effects'.

The view of Lotus was that gin drinkers wanted 'a pleasant warming aromatic taste or smack' as opposed to a simple alcoholic strength. Spirits which had been over-watered-down could therefore be perked up by the addition of chillies and cassia bark – Loftus approved of this and did not reckon it amounted to adulteration. It all sounds as if the retailer of gin needed to have the skills of a chemist and is a reminder of just how uncontrolled the spirits industry was in the Victorian era.

There was however one outlet where gin was always of a recognised strength and that was when it was used by the Navy. The reason given for this is that the gin, being inflammable, had to be stored in a safe place alongside the equally inflammable kegs of gunpowder. There was always a danger that barrels could get staved in as the ship rolled and it was important that if the gin spilt onto the gunpowder it would not prevent the gunpowder from being used. The sailors knew that this could easily happen if the gin had been diluted with water, so, in order to 'prove' that the gin was inflammable, they would place a few grains of gunpowder on a flat surface, then dribble gin onto the powder. Using a magnifying glass, the rays of the sun would be directed onto the mixture. As it heated the powder would either go off with a bang – in which case it was over proof, or with a quiet 'phut' – in which case it was proof. Fail to ignite and it was below proof, and hence would not be allowed on board.

Prior to the 1816 invention of the hydrometer by Bartholomew Sikes, this was the only way of testing the strength of spirits. Sikes was employed as an Excise Officer and after years of experimentation came up with a simple alcoholometric test. The hydrometer was floated in the sample being tested, giving a reading; by taking the temperature of the sample and then consulting a set of tables, the strength of the spirit could be accurately ascertained. It was a method used by HM Excise right up until 1980.

Historically, responsibility for testing was held by the Purser, known in naval parlance as the pusser. Pusser's rum and pusser's gin are names that are still in use today. The Navy being the Navy, they did not accept the definition of proof set down by Sikes – he accepted 100% proof as being just over 57% alcohol by volume, whereas the Royal Navy determined 'Navy Strength' as being 54.5% alcohol by volume.

It must be stressed: gin was never officially part of the alcohol allowance favoured by the Royal Navy. Rum was the drink of the British tar, and had been since the capture of Jamaica in 1655. Gin, on the other hand, was the drink of choice for the officers and back in 1793, the Plymouth distillery had secured the right to supply Navy Strength Gin. It meant that while the Able Seamen were knocking back their half a pint of rum every day the officers were drinking their own supplies of gin. How they must have wished they were in the Dutch Navy, which in 1864 dished out a generous gin ration three times a day, equivalent to a fifth of a bottle of Over Proof genever each and every day of the voyage. This was doled out not just to the European sailors, but also to 'African and Ambonese non-commissioned officers and troops, and for European women'.

It was thought that spirits, such as gin, were pure and that this purity could cure diseases such as malaria and scurvy. Royal Navy ships were therefore equipped with a wooden box containing two bottles of Navy Strength Gin together with appropriate glasses from which it could be drunk. This was called a Plymouth Gin Commissioning Kit. Initially, sailors were given lemon juice to ward off scurvy but this was replaced with a daily lime ration – giving rise to the expression 'limeys' to describe British sailors. When Rose's Lime cordial became popular this was seen as a simple way of introducing vitamin C to the diet, especially after Rear-Admiral Sir Thomas Desmond Gimlette suggested combining the cordial with gin, thereby creating what was known as the gimlet. In 1867, to fight the lack of vitamin C, Parliament had ordered that 'lime or lemon juice and other anti-scorbutics [were] to be provided and kept on board' and from 1876 lime cordial became part of naval rations. It is fair to point out that there is another theory that the gimlet was not named after the Rear-Admiral but was named after the small tool used to bore a hole in a barrel of spirits. Whatever its etymology, a gimlet consisted of lime juice (to immunise) plus gin (to fortify and to disguise the bitter taste) garnished with fresh lime.

Back in 1817, a pair of French scientists called Pelletier and Caventou developed a way of extracting quinine from the bark of the South American tree known as the cinchona. The bark had long been harvested for its medicinal properties, being known throughout the eighteenth century as Peruvian Bark or Jesuits Bark, and it was a staple apothecaries' ingredient. However, the French discovery enabled the quinine to be made in quantity and to be sold as a treatment for malaria.

Although quinine and fizzy water had been mixed occasionally it was not until 1858 that the name 'tonic water' was used, to describe a product made by Erasmus Bond, owner of the firm of Pitt & Co in Islington. It did not readily catch on, until five years later when it started to be offered as a tonic, digestive and fever medication for use in warmer climates. By 1863 it was being advertised in Hong Kong, as a mixer to be drunk with ginger brandy. This was at a time when laws were being passed in India requiring officers in the Indian army to take quinine, despite its extremely bitter taste. The officers discovered that the best way to mask the bitter flavour was to add sugar and soda water to it, and then to pour the mix into a glass of gin. The Gin & Tonic was born. In 1868, an article appeared in the Oriental Sporting Magazine referring to horse racing *aficionados* in Lucknow, India, ordering gin and tonic cocktails to go with their celebratory cheroots.

Other officers mixed their gin with Angostura bitters – known to settle the stomach during the long sea voyage out to the Indian sub-continent – giving rise to the pink gin always associated with naval traditions. Schweppes brought out their own ready-mixed 'Indian Tonic Water' in 1870. For troops serving in India, there was a mandatory allowance of neat spirits amounting to a pint of gin or arrack per man per day, despite calls to replace the ration with a more wholesome beer allowance. Meanwhile back in England, the tonic water was found to be an ideal mix with the now-fashionable 'Dry' London Gin, rapidly taking over in popularity from Old Tom.

These developments were happening alongside a general trend for new distillers to enter the marketplace. In 1829, the Chelsea Distillery was founded by John Taylor & Son. It was later acquired by the Burroughs family and re-named 'James Burrough, Distiller and Importer of Foreign Liqueurs'. James Burrough had previously acquired Hayman's Distillery, which had started in 1820. Its most famous achievement was the launch of Beefeater Gin in 1876. The Hayman family remained involved in the business until it was sold to the brewery giant Whitbread in 1987, but a year later Christopher Hayman bought back the fine alcohol division and re-launched Hayman Ltd, making London Dry Gin and also a type of Old Tom gin (sweetened with sugar and liquorice root, but with a hint of citrus and coriander seeds). Hayman also make a sloe gin and a navy strength gin, and are pioneers of a move to re-emphasise juniper berries as the most dominant flavour in gin.

In 1830, the young Thomas Tanqueray started the Bloomsbury Distillery. Here was a meticulous man who experimented endlessly with different botanicals, making notes in his diary of all the experiments. In 1898, the two firms of Charles Tanqueray and Alexander Gordon merged to form Tanqueray Gordon & Co and the following year Charles Gordon died, thereby bringing to an end his family's connection with the business. Production moved to Goswell Road in central London but the premises were largely destroyed during the Blitz and were not fully rebuilt until 1957. As production increased, the company out-grew the Goswell Road premises and the decision was made to relocate operations, initially to Laindon in Essex (1984) and then to Cameronbridge, Fife, in Scotland (1998). Nowadays Gordon & Co is owned by Diageo and is the world's largest producer of London Dry Gin. On several occasions, the company has experimented with producing sloe gin, orange gin and lemon gin, as well as a variety of ready-mixed cocktails. And who can argue with Ernest Hemingway, who described Gordon's as being his favourite gin, claiming that it could 'fortify, mollify and cauterize practically all internal and external injuries'?

Tanqueray, meanwhile, has largely concentrated on U.S. sales where it is the highest-selling gin import, using a product sold at 47.3% ABV. This is considerably stronger than the 43.1% version sold in the United Kingdom but there is also a premium brand, made using fresh as opposed to dried citrus, sold in Britain as Tanqueray Ten. It is quadruple distilled and aimed at the martini-drinking market and has an ABV of 47.3%. Tanqueray will forever be associated with the prohibition movement in the United States – see chapter 15. The company contributed a thousand dollars to a fund to fight prohibition, enjoyed a huge boom in sales as a result of its gin being smuggled into the States, and was reputedly the first gin to be poured in the White House when prohibition ended.

One date worth mentioning was 1840, being the year when, for the very first time, it was possible to buy a Pimm's Number One Cup – a concoction made with gin and a secret mixture of herbs fruit and liqueurs. It was the idea of James Pimm, a farmer's son from Faversham in Kent who came up to London and opened an oyster bar opposite Buckingham Palace. His clientele had been used to knocking back gin with their shellfish, but the introduction of the small tankard containing a refreshing concoction caused a sensation. Before long James Pimm was running five oyster bars and the Number One Cup was joined by Number Two (whisky-based) and Number Three (brandy-based) in 1851. Mary Pimm, wife of James, died in 1864 and the following year James sold the oyster bars and retired to Kent. The bars were franchised and flourished for a while, as did the drink bearing the Pimm name. Variants based on rum, rye whisky and vodka were added as Cups Four, Five and Six in the twentieth century but in the 1970s the drinks went out of fashion and Diageo, who own the name, now concentrate on the original gin-based summer drink synonymous with quintessential 'Britishness'.

The mid-nineteenth century saw a rapid growth in distilleries, with Boodles founded in 1847. Named after the famous gentleman's club in St James's, for many years Boodles gin was only sold in the United States, but in October 2013 Boodles gin was released in the UK, with a redesigned bottle and an alcoholic strength of 80 proof (40% ABV). The American version is stronger, at 90.4 proof – 45.2% ABV. It is unusual in not using any dried citrus, instead making use of nutmeg, sage, and rosemary along with five other botanicals including angelica root and angelica seeds. Much favoured by Winston Churchill, the gin is currently made at Greenall's distillery in Warrington.

Gilbeys followed in 1872, opening a distillery in Camden Town. The family had been involved in the trade of retailing wines and spirits for some years – Henry Gilbey was a wholesale wine merchant and his two younger brothers Walter and Alfred returned from the Crimea War in 1857 and started their own business in London's Oxford Street, selling wines and spirits, including London Dry Gin. They occupied premises built as the Pantheon, an eighteenth-century building designed for use as an opera house and assembly rooms, and nowadays the site of the Marks and Spencer flagship store. Their timing was perfect. It was a time when there was a prohibitive rate of duty payable on wines imported from France, so the brothers pioneered the import of colonial wines, particularly from the Cape region of South Africa. Business boomed, to the extent that within four years they were the third-largest firm of wine importers in the country. They brought in the sale of wine by the bottle, as opposed to a case of twelve, and more than any other firm brought wine drinking into the reach of what might be termed middle-class families. They prospered on the back of the introduction of off-licences, brought in by William Gladstone in 1860, and soon had an extensive network of retail contacts throughout Britain, all signed up on a 'tied' basis – in other words, restricted to selling only Gilbey products. The elder brother Henry was brought into the business and when gin distilling was added in 1872, production was established at the former LNWR site in Camden Town. It was to be another twenty years before the product was sold under the Gilbey name, and distilleries were opened in Canada and Australia. The company also moved into whisky production, having acquired three distilleries in Scotland for that purpose by 1905. The business remained in family ownership until 1962 when it merged with United Wine Traders to become International Distillers and Vintners. They in turn were swallowed up by Watneys in 1972 and in the same year Watneys was absorbed into the Grand Metropolitan Group and since 1998 has been part of Diageo. It was the end of the Gilbey family business and nowadays the gin, with its heavy citrus overtones, is made and distributed as part of the Jim Bean brand.

In 1883, Seagram's first appeared on the scene, adding the distillation of gin to the whisky which it had been making since the 1850s. Under the name Joseph E Seagram & Sons, it was based initially in Ontario in Canada. In 1928, the company was acquired by Samuel Bronfman, an extrovert character who guided the company through the trading difficulties of prohibition and then exploited the opportunities offered when prohibition ended in 1933. The company had hit upon the idea of getting its products into the United States by shipping spirits to French-controlled Saint Pierre and Miquelon, two islands off the coast of Newfoundland, where it was then picked up by bootleggers and smuggled into outlets in the New York and New Jersey areas. Subsequently, the U.S. authorities sought to recover 60 million dollars in unpaid excise duty but Bronfman managed to settle for $1.5million. Seagrams moved its operations to the U.S. and launched a gin aimed at the American market in 1939. Using botanicals such as angelica, cardamom, cassis and coriander, it is aged in oak barrels and is noted for its aroma and taste of candied orange and fresh oranges – but the product is not available for customers in the U.K. It may have called itself 'Seagram's ancient bottle-distilled dry gin' but in reality, it was never particularly ancient and its given date of 'since 1857' is misleading given that at that date Seagram's had nothing to do with distilling, and the distillery had nothing to do with gin! It hasn't stopped it becoming the best-selling American gin.

Bronfman died in 1971 at the age of eighty-two, one of Canada's wealthiest businessmen and a famous philanthropist. Not bad for someone who was born into a family with seven siblings, in what is now Moldova, and who was forced to become a refugee to escape persecution from the Russian authorities. His own children have had multiple marriages, been involved in a much-publicised kidnap and ransom payment, lost a fortune in business deals that involved losing control of the distilling side of the trade, and dabbled in the entertainment industry. As Samuel Bronfman remarked in an interview with *Fortune* magazine in 1966: 'Shirtsleeves to shirtsleeves in three generations. I'm worried about the third generation. Empires have come and gone'. It was a prophetic comment and by the turn of the century the entire business built up by Samuel had been broken up and sold to the likes of Coca Cola and Pernod Ricard, and today the right to the Seagram Gin name belongs to the Diageo conglomerate.

***

In the United States, consumption of 'dry' gin did not really become widespread before 1850. Indeed, it seems that the majority of juniper-based spirits imported into the country were actually genever, imported from Holland. After all, the Dutch had always enjoyed a close trading relationship with the American colonies and this remained strong long after the American War of Independence. It was in America that developments were taking place which would transform the history of gin. The level of alcohol consumption had long been excessive. In 1830, the average American was drinking seven gallons of liquor every year – that is, more than one and a half bottles of spirits every week for every single man woman and child over the age of fifteen. But changes were afoot – a move away from sheer quantity towards flavour and variety. The preface to an 1862 book by Jeremiah ('Jerry') Thomas suggested that 'a relish for "social drinks" is universal; that those drinks exist in greater variety in the United States than in any other country in the world and that he, therefore, who proposes to impart those drinks … is a genuine public benefactor.' It continued, but without giving a date for the reminiscence, as follows:

> We very well remember seeing one day in London, in the rear of the Bank of England, a small drinking saloon which had been set up by a peripatetic American, at the door of which was placed a board covered with the unique titles of the American mixed drinks supposed to be prepared within that limited establishment. The 'Connecticut eye-opener' and

'Alabama fog-cutters' together with the 'lightning-smashes' and the 'thunderbolt-cocktails' created a profound sensation in the crowd assembled to peruse the Nectarian bill of fare...

So, even as far back as the mid-nineteenth century, the British were following in the footsteps of American bartenders and then presumably adapting the recipes to suit British tastes. It was a case of imitation being the sincerest form of flattery and it was to be repeated throughout the following century. The spectacular emergence of the bartender, the man who served the gin, helped fuel the popularity of gin as a basis for a huge variety of mixed drinks. No one was more influential than Jerry Thomas. Here was a real showman, someone regarded as the godfather of bartenders, and his book *How to Mix Drinks, or, the Bon-Vivant's Companion* is recognised as the very first to be published in America on the topic of cocktails. Early on in his career, Thomas realised that mixing drinks was like a theatrical production. Sporting diamond rings (plural), diamond cuff-links and a diamond tie-pin, he gave a dazzling performance, the highlight of which was his skilful demonstration of pouring flaming brandy back and forth between two metal cups, in a blazing arc. This was part of his signature cocktail, known as the Blue Blazer. He was a flashy dresser and someone who was proud to be a member of the American Fat Men's Association, larger than life and subtle as a sledgehammer. If you want to know who first became famous for juggling glasses, and for mixing jugs and bottles, look no further than Jerry Thomas. Known as 'The Professor', he surely learnt a thing or two from working in a saloon next door to the American Museum premises of a certain circus impresario known as P. T. Barnum.

He had been born in New York State at Sackets Harbor in around 1830 and as a young man had travelled to California to try his hand at gold prospecting. He had then worked his way back across America in bars and saloons in St. Louis, New Orleans, Chicago and Charleston. Along the way, he experimented with inventing new drinks and new ways of presentation and by the time he had got back to New York he had built up a following as a truly inspirational character. Drinks moved away from the communal punch-drinking of years gone by, to be replaced by a host of individual concoctions involving fruit and ice, whether shaved, crushed or in cubes. He produced the Collins, the fizz and the sour, as well as gin slings, crustas, toddies and sangarees, some of them listed in Appendix 2. He developed a sour, sweetened with orange cordial or grenadine, known then as a daisy. When the drink moved down to Mexico, it developed a natural affinity for tequila, evolving as the modern-style margarita. Why margarita? Because 'daisy' translates as margarita in Spanish. Later editions of his book were published after his death and featured drinks with names such as 'Manhattan' and 'Martinez'. They may appear to have little in common with their modern namesakes, especially Martinez as a precursor of martini, but that is all part of the way that gin has evolved over the years. One story is that Thomas created it as a celebratory drink for successful gold prospectors in the Californian mining town of Martinez, some time in the mid-1880s. The original Martinez was far from 'dry'. It combined Old Tom, i.e. sweetened gin, with an equal quantity of sweet vermouth, to which a teaspoon of maraschino liqueur would be added. Either Angostura or orange bitters would then be used to give a drink which might possibly have shaken James Bond, but certainly would not have stirred him in the slightest …

While it may be very different to modern martinis, Jerry Thomas is generally credited with being the creator of the martini, which, when all is said and done, comes in many different forms. You want a dirty martini? Add some salty brine from a jar of cocktail olives. Want it not just dirty, but filthy? Add even more olive brine to give a real smack of salt. You want it dry? Mix six parts gin to one part vermouth. You want it wet? Halve the gin so it is a three-to-one mix. You want it with a twist? Get the barman to twist a strip of lemon or orange peel over the drink before serving, so that a little zest is added to the drink – or ask him to leave it in the cocktail as a garnish for even more citrus flavour. And as for the 'shaken or stirred' conundrum – it is simply a matter of taste. Stirring the mixture of gin and vermouth with ice, for perhaps a minute, ensures that the flavours are truly mixed into a velvety blend – a case of the 'marriage' being consummated! Shaking the mixture in a cocktail shaker breaks up the shards of ice, diluting the mixture. And then there are other variants. Add a small pickled onion, rather than an olive garnish, and you have a Gibson Martini. Add a slug of single malt to your martini and it can be described as 'burnt'. And a 'Perfect Martini'? It is actually a technical name, rather than an aspiration for perfection, and means that the vermouth which is being used is a fifty-fifty mix of sweet and dry vermouth.

Jerry Thomas died 'of apoplexy' in 1885 at the age of fifty-five, at which point *The New York Times* said of him that he was 'at one time better known to club men and men about town than any other bartender in this city, and he was very popular among all classes'. By that time he had either gambled away almost all his money, or lost it on the Stock Exchange, which must have seemed to be much the same thing to his widow and two young children who outlived him.

One man who followed in the shoes of Jerry Thomas, and who was a great rival, was Harry Johnson. The two crossed swords, metaphorically, on a number of occasions. Johnson had been born in Prussia, became a sailor, but went ashore in San Francisco in 1861 having broken an arm and a hip. He worked his way up from being kitchen-boy to become manager of the city's Union Hotel and while there first encountered Jerry Thomas. He later worked in Chicago before moving to New York where he took over a bar with which Thomas had previously been associated. Thomas was horrified that his own reputation was being linked in any way with the Prussian upstart and ended up pouring an entire cocktail bowl full of egg-nog laced with hot brandy and rum over the floor of his rival's bar, complaining that any professional would know that this Christmas-time drink was only ever served when the temperature outside dropped below zero. In 1882, Johnson published a book under the title *New and Improved Bartender's Manual, or How to Mix Drinks in the Present Style*. It listed the liquors required in a well-run bar-room: brandy, rum, whisky and arrack, and Old Tom Gin and Holland Gin.

It was unusual in that it contained a whole series of advice to bartenders about how to run a successful bar – how to maintain stock control, how to train staff, how to look after liquor and so on. It also set out literally hundreds of cocktail recipes. On being told that Thomas claimed that his book was the first book on cocktails to be published, Johnson claimed that his 1882 book was a re-issue of a book he had first published in 1860, two years prior to the seminal work of his rival. It seems an unlikely claim, since that was when he was still a sailor, and no trace of the early work has been found. He died in 1933, a hugely influential figure linking the Victorian tradition of bartending to the flamboyant cocktail mixers who emerged after the Prohibition era.

There is one final bartender with aspirations to be a cataloguer of the Victorian drinks world, and that is William 'Cocktail' Boothby. Operating in San Francisco as a wheeler-dealer (part-time real estate agent, full-time hustler, occasional bartender, vaudeville dancer and purveyor of patent medicines) he brought out a book entitled *Cocktail Boothby's American Bartender* in 1891. Various reprints followed and, after the earthquake which demolished so much of the city of San Francisco, a completely new version of the book emerged in 1908 under the title of *The World's Drinks and How to Mix Them*. Boothby ended up as head bartender at the Palace Hotel bar, the finest in the city once it was rebuilt and he continued to add recipes to subsequent editions. Most unusually, he gave credit to the other bartenders who had created those drinks. In doing so he saved many of those early mixologists from obscurity and helped satisfy the modern appetite for recreating 'genuine original' cocktails.

Jesuit's Bark, Cinchona, Peruvian Bark – all names given to the anti-malarial plant known as quinine and featured in the tonic waters launched in the second half of the eighteenth century.

Chapter 14

Gin Magnates and their Money

The success of the early gin-magnates inspired some interesting examples of philanthropy. One intriguing character was Felix (later, Sir Felix) Booth, mentioned earlier in connection with the development of Booth's distillery. He used some of his very considerable fortune to play a significant part in Arctic exploration. His contribution has to be seen in context: the Napoleonic Wars were over, and very real questions were being raised about whether we needed a Royal Navy. After all, Britain ruled the waves. With unchallenged superiority, naval strength had dropped to just thirteen ships of the line. Manning levels plummeted from 130,000 to 20,000 and the Admiralty was desperate to be seen to be relevant and necessary. Exploration was seen as the answer, and in particular, Arctic exploration linked to the establishment of a North-West Passage, providing a route between the North Atlantic and

The paddle steamer *Victory* fitted out and ready to sail to the Arctic.

the Pacific Ocean. For centuries there had been attempts to prove that such a route existed – small wonder, when you think how significant this could be by cutting many months off the journey from Europe to the Far East. A number of expeditions were sponsored by the Royal Navy, in particular, one headed by Sir John Ross, onboard the *Isabella,* supported by a smaller vessel, the *Alexander*, commanded by William Perry. In 1818, the ships sailed to Greenland and crossed the Arctic Circle. Having explored Baffin's Bay the ships entered Lancaster Sound, with the *Isabella* some nine miles in the lead. Confronted by appalling visibility, Ross claimed that when the fog briefly rolled back he could clearly see that there was no way out of the inlet and that all further progress was blocked by a range of mountains, which he called Croker's Mountains, in honour of the First Lord of the Admiralty. So he turned around, went back to where Perry was sailing the *Alexander* and in effect, said 'Time to go home.'

The problem was that Perry never saw the Croker's Mountains, and was convinced that Ross had thrown in the towel too soon. When the explorers returned to England, Perry wasted no time in explaining to his superiors that Ross had chickened out of his mission. To the chagrin of Ross, Perry convinced the Admiralty that he, Perry, should lead a follow-up voyage. Off he went in 1819, and sure enough, found no sign of the Croker range of mountains. He returned, very much the flavour of the moment, to a hero's welcome, leaving the reputation of Ross in absolute tatters. In vain, Ross begged to be allowed to have the chance to lead another mission, but the Admiralty was having none of it. He had embarrassed the navy; he had made the Admiralty a laughing stock; he was a coward.

But Ross was not one to give up and he approached Sir Felix Booth for sponsorship. Booth enthusiastically placed his faith in Ross, underwriting the entire cost of the voyage. It was to cost Booth £10,000. It enabled Ross to purchase and equip a paddle-steamer, called the *Victory* for £2,500. Up until then, the *Victory* had plied the route between Liverpool and the Isle of Man as a mail-ship. It was to be the first time a steam-powered ship had been used to explore the route of the North-West Passage. Off went Ross in 1828 but made slow progress as he inched westwards – often having to hoist sails rather than use the steam-driven paddles. On 6 August 1829, he entered Lancaster Sound, the scene of his previous humiliation, and then disappeared from view for four long years. Winter after winter his ship was iced in and exploration was painfully slow. New features and harbours were named after his sponsor, giving rise to 'Felix Boothia Peninsula' and 'Felix Harbour'. Remarkably, Ross managed to maintain discipline onboard the ice-locked vessel, ensuring that the crew kept fit with regular exercise, holding literacy classes, teaching mathematics and so on. In 1831, he sent his nephew James Clark Ross on an overland trip due north, hoping to find an open passage of water. Nothing was found, but on 1 June 1831, James Clark Ross reached the magnetic North Pole. He constructed a cairn, claimed the land in the name of the British Crown, and headed back to tell his uncle. That year *Victory* only managed to sail eleven miles in the entire year, before succumbing once more to an ice-bound winter. Provisions were dropping to a dangerously low level, signs of scurvy were evident in the crew, and the sled dogs were dying of starvation. The decision was made to abandon *Victory* and to half-sail, half-drag the lifeboats back to where they came from. It was an extraordinary feat of hardship and perseverance, and was met by a suitably extraordinary piece of good fortune: they were rescued by the *Isabella*, the ship on which Ross had sailed fourteen years earlier. He had failed to locate the fabled North-West passage but had mapped an area of over half a million square miles, significantly narrowing down the search area for subsequent explorers.

Ross returned to Kingston upon Hull in October 1833, his reputation fully restored. He was presented to King William IV, he was knighted, he was greeted by cheering crowds wherever he went. And the restoration of his good name was entirely down to the encouragement and generosity of one man – Felix Booth, who was, in turn, made a baronet in recognition of his generosity. Small wonder that when Ross went back to the arctic in 1850 as an old man – he was seventy-two – he named the ship on which he sailed *Felix*. Ross died in London in 1856 and is buried in Kensal Green Cemetery having outlived his sponsor by six years.

Sadly for Sir Felix, his philanthropy was not always so appreciated. One of the people he tried to help was his godson, born to his second cousin, and who was also called Felix Booth. Young Felix was born in 1805 and seems to have felt that life owed him a living. He asked Sir Felix for a job, and was given a position working in the distillery. He was not best suited to the position, given that his only skill lay in drinking the profits. He was sacked, but then asked Sir Felix for different employment. He was given a position looking after the poultry on a farm owned by Sir Felix. This involved free board and lodging along with profits from the poultry business but this was insufficient to satisfy the ungrateful godson. He then decided that he wanted to run a shop, and held out the begging bowl. Again, Sir Felix coughed up the readies, only to find that a year later his godson wanted more money for stock. Sir Felix declined, because his godson was unable or unwilling to produce any accounts showing where the earlier money had gone. It left one very ungrateful young man determined to cause the maximum amount of damage to his elder relative. Aware that Sir Felix seemed to be offering financial help to someone employed by him as a confidential secretary, Felix tried to blackmail Sir Felix, alleging that Sir Felix was having a homosexual affair. Sir Felix declined to pay up; the allegation was made public and Sir Felix was forced to face a very painful allegation of something which was not just a criminal offence, but one which carried the death penalty. The young Felix was charged with blackmail, and sought to justify the allegation by 'naming and shaming' the recipient of Sir Felix's largesse as being a Mr Marr. It totally backfired when Sir Felix publicly acknowledged that Mr Marr was his natural son, the result of an affair with a Scottish woman three decades previously. He was simply doing what any father would do in the circumstances, giving his son a decent start in life. Young Felix was found guilty of blackmail, sentenced to twenty years transportation, and disappeared from public view. Newspapers, particularly in the North of England, were awash with the story. Poor Sir Felix – he never deserved the humiliation and pain caused by somebody he had bank-rolled. Sir Felix died in Brighton in January 1850, unmarried, and the baronetcy passed to his nephew J Williamson Booth.

***

The distillery firm of Nicholsons has been mentioned – it was William Nicholson, a keen cricket aficionado and sportsman, who played a major part in acquiring the ground known as Lords. The field at St John's Wood had originally been leased to the bowler Thomas Lord, who made it available to the Marylebone Cricket Club, otherwise known as the MCC. When the lease approached its term date, the MCC were desperate to secure funds so that the freehold could be purchased, thereby safeguarding Lords as the spiritual home of English cricket. They had missed their chance in 1858 when the freehold had been snapped up by Isaac Moses, a successful retailer of ready-made clothes, who owned the largest clothing emporium in London and who astutely paid £5,910 for the freehold. The MCC were not in a financial position to pursue a bid, but eight years later Moses indicated that he was willing to sell his freehold interest in the land for roughly three times what he paid for it. The MCC had no such cash reserves, and raising the money by subscriptions and donations would take time. Step forward William Nicholson, a cheque for £18,333 6s 8d in hand. Although it was a loan, it gave the club the chance to buy the land without having to wait to raise funds. The MCC made him president of the club and in 1897, when they needed to finance the construction of a new pavilion, they again turned to Nicholson, who responded with another loan, this time of £21,000. The story goes that whereas the MCC had originally used blue as its colour, in recognition of the magnanimous generosity of William Nicholson they changed to the colours found on Nicholson gin bottles – red and yellow. This somewhat garish colour combination is still used by the MCC, where it is colloquially referred to as 'eggs and bacon'.

In 1873, J&W Nicholson & Co acquired the Three Mills site in Bow, London, introducing innovative milling machinery. William Nicholson had fourteen children and one of them, his son Geoffrey Maule Nicholson, was made Managing Director. He met a desperately sad ending. For a while the distillery had used water from a local well but had discontinued the practice when the Council ran a mains sewer across the site, apparently causing the well to dry up. After the passage of a few years, the young Mr Nicholson decided to see if there was any chance of resurrecting the well and instructed a labourer to carry out an inspection, under his supervision. The labourer, by the name of Thomas Pickett, went down a long ladder with a measuring pole, hoping to measure the depth of water. When passing the pole to another man, Pickett was suddenly overcome by poisonous gasses and collapsed into the water. Godfrey Nicholson immediately lowered himself down to try and rescue Pickett but he too was overcome by fumes and disappeared. The tragedy deepened as a third and fourth rescue attempt was made, each one resulting in another man dying. Eventually, the Fire Brigade arrived and recovered the four bodies, and today there is a sculpture entitled Helping Hands recording the tragic events of that summer's day in July 1901, near the spot where the well had existed. The body of Geoffrey Nicholson was buried at Holy Trinity Church, Privett, in Hampshire, his valour commemorated by a stained-glass window and a marble plaque. The three workmen were buried in Woodgrange Park Cemetery, without any visible memorial, and the site is now largely derelict and untended.

The family distillery business expanded despite the tragedy and distilling capacity was increased so rapidly that by the end of the Edwardian era the company was one of the largest distillers in the world. By the 1930s Nicholson's Gin featured in many of the main cocktail mixing books which proliferated at that time. Production ceased following the outbreak of the Second World War and Nicholson's Gin then disappeared from the scene. The assets of the company included a chain of public houses and when these were acquired by Allied Breweries it was clear that there was no interest in going back to gin production. However, the brand was revived in 2017 by Tim Walker and Nicholas Browne, cousins and direct descendants of the original founders.

***

The Hodges' distillery in Lambeth was mentioned in Chapter 12, with its two master distillers called Thomas ('Old Tom' Chamberlain and 'Young Tom' Norris). The distillery was pre-eminent in the first half of the nineteenth century, giving rise to ballads and songs along the lines of:

> The Gin! the Gin! Hodges' cordial Gin!
> It fairly makes our head to spin:
> It gives us marks, and without bound,
> It turneth our head completely round;
> It plays with our eyes, it mocks our brain,
> And sends us rolling in the drain…

Following the death of the founder, the distillery passed into the hands of Captain Frederick Hodges, a remarkable if somewhat eccentric man given to bouts of considerable generosity. You get the unmistakable impression that if, as a boy, he had been asked what he wanted to do with his life, he would not have answered: 'I want to be a gin distiller' but instead would have said: 'When I grow up I want to drive a shiny fire engine.'

Perhaps because of the memory of the conflagration which destroyed the Langdales Distillery during the Gordon Riots, the good captain was preoccupied with devising ways of putting out fires throughout London. The distillery was in a high-risk area, with neighbouring factories including the Price's Candle factory and Burdett's distillery. At his Lambeth premises, he had his own works fire brigade – larger and better equipped than the 'official' brigade known as the London Fire Engine Establishment (LFEE). The LFEE had grown as a composite grouping made up of the individual brigades maintained by certain insurance companies. For over a century these separate brigades had protected the City, but were limited to putting out fires affecting premises actually insured by the company in question. For instance, the Hand-in-Hand brigade would not put out fires in a building insured with the Atlas company, and no one would put out fires on uninsured premises in case they never got paid for their services. This made no sense where flames might easily spread from one building to another, so the LFEE was formed in 1833 representing the major insurers including the Alliance,

Atlas, Globe, Imperial, London Protector, Royal Exchange, Sun, Union and Westminster insurance companies. By 1850 the LFEE had eighty full-time firemen spread across nineteen fire stations.

The LFEE was headed by Superintendent James Braidwood, a man who despised steam-powered fire-fighting equipment, instead using hand-cranked machines which would be pushed into position right near the heart of the fire. Hodges, on the other hand, liked the new-fangled machines which enabled the operator to fire a jet of water from some distance away. In 1854, Hodges acquired 'two powerful engines' supplied by Shand and Mason, in nearby Blackfriars. He also owned two barges converted to being fire engines, which could be floated on the Thames alongside any fire so that the flames could be doused, using water pumped straight from the river. The LFEE on the other hand had only one such fire-fighting barge.

So enthusiastic was Captain Hodges that he constructed a unique look-out platform at the distillery premises in Church Street Lambeth, 120 feet up in the air, giving a vantage point from which his men could scour the city skyline looking for fires. In the days before sky-scrapers, it must have given an unparalleled view of London and the villages beyond. A man would be hauled up the structure using a pulley and would then be expected to spend his entire watch on this high perch. When it was not in use, the observation pole was used to fly the flag or, as Captain Hodges put it: 'It became at once an ornament for miles around and on high days and holidays waved a Union Jack, 30 feet in the hoist and 60 feet in the fly.'

So successful was this look-out system that Hodges machines were invariably on-site to commence fire-fighting before the LFEE brigade arrived. It must have demoralised James Braidwood and his men, who kept losing out on the reward doled out by the insurance company for the first brigade to reach a blaze.

It is easy to think that after the Great Fire of London in 1666 Londoners were safe from flames sweeping through entire neighbourhoods, and that fires were limited to individual premises. Not so, and on 22 June 1861 a blaze broke out in Tooley Street, south of the River Thames near London Bridge. The fire started in a warehouse where a huge quantity of inflammable materials was being stored, including bales of hemp and jute, cotton, wooden boxes of tallow, piles of cotton and sacks and sacks of spices, teas and sugar. The cotton may have been damp, but the conflagration fuelled by the tallow caused the cotton to combust in a fireball which soon spread the flames down towards other warehouses by the river. Scovell's wharf, the adjoining Cotton's wharf and the Hay's and Chamberlain's wharves all went up in flames.

First on the scene was the Hodges' brigade bringing with them one of his steam-powered fire engines. It was donated to Hodges by subscriptions raised by grateful parishioners in Lambeth, and is now in the Museum of London. He also brought up the two fire barges but their attempts to bring the fire under control were hampered by the receding tide, leaving the fire barges out of range for the pumps to reach the shore.

Braidwood's brigade also arrived, and hand-operated parish pumps were brought to the scene, manned by local but often untrained operators. The response of the various factions under the control of Braidwood was haphazard and sadly when Braidwood went forward to inspect the seat of the flames, a warehouse wall collapsed and killed him instantly, alongside one of his officers. They were not the only two to die in the inferno: four men in a boat trying to collect tallow floating on the water were suddenly engulfed in flames when the oily surface of the water ignited. They all perished.

The fire took three days to be extinguished. The body of Captain Braidwood was recovered and given a hero's burial. The funeral procession stretched for one and a half miles, and all the churches throughout the City of London tolled their bells in recognition of his bravery. The insurance companies faced huge losses – estimated at nearly two million pounds – to rebuild warehouses and factories along a quarter-mile stretch of the banks of the Thames. Parliament then formed a select committee to look into the lessons which could be learned from the disaster. The result, three years later, was an Act of Parliament setting up the London Fire Brigade. No longer were residents left to worry about whether they or their neighbours were insured before the brigade would come to put out their flames, or save their cats stuck up a tree, or rescue them from the floods. But it took the perspicacity and drive and generosity of men like Hodges, as well as the personal bravery of men like Braidwood, to bring about the change.

That wasn't quite the end of Hodges: he sold the distillery to Messrs Dunn and Vallentin and retired to live in Margate where he was described as being 'a bit of a nutcase'. He bought a three-wheeler steam engine and terrorised the residents of Margate by driving it around, whistles blowing and bells ringing, knocking down lamp-posts and railings and causing horses to bolt in fright. The machine had originally been built by Garrett, Marshall & Co., of Leeds, and had been exhibited at the Leeds Royal Show. It was a real leviathan: weighing five tons and carrying nine people it could manage an impressive 15 mph. One engineering magazine apparently referred to it as 'probably the most remarkable locomotive ever made' and Hodges bought it in September 1864. The machine was called *Fly-by-Night* and the impetuous Captain Hodges liked nothing more than taking it for a spin, being hauled before the magistrates on no fewer than six occasions in as many weeks, presumably for causing a public nuisance.

The local newspaper recorded the fact that on one of these occasions Hodges tore along the seafront aboard the *Fly-by-Night* and as he turned the corner came face to face with a cart belonging to Mr Wilson, a local farmer. It was being drawn by a fine grey, which bolted towards the cliff edge. The cart was smashed to smithereens and the terrified horse was left so traumatised that it was subsequently declared unfit to work again. Mr Wilson survived, but cannot have been best pleased on hearing that Hodges decided to round off his day of causing pandemonium by holding a rather noisy fireworks display, accompanied by the firing of cannon, commencing at nine that very evening. In the end, Hodges donated the *Fly-by-Night* to the local fire brigade for them to convert into a dedicated fire engine, and peace was restored to the streets of Margate.

'The Drunkard's Progress; from the Pawnbrokers to the Gin Shop; from thence to the Workhouse; thence to the Gaol and ultimately to the Gallows.'

Chapter 15

Prohibition – Before, During and After

The period from the mid-1800s to the end of the Great War in 1918 was marked in Britain by a battle between the Temperance Movement and those who wanted to permit alcohol consumption. The battle lines were further complicated by those who wanted to achieve their temperance aims through the enforcement of the law and those who wanted to develop abstinence through encouragement and education. The first British organisation to call for legal abolition of alcohol sales and consumption was founded by John Dunlop in Glasgow in 1829. Four years later Joseph Livesey formed the Preston Temperance Society where, inadvertently, the phrase 'teetotal' was first coined. Various stories exist as to how the word came about: one was that a member of the Preston society was Richard Turner, a man who suffered from a speech impediment. He supposedly stuttered the word 'total' when calling for total abstinence in 1833. From then on, 'teetotal' was taken to mean complete abstinence as opposed to any form of partial or occasional avoidance of alcohol. It covered all forms of alcohol – spirits and ales – and was quickly incorporated into a pledge signed by all members. Others trace the expression to the placing of the letter 'T' alongside members willing to espouse Temperance. Britain was some years behind America – in 1833 when the first British temperance society was formed there were already five thousand such groups operating in the United States. A strong temperance movement developed in Scandinavian countries with the first group emerging in Norway in 1836 and in Sweden the following year.

Back in Britain, 1847 saw the formation in Leeds of the Band of Hope, aimed at protecting young children from the dangers of alcohol. Supporters were asked to sign a pledge to abstain 'from all liquors of an intoxicating quality, whether ale, porter, wine or ardent spirits, except as medicine'. Other independent groups then came together under the banner of the United Kingdom Alliance for the Suppression of the Traffic in all Intoxicating Liquors, formed in 1853 in Manchester. The idea had been promoted by Nathaniel Card, a Quaker cotton mill owner who sought to emulate law-makers in the American state of Maine, who in 1851 passed a law prohibiting the sale of alcohol.

Woman's Holy War, an 1874 lithograph showing female members of the Temperance League going into battle against the scourge of strong liquor.

The United Kingdom Alliance appeared to have an early success with the passing of the sale of Beer Act in 1854, which restricted Sunday opening hours. But the change in the law proved widely unacceptable to the general population and was quickly repealed. Within five years, pressure on MP's led to a Bill being drafted to outlaw alcohol sale and consumption but it never got off the ground and was heavily defeated in the House of Commons.

This was happening at a time when tastes were becoming more sophisticated – at least in some quarters. For instance, when the Great Exhibition opened in 1851, the Food and Beverage contract was originally offered to the renowned French chef and mixologist Alexis Soyer, on condition that this was to be alcohol-free. Soyer declined and instead opened his *Gastronomic Symposium of All Nations* in Gore House opposite the gates of the Great Exhibition in Hyde Park, a site which is now occupied by the Royal Albert Hall. A thousand people a day crammed into his premises to sample the delights of fine food, accompanied by fireworks and music and, most importantly, a selection of forty different shots and cocktails. Although Soyer lost heavily with his experiment, it nevertheless showed that there was an appetite for cocktails. Whereas the working-class poor were still aiming to get drunk for the minimum expense, to alleviate the hardship and monotony of their lives in Industrial Britain, the better-off middle classes were looking to taste new and exotic drinks served in pleasant surroundings.

In 1872, the government of William Gladstone decided to tackle some of the worst excesses of drunkenness by specifying that, in the towns, public houses must close by midnight and by 11.00 p.m. in rural areas. The Licensing Act of that year also granted magistrates the power to ban alcohol sales in an entire area. That did not go down well with the man-in-the-street, who up until then had regarded Gladstone as 'the People's William'. Mind you, he was also given the acronym of G.O.M. – standing either for 'Grand Old Man', or 'God's Only Mistake', depending on your political persuasion. But for Joe Public, forcing places to go completely 'dry' was never going to be popular. There was widespread disquiet, falling short of outright rioting, but the underlying sentiment was that people would not tolerate this interference with their personal freedoms. Gladstone surprised everyone by calling an election, keen to get a new mandate for his reforms. The voters did not oblige, and sent Gladstone packing from office. Writing to his brother Robertson Gladstone, William explained his defeat: 'But more immediately operative causes have determined the elections. I have no doubt what is the principal. We have been borne down in a torrent of gin and beer.'

Undoubtedly one of the most significant obstacles to prohibition was the amount of revenue brought in by the trade in alcohol. By 1870 it is estimated that one-third of all government income was derived from taxing alcohol in one form or another. The government neither wanted to lose that income nor to be forced to spend that income in 'tidying up' after the inebriated poor. This is reflected in the low response to the Habitual Drunkards Act of 1879, which enabled Local Authorities to set up homes where alcoholics could be treated. The idea had been encouraged by Dr Norman Shanks Kerr, who called alcoholism a disease – and a treatable one at that. In Parliament, a special committee headed up by Dr Donald Dalrymple, MP for Bath, tried to introduce a Bill aimed at forcibly confining habitual drunkards in reformatories, where medical care could be given alongside moral and spiritual guidance. Apart from isolating the inebriate from any source of alcohol, treatment would include such experiments as applying mustard plasters to the body to draw out the toxins. But Parliament had its hands full with more pressing demands on its time, such as improving factory conditions and ending the appalling consequences of child labour. The Bill never progressed, especially as there was strong opposition to it from the influential brewing and distillery trades. However, the pressure for reform did lead eventually to the passing of the Habitual Drunkards Act, but the legislation failed in its mission because the government did not commit any funds to making it work. Councils were empowered to run retreats for alcoholics but no money was committed by the government to cover the running costs of such homes, meaning that the only people who could afford to use the facilities were the alcoholics from well-off families. The working-class poor, for whom the facilities were designed, simply could not afford to stay.

The retreats were designed for two different categories: those who were to be admitted of their own volition; and those who were sent there because of their criminal convictions. A habitual drunkard was defined as someone 'who cannot be certified as a lunatic, but who due to habitual intemperate drinking is dangerous to him or herself or incapable of managing their affairs'. Subsequently, the Inebriates Act of 1898 extended the range of people eligible to stay at the retreats to include anyone convicted of drunkenness four or more times in the year, and inebriation covered not just consumption of alcohol but also drug addiction provided that the drug in question was taken orally (and hence laudanum was included, but not opiates administered by injection). In practice, the highest category of people being treated were addicted to spirits, including gin, then beer, then wine and then narcotics of one kind or another. By 1900 not a single purpose-built residential unit had been built and although a few councils took over existing buildings, the numbers being treated were comparatively small. By 1904 over 90% of people in the retreats were women, even though females accounted for only 20% of the inebriates eligible for admission by reason of their having received multiple convictions. By the Mental Deficiency Act 1913, the vast majority of inebriates were reclassified as being mentally defective and by the 1920s all of the retreats had either been closed or turned into mental asylums.

The Temperance Movement was gathering strength, not just in Britain but in much of the rest of Europe and especially in America. Supporters of prohibition must have seen the evils of drink all around them: in Britain, new gin distilleries were opened. As mentioned, 1872 saw the launch of Gilbey's gin followed by Beefeater gin in 1876. In Canada, Seagram's launched their gin in 1883, a dozen or so years after the Fleischmann Brothers had started distilling dry gin at their newly opened distillery in Ohio. The merger of Gordon's and Tanqueray's in 1898 led to the creation of a leviathan with a worldwide reach. In France, the consumption of absinthe exploded from 185,000 gallons in 1875 to 9,500,000 gallons by 1910. A rise in mental illness in France was blamed on this spirit, which was made in much the same way as gin, but with different botanicals and without the juniper. Ultimately the drink's popularity led to a presidential decree in 1915 banning absinthe altogether, even though there is evidence to suggest that rampant syphilis, epilepsy and pre-existing medical conditions were more potent factors.

Back in the last decades of the nineteenth century, groups opposed to alcohol started to gain a bigger foothold. The Quakers and the Methodists had always been opposed to the evil effects of drink; now they were boosted by the foundation of the Salvation Army in 1864. Its founder, William Booth, had previously been an itinerant Methodist preacher. First and foremost a Christian group, it launched its mantra of the three 'S's – defined by William Booth as 'the way in which the Army administered to the "down and outs": first, soup; second, soap; and finally, salvation'. William concentrated on gaining support from the most needy recruits – the gin drinkers, the whores, the drug addicts – while his wife targeted the wealthy sponsors for financial assistance. Abstaining from alcohol was central to membership and therefore it was not surprising that the early meetings were opposed by the so-called Skeleton Army. Backed by local publicans they sought to disrupt meetings, hurling rocks and rubbish at their rival Salvationists. Their opposition failed and in time the Salvation Army became influential lobbyists in Parliament.

The Church of England Temperance Society was formed in 1862 with its Roman Catholic equivalent, the League of the Cross, following in 1873. Another group, allied to the Liberal Party, was the National Temperance Federation, founded in 1884. These various groups developed close links with counterparts in America, where the World's Woman's Christian Temperance Union had been formed in 1883. In 1909, a world prohibition conference was held in London and the upshot was the formation of the International Prohibition Confederation. At the end of that year, the chairman issued a statement saying that the year 1909 broke 'all records as a twelve-month period of anti-alcohol reform'. He went on to say:

> In addition to gains in thousands of cities throughout America the twelfth world's congress against alcoholism, held in London, revealed a unity that promises greater progress for the ensuing year … In the United States exists a strong trend toward abolition of the liquor traffic. Despite claims of a reaction made by the liquor press, the records show that in no twelve months during the past fifty years has there gathered such a progressive force or been such a substantial gain for national prohibition.
>
> The chief handicaps to the enforcement of prohibition are the need of federal protection of dry territory against interstate liquor traffic and the treacherous alliance with the outlawed liquor traffic of politicians and party machines unfriendly to prohibition. Last November the Prohibition party polled an increased vote in every state except Rhode Island, Massachusetts, New York, Pennsylvania, Nebraska and Indiana. As a result, the party is going into the congressional campaign of 1910 with vigorous agitation and organization in many sections of the country.

Georgia and Oklahoma had adopted statewide prohibition in 1907 and were followed by Mississippi and North Carolina the following year. Tennessee went dry in 1908 and by 1914 no fewer than thirty-three states had embraced statewide prohibition.

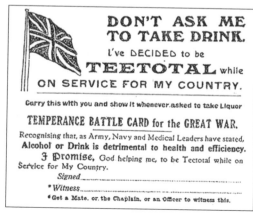

DON'T ASK ME TO TAKE DRINK.

I've DECIDED to be **TEETOTAL** while ON SERVICE FOR MY COUNTRY.

Carry this with you and show it whenever asked to take Liquor

TEMPERANCE BATTLE CARD for the GREAT WAR.

Recognising that, as Army, Navy and Medical Leaders have stated, **Alcohol or Drink is detrimental to health and efficiency.**

I Promise, God helping me, to be Teetotal while on Service for My Country.

Signed...

* Witness..

* Get a Mate, or the Chaplain, or an Officer to witness this.

In Europe, the outbreak of the Great War in 1914 caused a real headache for the British authorities, battling not only with Germany, but also with alcoholism in the armed forces and a vociferous prohibition movement. David Lloyd George was the Munitions Minister in 1915 when he mentioned the problem of alcohol, saying that 'Drink is doing us more damage in the war than all the German submarines put together'. On 15 March 1915, he told the Shipbuilding Employers Federation that Britain was 'Fighting Germany, Austria and Drink, and as far as I can see the greatest of these three deadly foes is Drink'. Lloyd George was no teetotaller himself, but he helped launch a campaign for total abstinence for the duration of the war. King George V was persuaded to give his support, issuing a statement that 'no wines spirits or beer will be consumed in any of His Majesty's houses after to-day, Tuesday April 6th, 1915'. Other countries followed, with Tsar Nicholas II closing down 400 state vodka distilleries in Russia. It didn't stop people drinking: it simply drove vodka production underground and its only effect was that the Russian state suddenly lost a third of its income from tax revenue.

In Britain, the Defence of the Realm Act was passed four days after the outbreak of war in August 1914. It enabled rules to be passed covering an enormous range of prohibited activities – everything from flying a kite to lighting bonfires and whistling in the street. It introduced British Summer Time and it sought to reduce alcohol consumption out of fear that it was undermining the war effort. Restrictions on the opening hours for public houses were introduced, 12.00 until 14.30 at lunchtime and, later, 18.30 to 21.30 at suppertime. Before this, pubs had been permitted to open from five in the morning until just after midnight. The 'afternoon gap' was to remain in one form or another until the Licensing Act of 1988.

Rules imposed under the Defence of the Realm Act – or DORA as it was generally termed – included taking a swipe at what was known as 'treating' – the custom whereby a person entering a public house was encouraged to buy drinks for those present. A 'No Treating Order' laid down that any drink ordered had to be paid for by the person drinking it, thus dissuading the purchase of rounds of drinks. The maximum penalty for defying the government order was six months' imprisonment. It led to some surprising results, with a report in the Morning Post in March that 'at Southampton yesterday Robert Andrew Smith was fined for treating his wife to a glass of wine in a local public-house. He said his wife gave him sixpence to pay for her drink. Mrs Smith was also fined £1 for consuming and Dorothy Brown, the barmaid, £5 for selling the intoxicant, contrary to the regulations of the Liquor Control Board.' Buying drinks on credit was banned, along with the consumption of alcohol on public transport

This left the government with very particular concerns at the juxtaposition of alcohol consumption and munitions production. Large munitions factories were being built, for instance, the Royal Small Arms Factory at Enfield near London, and there were obvious concerns that workers who were drunk could cause catastrophic accidents. The government toyed with the idea of nationalising the entire drinks industry, or of introducing prohibition, but in the end, settled for a measure of state control. A Central Control Board was set up and five public houses were compulsorily acquired near the Enfield works, so that they could be run on State lines with beers at reduced strength, with controls on advertising, and with limits on alcohol being sold to factory workers. A similar attempt was made to control drinking near the Cromarty Firth naval base, where over a dozen pubs were brought under state control. Then the CCB decided to go all out, and tackle the outbreak of drunkenness in the area north of Carlisle where an enormous munitions factory was being constructed. Some 15,000 people were involved in constructing and manning the factory, which stretched for six miles and crossed the border into Scotland, near Gretna. It was an area where vast amounts of nitro-glycerine and cordite were being stored and made into ammunition, and the sudden influx of new workers into the area had caused cases of drunkenness and anti-social behaviour to soar. The government bought up five breweries and 363 public houses covering an area of three hundred square miles in what became known as the Carlisle Experiment. All off-licences in the area were revoked and a ban on all alcohol advertising was introduced. Bottles of spirits were not even allowed to be displayed so as to be visible from outside the premises. The CCB set up a State Management Scheme which prohibited the sale of spirits 'chasers' to accompany beer, required gin and other spirits to be sold in glasses that were large enough to be heavily diluted with mixers or water, and incentivised the managers to concentrate on the sale of food. A third of the pubs were closed down altogether, and the others were improved with new amenities such as dining rooms, reading rooms, games rooms and so on. The level of control may seem extraordinary – twenty-six of the pubs were designated for the sale of state-made meat pies! From 1917 a 'no spirits Saturday' was introduced. No gin, whisky or brandy on a Saturday led to arrests for drink offences over the weekend coming to an almost complete halt. Looked at in the context of its very specific objective – to reduce alcohol-related sickness in the workforce and to prevent accidents caused by drunkenness – it was a success. As such, it remained in force for many years, with the last state-controlled public house being sold off as recently as the 1970s.

Nationally, alcohol-related crimes plummeted. At the time when war broke out in 1914, there were over 67,000 cases in London leading to a conviction for being drunk. Three years later this number had slumped to just over 16,500. In part this was a reflection on higher prices for spirits resulting from tax hikes – gin and whisky were five times as expensive after the war as they were beforehand. This may be one of the factors behind a decline in support for the temperance movement in Britain – the peak had passed. Elsewhere in the world prohibition was tried, but in each case was subsequently abandoned. Iceland went dry between 1912 and 1932; Russia followed suit between 1914 and 1925; Finland followed from 1919 to 1932, and Norway from 1919 to 1927. Canada had started to dabble in prohibition in 1907, but a number of states withdrew in the 1920s and the final state to abandon it was Prince Edward Island in 1948. Elsewhere, referenda were held in New Zealand in 1919 and in Australia in 1930, but in each case failed to produce a majority in favour of going dry.

Then, of course, there was the United States, where prohibition was in force between 1920 and 1933. It is worth remembering that by the time America entered World War I, twenty-one states were already dry and peace brought added impetus to the temperance movement. Prohibition came about through the Eighteenth Amendment to the US Constitution, ratified in January 1919 and coming into force one year later. What it did not do was ban the purchase or consumption of alcohol – it banned its manufacture, distribution and sale. In order to work, enabling legislation in the form of the Volstead Act was passed, named after Congressman Andrew J. Volstead who chaired the Senate Judiciary Committee and who promoted the legislation. It was to have consequences that no one could ever have imagined. On one level it promoted speakeasies – illegal drinking joints which, unlike the saloons which they replaced, served both men and women. In the speakeasies, spirits took the place of beer so that by the end of the decade consumption of gin, brandy and whisky accounted for two-thirds of all consumption of alcohol.

It was the era of bathtub gin – a phrase that appeared in the 1920s and was used to describe low quality alcohol which was made without involving botanical distillation. Instead, cheap grain alcohol would be mixed in a large domestic container – such as a bath – with a variety of herbs and flavourings, including juniper berry juice and glycerine. Why gin rather than any other spirit? Because it was simple to make and did not, for instance, require any form of ageing, or maturing in barrels. The result was often a drink with a very rough taste and it became fashionable to mask the unpleasant flavour by disguising it. By combining the drink with various mixers, it became a form of cocktail. In time, the cocktail spread from the speakeasy to the private home, and from there fostered the cocktail party. So, instead of weaning the population off spirits, prohibition gave a huge boost to what has been described as the first Cocktail Age. Trends in the United States then crossed the Atlantic, particularly thanks to liners such as Cunard's *Mauretania,* which held the record for the fastest Atlantic crossing for the two decades up to 1929. Known as the Blue Riband, the accolade of being the fastest liner then passed to a succession of European rivals before the *Queen Mary* claimed the crown back for Cunard in 1938. Ocean cruising, elegant parties, big band jazz and gin cocktails – what more could the fashionable well-to-do ask for in the inter-war period?

Back in the States, prohibition may have driven consumption out of sight but it also spawned a rapid increase in the number of drinking joints available to the public. In New York alone the Commissioner of Police estimated that there were 32,000 speakeasies, more than double the number of saloons and drinking dens that existed ten years earlier. Speakeasy operators were involved in a constant battle with the authorities to disguise their activities and corruption was rife. In Pennsylvania, the Prohibition Director was involved in a conspiracy to 'liberate' 700,000 gallons of alcohol from State storage. It emerged that he had control of some four million dollars in a slush fund which he could use to bribe officials. In the White House, President Harding kept a stock of bootleg alcohol despite having voted in favour of prohibition while he served as a senator. Even Andrew Volstead, who promoted the legislation which enforced prohibition, was not averse to drinking alcohol, while it was said that the Speaker of the House of Representatives used his own private still to manufacture illegal spirits. Perhaps most amazing of all, congressmen allowed George Cassiday, known as the Man in the Green Hat, to operate from within the Congress building. Allocated an office in the basement of the House Office Building, Cassiday supplied illegal alcohol to an estimated two-thirds of the members of Congress. In the days before terrorist threats, no one was worried about people coming into the building. They were only concerned with preventing items from being stolen. It was therefore easy for Cassiday, wearing his trademark green fedora, to walk into his office with two suitcases. Both would contain forty bottles of spirits, each holding one quart. He would distribute these throughout the day to thirsty congressmen and when he was arrested and barred from the building he simply turned his attention to the Senate. He made use of a room in the Senate Office building and was able to supply senators with his illegal hooch. He was arrested a second time and sentenced to a spell in prison, but never actually spent a single night behind bars. Every morning he would sign himself in, and every night he would sign himself out and return to his home. It was an example of how the law was placed in a ridiculous light. Hypocrisy was rampant everywhere – not least in the police force, where some officers happily spent their day arresting law-breakers before spending their off-duty hours promoting their own racket selling hard liquor. Politicians served alcohol at their house parties, giving rise to the comment by Al Capone: 'When I sell liquor, it's bootlegging. When my patrons serve it on a silver tray on Lakeshore Drive, it's hospitality.'

It reached the stage where the hypocrisy and the counter-productive consequences of Prohibition meant that legislation to repeal was inevitable. On 6 December 1932, Senator John J. Blaine of Wisconsin tabled a Twenty-first Amendment, aimed at repealing the Eighteenth Amendment in its entirety. It passed through both Houses but took an entire year to be ratified by sufficient states (thirty-six) to bring national prohibition to an end. It heralded an upsurge in interest in the way spirits were offered for sale to the consumer – and that meant cocktails.

During Prohibition, the cocktail spotlight had moved away from the speakeasies in New York, serving bath-tub gin into tea cups with saucers, and crossed the Atlantic to the fashionable hotels like the Ritz, the Savoy and the Dorchester. Here, in these *Grandes Dames* of the hotel world, with their opulent art deco interiors and Manhattan-inspired bars, cocktail drinking was preserved and developed. One of the men who claimed to have left the United States after serving one of the very final drinks before Prohibition cut in was a man called Harry Craddock. Finding himself out of a job as a barman in America he had caught a ship sailing for Liverpool. Craddock was originally British, having been born at Stroud in England in 1876. He had emigrated to the States in 1897, had acquired American citizenship, served in the US Armed Forces, and worked at Cleveland's Hollenden Hotel and at the Knickerbocker Hotel in New York. He had also been barman at Hoffman House, which was a fine colonial building dating back to 1679 and which housed a bar and restaurant at Kingston, New York. In other words, Harry Craddock had a solid grounding in designing and serving American cocktails in fashionable venues – and he spoke with a thoroughly American accent. Those attributes ensured that he soon found employment back in Britain, initially in Bristol, before moving to the Savoy in London. There, at the American Bar, the Savoy had developed a venue to showcase American style and pazazz, and Craddock was exactly the right person in the right place at the right time to make his mark. It was a case of America's loss being Britain's gain.

The Savoy had already earned a reputation for being host to the leading figures of the age – film stars rubbed shoulders with princes and nowhere was the ensemble more glittering than at the American Bar. Previously it was the domain of the remarkable Ada Coleman, known to all as 'Coley'. She had been made head bartender at the Savoy in 1903 and her personality, her skill as a hostess and as a maker of cocktails helped popularise the American Bar so that it attracted the likes of Mark Twain, Marlene Dietrich and Charlie Chaplin. Other habitués included the Prince of Wales and the wealthy American philanthropist James Buchanan Brady, known as Diamond Jim. Another visitor was the actor-manager Sir Charles Hawtrey (no relation to the comic actor who subsequently chose to copy his name). Sir Charles was aware of Coley's interest in developing new cocktails and asked her to devise a drink for the occasion: 'Coley, I am tired. Give me something with a bit of punch in it.' Coley later recalled: 'It was for him that I spent hours experimenting until I had invented a new cocktail. The next time he came in, I told him I had a new drink for him. He sipped it, and, draining the glass, he said "By Jove! This is the real hanky-panky!"' The Hanky-Panky, made with gin, sweet vermouth, and a couple of dashes of Fernet Branca became her signature cocktail and enhanced her reputation as the Queen of Cocktail Makers.

The Savoy closed the American Bar for refurbishment in 1925 and Coley decided it was time to retire and to make way for Harry Craddock, who had been waiting in the wings and was clearly destined to take over her crown as London's leading bartender. Off went Coley into retirement, lauded as having served a hundred thousand customers and having poured a million drinks. In came Craddock with his card index of cocktails which, over the years, gained over two thousand entries. Some 750 of these were featured in his 1930 book *The Savoy Cocktail Book*, a publication that used his name but brought him not one penny in royalties. The book is still in print, is regarded as a bible for modern mixologists, and contains recipes for drinks such as the Hanky-Panky. It also contained the earliest printed recipe for the Singapore Sling. Made famous at Raffles Long Bar in Singapore, there are innumerable variants, but the Craddock version features gin mixed with Grand Marnier, cherry liqueur, herbal liqueur, pineapple, lime, bitters and club soda. The Savoy Cocktail Book also features Craddock's own creations, the Corpse Reviver #2 and the White Lady. The Corpse Reviver #2 is a gin-based cocktail intended to act as a hangover cure and general reviver, but with the added description in the Savoy Cocktail Book that 'Four of these taken in swift succession will un-revive the corpse again'. As for the White Lady – otherwise known as a Chelsea Sidecar and sometimes as a Delilah – Craddock made it with gin, Cointreau, and fresh lemon juice.

Others would maintain that the original White Lady was devised by another Harry – Harry MacElhone in 1919 at Ciro's Club in London. He originally made the drink using crème de menthe but replaced it with gin when working in Paris in 1929 at a venue called Harry's New York Bar. This legendary venue had originated as a bar in Manhattan. It was dismantled and re-assembled in Paris in what were formerly bistro premises, near the Avenue de l'Opéra. Harry MacElhone bought the bar in 1923, endowed it with his own name and was soon attracting the likes of Ernest Hemingway, Humphrey Bogart, Coco Chanel, the heavyweight boxing champion Jack Dempsey and the Irish playwright Brendan Behan. Other famous visitors were the playboy Aly Khan and the actress Rita Hayworth, who subsequently married Aly Khan. Here, at Harry's Bar, numerous drinks were popularised. French 75 (otherwise, 'soixante quinze') involved mixing gin with champagne, while Monkey Gland was a cocktail made by mixing gin with orange, grenadine and absinthe. Harry's Bar also laid claim to creating vodka-based drinks such as the Bloody Mary and also deserves to be remembered as the place where George Gershwin composed the jazz-inspired orchestral piece *An American in Paris*. Harry MacElhone ruled supreme in Paris until his death in 1958, leaving the bar to be run by his son and, later grandson, establishing it as a Parisian landmark and a firm favourite with tourists.

It needs to be distinguished from Harry's Bar in Venice, which was a quite separate phenomenon. Founded in 1931 by barman Giuseppe Cipriani and named after his customer Harry Pickering (who put up the money), it quickly became the haunt of the rich and famous such as Ernest Hemingway, Alfred Hitchcock, Orson Welles and Aristotle Onassis. The American novelist Truman Capote, the inventor Guglielmo Marconi, actors Charlie Chaplin and James Stewart and the American socialite Peggy Guggenheim all frequented Harry's Bar when in Venice. Nowadays it is famous for the creation of the cocktail called the Bellini, made using Prosecco and peach puree. The bar has also become known for the dryness of its Martinis, with the Montgomery Martini, named after the Field Marshall, being fifteen parts gin to one part dry vermouth.

While all this was happening on the continent, the first Harry, the Harry Craddock who ruled the roost at The Savoy, developed his style and reputation, earning the title of 'dean of bartenders'. He formed the United Kingdom Bartenders Guild in 1934 and four years later was tempted away from the Savoy to become head barman at The Dorchester. He retired in 1947 and when he died in 1963 he was completely destitute, despite the fame and success of the book which he had inspired. Ironically, his precursor at the Savoy, Ada 'Coley' Coleman, outlived Harry and died three years after her successor, at the ripe old age of ninety-one.

The cover on the first edition of the *Savoy Cocktail Book* containing Harry Craddock's choice of mixed drinks.

Chapter 16

The Modern World of Gin

In the aftermath of Prohibition many films popularised gin, none more so than the film *Casablanca*. There, Yvonne, an ex-girlfriend of the character played by Humphrey Bogart, orders a 'French 75' when she turns up at Rick's Bar with her new Nazi partner. The drink, a mixture of London Dry Gin and French champagne, got its name from a French 75mm artillery gun –

presumably because it gave a terrific kick and was extremely rapid acting. But if that film showed that gin was a man's drink, the book behind the 1961 film *Breakfast at Tiffany's* showed that it was also a drink for women. The Holly Golightly character, played by Audrey Hepburn, gives the impression that she is able to drink most of the men under the table, even though it is only in the original book by Truman Capote that she displays her penchant for the drink White Angel ('one-half vodka, one-half gin, no vermouth').

By 1961 gin had a very middle-class, middle-aged image. 'Gin' meant Gordons and it also meant tonic – which meant Schweppes. Respectable families might host cocktail parties, where their genteel guests would be offered spirits-with-a-mixer (Gin & Tonic, Brandy and Soda, Whisky and Ginger Ale, etc). The host and hostess might offer a punch that may or may not have included gin. So, drinking gin was respectable, but it certainly wasn't exciting and it definitely did not appeal to the under-thirties market. Gin as a drink still sold, but it was a decidedly dated drink, not for the young at heart. It was looking as though it would forever be associated with Queen Elizabeth, the Queen Mother, who famously enjoyed Gin and Dubonnet. Made with 30% gin, 70% Dubonnet and a slice of lemon under the ice it was apparently a favourite tipple at Clarence House. Gin summoned up an image of retired army colonels, of lonely drinking in hotel bars and of furtive visits to hide the empty bottles in someone else's rubbish bin.

Gin certainly received a boost in the mid-Sixties when Frank Sinatra and the Rat Pack took to knocking back Tanqueray Martinis in the Buena Vista Social Club in San Francisco. Sales of Tanqueray apparently doubled in a single year (1964) without a dime being spent to promote or advertise it. Subsequently, Tanqueray sought to revive its popularity with its launch in 2000 of Tanqueray No. Ten. Named after the Tiny Ten distillery in which it is made, it is distilled four times and includes the traditional botanicals of juniper, coriander, angelica and liquorice, alongside whole citrus fruits, including limes, oranges and pink grapefruit.

Gin had vague connotations for the young with something unsavoury, with its connection with hot baths, metal coat hangers and unwanted pregnancies. The film *Saturday Night and Sunday Morning*, which came out in 1960 and starred Rachel Roberts as the pregnant Brenda did nothing to dispel the connection between gin and at-home abortions. Also, by the Sixties cocktail parties were no longer as fashionable as a bring-a-bottle party – where the chances were that the bottle would have been a cheap bottle of wine, or else beer, such as the infamous Watneys Party Four (1964) and Party Seven (1968). Gin seemed destined to be relegated to being the secret drink of lonely widows, offering solace and an antidote to loneliness.

If people wanted spirits they were more likely to turn to something 'exotic' like a Bacardi-and-coke, or would look for a different form of high by dabbling with something far more exciting, be it cannabis, cocaine or LSD.

So why didn't gin end up as a footnote in the history of long-gone drinks? Why was it not relegated to the likes of shrub, or mead, or become indelibly linked to a particular period of history, such as 'the original champagne perry', launched in 1953? Still available in Britain, Babycham had its heyday in the 1960s and 70s. You can still buy it but it is hardly a shadow of its former glory. How come gin has not languished similarly?

The whole idea of mixing drinks received a boost with the 1988 Touchstone Production film *Cocktail* starring a young Tom Cruise. No matter that Cruise himself said in 1992 that the film 'was not a crowning jewel' in his career. Slated by the critics and a winner of the Golden Raspberry Award for the worst picture of the year and another for worst screenplay, the film was a huge hit with the public across the globe, grossing $170,000,000. The film follows the story of a New York business student who takes up bartending to make ends meet – and who learns all the skills of a cocktail showman along the way. He has the flair and visual ostentation of Jerry 'The Professor' Thomas mentioned in chapter 13, the man who was the first bartender to pour flaming streams of spirits from one container to the other while making a Blue Blazer. In the film, the Tom Cruise character and his colleagues are expert jugglers, tossing cocktail shakers and drinks bottles through the air with precise timing. The film helped increase the popularity of what is called 'flairing' or 'flair bartending', with competitions and exhibition matches being held, especially in America. The skills, the showmanship and the sense of fun associated with ordering mixed drinks were what gin needed to stop an inevitable slide into staid obscurity.

It was picked up again in 2000 with the film *Coyote Ugly* – another movie that acquired cult status despite being panned by the critics. It too centres around the antics of a popular bar in New York, but this time with lots of dancing on the bar by girls in wet T-shirts. In short, it helped demonstrate that bartending could be a branch of showmanship. If the Victorian gin palaces had been about shuffling along in a line knocking back a shot of gin and leaving silently by a side exit, this was the exact opposite: drinking at a bar was fun, noisy, exciting and sexually charged. It showed that films could help put the 'spirit' back into 'spirits' and that mixing and serving drinks could be a skill that could be developed as a form of entertainment. The International Bartenders Association had been formed back in 1951, with an annual congress of members, and has been hosting a World Classic Cocktail Competition since 1955. But the past few decades have seen a move towards emphasising the drinks-mixing qualities of a good bartender and the idea of a mixologist has emerged. The Merriam-Webster's dictionary dates 'mixology' to 1872 and defines it as 'the art or skill of preparing mixed drinks'. Meanwhile, the Oxford English Dictionary defines 'mixology' as 'the skill of mixing cocktails or other drinks', and so it follows that a 'mixologist' is a person who possesses these skills. That does not necessarily mean that he or she has the skills to manage a bar, keep stock, serve half a dozen customers at once, and maintain crowd control, but he or she does know how to blend flavours, how to create the perfect drink for the occasion. A mixologist will also be expected to understand why some flavours work and why some do not. A mixologist will know how the various cocktails developed over the years and be a sort of cocktail historian. Indeed, the mixologist may not even be in the public eye, but work away behind the scenes creating new cocktails and new flavours on behalf of the distillery companies. Whether there is a real distinction between a good mixologist and a good bartender is debatable, but it is an indication of how the spotlight has fallen on the man or woman producing the cocktail. The cocktail is more than a drink. It has become an experience.

Other films helped secure the image of gin as a drink with caché and style. In the 2006 movie *Casino Royale*, James Bond is very specific about ordering a cocktail that includes Kina Lillet. Kina Lillet was created at the end of the nineteenth century in France, where wine-based tonics were popular. Known as *quinquina*s, they were flavoured with bitter-tasting quinine. Bond's drink, which he calls the Vesper, echoes a U.S. advertisement from the 1950s: 'Everyone enjoys a gin and Lillet'. It is not a slogan which will catch on in Britain – where 'Lil-let' describes something altogether different! What *Casino Royale* does do is show how the portrayal of particular drinks in films can create an image that is priceless to manufacturers. Obviously, product placement has been around for many years – some argue that it dates back to the very earliest silent movies, while others point to a painting by Edouard Manet entitled *A bar at the Folies Bergère*. Dating from 1882, it shows the distinctively marked bottles of Bass beer placed at either end of the counter.

What is certain is that the power of product placement and endorsement by celebrities can be very effective, as evidenced by the fact that when Daniel Craig appeared in *Skyfall*, he not only swigged a Heineken beer instead of sipping a martini, but also appeared in an accompanying advertising campaign for Heineken. The Dutch brewery company invested millions of dollars in a joint promotion when the film came out in 2012.

The Great Gatsby starring Leonardo DiCaprio came out in 2013 and not surprisingly features gin drinking, given that a gin rickey was a favourite tipple of author Scott Fitzgerald. Made with gin, lime and Club Soda it echoed a tradition that helped position gin in the eyes of the public – sophisticated, cool, aspirational.

A number of quite separate developments came into play, around the turn of the millennium. First up was a gate-crasher to the party: Hendrick's Gin. Do not be fooled by the date of 1886 on the bottle, or by the quirky, mock Victorian advertising. This is a thoroughly modern product, launched by William Grant & Sons who, though founded in 1886, had spent over a century manufacturing whisky and had not tried to touch gin manufacture with a barge pole. But when they did launch Hendrick's Gin it was to have huge importance to the subsequent explosion in 'ginterest' – an interest in all-things-gin. For a start, it was not a London Dry Gin, and it used a new range of botanicals. These were added after the distillation process. Yes, it is still recognisably a gin, with its base firmly in the use of juniper berries, but the flavours added after distillation include cucumber and rose petals. Absent are the citrus notes – and therefore there is little point adding lemon to your tonic because there is no significant citrus flavour to enhance. Instead, 'ice and a slice' with Hendricks is likely to mean a slice of cucumber. Granted, not everyone is a fan of cucumber: Samuel Johnson remarked that 'It has been a common saying of physicians in England, that a cucumber should be well sliced, and dressed with pepper and vinegar, and then thrown out, as good for nothing'. But for aficionados, the cucumber gives a crisp, invigorating flavour and it quickly caught on, aided by some brilliant advertising worthy of Monty Python's Flying Circus. In 2008, eight years after its launch, Grant's sold more than 100,000 nine-litre cases of Hendrick's for the first time. By 2017 the company were selling over a million cases of Hendrick's gin each year – not a bad rate of growth for a relative newcomer when set against established manufacturers such as Gordon's (just over five million cases) Bombay Sapphire (four million cases) and Tanqueray (three and a half million). It is a growth rate that has continued for all the leading manufacturers and within two years the sales of Hendrick's gin had increased by nearly fifty per cent, while Gordon's had grown to nearly six and three quarter million cases per annum. As of 2019, the biggest growth was from Diageo's Tanqueray – up nearly 12% in the year to 4.5 million cases.

What Hendrick's has shown is that in a growing market there is always going to be room for innovation, and it helped pave the way for the explosion of craft gin-making which has been the hallmark of the industry in recent years. Where Hendrick's led, others have followed. Many of them have no wish to be market leaders, or sell in supermarkets across the country: they are simply supplying a local niche market for innovative products. It has led to an explosion of interest in gin and the market has grown to accommodate large and small manufacturers alike.

A totally unrelated event occurred in 2004 which proved to be significant; the launch of Fever-Tree Tonic, with its slogan 'If three quarters of your gin and tonic is the tonic, make sure you use the best'. Up until then the market for tonic water had seemed to consist either of Schweppes or of over-sweet supermarket own-brands, tasting vaguely of grapefruit and not at all of quinine. Fever-Tree got drinkers thinking about the botanicals in their gin, about how to enhance the flavours. Before long they were producing more than a dozen mixers for a range of different spirits, from Cucumber Tonic Water to Sicilian Lemonade, Elderflower Tonic, Mediterranean Tonic and Aromatic Tonic. The company even produces a Fever-Tree Tonic Pairing Wheel, showing the different qualities of using certain gins with particular tonics, topped off with specific garnishes. It helped transform the gin-drinking market, attracting a new breed of customer a world away from the retired army colonel sitting at a table in the corner of the bar – who had never once thought of changing either the make of gin or the type of tonic, and for whom 'revolutionary' would mean trying a slice of lime instead of a slice of lemon. A new breed of G&T drinkers emerged, knowledgeable about what they were drinking and wanting to pair their drink with a choice of rosemary, cucumber, grapefruit, thyme or orange peel. It encouraged an interest in the botanicals in the gin itself, and before long the gin-bore, blathering on about polyphonics, congeners and 'respectfully harvested botanicals' could be added to the wine-buff and the whisky-connoisseur as people to avoid if you just wanted to be able to drink in peace, in silent contemplation.

One more push was needed in Britain before the craft gin market could emerge into the sunlight: the overthrow of a piece of legislative control dating back to the Gin Acts of the eighteenth century. In a bid to stop cellars and spare rooms being used to distil alcohol, Parliament had enacted that distilleries could not get a licence unless the still had a capacity of at least 1,800 litres. It meant that whereas the drinks giants such as Diageo, or Pernod Ricard, had the size of operation where they could afford to develop a new product in large quantities, backed with a ready-made marketing arrangement with outlets nationwide, there was no way that any newcomer could 'start small' and grow the business on the back of a good reputation. Enter two men, friends from childhood, by the name of Sam Galsworthy and Fairfax Hall. Gin-lovers and perhaps gin-dreamers, they combined resources with drinks aficionado and master distiller Jared Brown and developed the idea of buying a copper beauty called Prudence, swan-necked and holding a mere 300 litres, and using her to launch the first new London Dry Gin to be made in the capital for the best part of two centuries. The trio managed to persuade the government to change the rules and grant a licence for their diminutive operation and in 2009 they launched Sipsmiths on an unsuspecting market. The quantities may have been distinctly limited at first, with the operations being carried out in a small garage in Hammersmith, but the enterprise grew rapidly and by 2014 it had outgrown its first home and moved to leafy Chiswick, where Prudence was joined by her 'sisters' Patience and Constance. Sloe gins and flavoured vodkas followed, along with all manner of innovative products including the 2017 launch of its London Cup. Described as a blend of Earl Grey tea with borage, lemon verbena and other botanicals, it was stated to have 'aromas of burnt orange, cucumber, caramel and tea leaves', while the taste is apparently 'reminiscent of marmalade and cherry with herbaceous notes, leading to a scorched oak finish'.

By 2016 the company had been acquired by Beam Suntory, albeit with the founding trio of Galsworthy, Hall and Brown remaining at the centre of operations. And some things don't change: the distilled spirits are diluted to a drinkable strength using Lydwell Springwater. One of the sources of the River Thames, the springwater is still brought up from the Cotswolds by tanker, thereby ensuring a connection with centuries-old gin manufacture in the heart of the City.

It wasn't just that Sipsmiths burst onto the scene, but that the company made it possible for all the other little guys to come out and play. The lifting of the size limit meant that people could become part-time distillers, producing a product to match local demand. Local distillers could bring out commemorative gins to mark special occasions, leading to the stage where in 2020 the Otterbeck Distillery in Yorkshire was able to launch a Captain Sir Tom Moore gin to commemorate the life and achievements of the centenarian fund-raiser. And if you are interested, it's described as being 'softly herbaceous with thyme, rosemary and juniper, plus a splash of lemon zest'. Elsewhere, gins which are only made when specific botanicals can be harvested started to appear. Gins with an affinity to a particular place developed and before long the consumer was faced with a baffling plethora of new gins.

It is worth mentioning that HM Revenue & Customs still insist on small-scale distillers applying for a licence. Indeed, the regulations confirmed in January 2021 (i.e. post-Brexit) say:

> [HRMC] may refuse to issue a licence where the largest still to be used has a capacity below 18 hectolitres. However, we'll consider applications for a distiller's licence providing

you use the still for the commercial production of spirits. You must submit a business plan to support your application for commercial production.'

Even if a distiller wants to operate on a very low-key basis he or she will still need approval of plant and process, together with proper warehouse and warehouse-keeper approvals, along with the actual licence, before production of spirits can take place.

The reduction in still size has meant that it is now possible for gin schools to operate, where students can make their own selection of dried botanicals, place them in a half-litre still with pure spirits and watch as the distilled, highly-personalised product drips through into a bottle where it can then be diluted, labelled and handed to the happy student at the end of the session.

Gin Clubs, sipping societies, pairing suggestions for gins with different meals – the list of ideas promoting gin seem endless. There has also been an extraordinary variety of new tastes launched on the market. You want a Jaffa Cake flavour? You got it. You want your gin to taste of marshmallows? Not a problem. You can get parma violet gin and you can get gin made from wild mushrooms. You can get seaweed gin. You can even get a Stormtrooper Gin and drink a Darth Vader cocktail, which seems to be equal measures of gin, rum, vodka, tequila orange liqueur and Jägermeister – diluted with a little ice. Perhaps you feel that your gin is a little lacking because it is made using a mere dozen botanicals? Try Monkey 47. The number refers to the forty-seven botanicals used in its manufacture, mostly sourced locally in the Black Forest. No, it doesn't explain the 'monkey' bit, but there you go.

You want a gin cocktail to match your favourite TV programme? Try A Game of Thrones cocktail. For lovers of the TV series about a Birmingham crime family in the early 1900s, there is a well-reviewed gin from Sadlers known as Peaky Blinders Spiced Dry Gin. The Master of Malt tasting notes describe it as having a nose of 'ripe orange, oak-y cassia and perhaps even a hint of coffee bean' along with a palate of 'ginger and black pepper' and a finish of 'oily juniper and a hint of eucalyptus'. You watch the programme: you drink the gin.

Your fascination with Snoop Dogg has no limits? Well then, it means that you will want to knock back the gin which carries his endorsement. It is sold by the name of Indoggo, and has a strong strawberry flavour. And you can buy gin from every locality – nowhere seems to be remote from a distillery, with at least 220 gin distilleries operating in England alone in 2019 – up by 62 from the year before. Indeed, the number of distilleries throughout Britain has gone up from 184 to 445 in the five years from 2014.

These distilleries produce an awful lot of gin between them, with more than 82 million bottles of gin sold in the UK in 2019. Sales were worth £2.6 billion in the year to June 2019, while exports of gin totalled £672 million, according to HMRC figures. Subsequent figures will no doubt be affected by pub closures caused by the Covid pandemic but there is nothing to suggest that our passion for drinking gin is likely to evaporate any time soon.

What, then, are likely to be the trends? Drinking patterns always go in cycles but it is highly probable that the appetite for gimmicky flavours will continue for a while. We may well end up with a scenario where TV 'stars' – 'C' list celebrities – have not just a signature perfume, but also their own signature gin. More films will be launched in conjunction with special edition gins and there will be more dinners with pairing recommendations. But at the same time, we can perhaps expect some of the more exotic drinks to spin off and cease to be caught in the gin category – simply because they no longer have a sufficient connection with juniper to be classed as gin. The opening chapter of this book starts with the words 'If it's not made with juniper berries, it ain't gin …' and this echoes the legislation which defines gin. Britain has left the European Union, but there is no suggestion that the country will walk away from a definition that says that juniper has to be the predominant flavour. Or, if you want to be pedantic and quote Annex II, Section 22, Subsection (a)(i) of Regulation (EC) No 110/2008 of the European Parliament:

a) Gin is a juniper-flavoured spirit drink produced by flavouring organoleptically suitable ethyl alcohol of agricultural origin with juniper berries (Juniperus communis L.).
b) The minimum alcoholic strength by volume of gin shall be 37.5%
c) Only natural and/or nature identical flavouring substances as defined … shall be used for the production of gin *so that the taste is predominantly that of juniper* [own italics].

Surely it is time for some of the more exotic flavours to be renamed – as vodka (which has no such ruling as to predominant flavour) or simply as flavoured spirits. It is a move that was urged by Hayman's Distillery, when they launched their campaign to 'Call time on fake gin', in 2018. As their website states: 'While botanical innovation and experimentation has long been linked to gin's success, we believe that a small number of producers are today creating spirits that have strayed too far from what makes gin 'gin'. Such products undermine the work that the vast majority of distillers complete and run the risk of misleading consumers by blurring boundaries between gin and other spirit drinks.'

Britain is no longer in the E.U., but the country is unlikely to choose to adopt a different definition of gin – not when it has also been adopted in the United States. It is more a question of whether the definition is going to be enforced. Cue proceedings under the Trade Misdescription Act of 1968 …

Interestingly, there has been a recent spate of non-alcoholic and low alcohol drinks, made to mimic gin with its juniper flavours. However gin-like the flavour and however strong the notes of juniper, the manufacturers are unable to use the word 'gin' because they fall foul of the above rule on 37.5 ABV. Both Gordon's and Tanqueray have introduced drinks in almost identical bottles to their full-strength versions, without the word gin, and simply emphasising the 0% figure on the label. Both refer to a 'heavily guarded secret' used in the manufacture but it is hard to escape the conclusion that the 'secret' is the addition of … more water! It is made the same way as the normal spirit, with the distillate capturing the flavours of the botanicals. However, whereas the standard-strength gin is then diluted by roughly half, to bring it down to a level that is drinkable, with the 'zero-gins' it is heavily diluted and excess alcohol removed. One can easily imagine that many consumers will be keen to have a non-alcoholic drink which leaves them able to partake in the 'gin experience' – tasting it with different mixers, serving it with different garnishes, in short, joining in without having any of the effects of imbibing alcohol.

One other trend looks to be the popularity of 'gin in a tin'. Perhaps as a result of Covid lockdowns and restrictions on attending pubs, people are looking to ready-mixed cocktails, which can be bought, stored at home and used when required. It is a huge market and it looks set to grow. There is even a move to combine 'gin in a tin' with a celebrity endorsement, as with the late Shane Warne's 'Seven Zero Eight; gin (named after the number of Test wickets taken by the Aussie bowler). He produced a pre-mixed drink selling in Australia with a lower alcohol content called '23' (a reference to the strength of the alcohol). In Britain it should not be sold as 'gin' because it is half-strength, but who is to say that the definition of 'gin' will not change in line with pressure on people to reduce their alcohol consumption?

The more serious student of gin will continue to look for drinks showing the 'original authentic taste' of gin – and that may mean demanding genuine Genever, either new style or old. It also means renewed interest in that 'missing link' in gin's history, Old Tom. It is seen as a sort of halfway step between Genever and London Dry and if a connoisseur wants to know how the original Victorian-era cocktails tasted, it is Old Tom which provides the answer. Other trends are towards storing the gin for a period of time – typically six months – in oak barrels. We could well see a move towards vintage gins.

As craft gin distilleries produce more and more limited edition gins – for instance to mark special celebrations, anniversaries and so on, or to mark harvests of locally-grown botanicals – there will be more and more opportunities for people to collect different gin bottles or even sets of gin bottles. Themed collections – gins named after people, or featuring animals, or linked to particular countries – could easily lead to beautiful bottles being collected and traded in the same way as postage stamps from around the world.

Gin lovers, like beer lovers, seem willing to enhance their overseas journeys by looking out local drinks from wherever they visit. We can expect to see this trend develop as international travel recovers from Covid: it doesn't matter whether you go to Japan, or Brazil, or South Africa, or Estonia – all have their own gin distilleries. And surely, no self-respecting gin aficionado will want to miss out on the chance to display a bottle of gin from Angola, redolent as it is of piquant baobab, spicy nutmeg and strawberry fruitiness. Gin is truly a drink that has conquered the world.

Appendix 1

EXTERIOR OF A LONDON GIN-PALACE.

Synonyms for Gin and words associated with Gin – mostly eighteenth century:

BLUE TAPE. Gin.
BLUE RUIN. Gin.
BLUE RI[B]BAND. Gin.
BLUE LIGHTNING. Gin.
BOB. Gin.
BOWSING KEN. A gin-shop (also an ale house).
CLEAR CRYSTAL. Undiluted gin.
COLD CREAM. Gin.
COCK-MY-CAP. Gin.
COLIC & GRIPE-WATERS. Gin.
CREAM OF THE VALLEY. Gin.
CRANK. Gin and water.
CUCKOLD'S COMFORT. Gin.
DEVIL'S LEFT HAND. Gin.

DIDDLE. Gin.

DOROTHY ADDLE-BRAIN. Gin

DRAIN. Gin: So-called from the diuretic qualities imputed to that liquor.

DRAM. A glass or small measure of any spirituous liquors, which, being originally sold by apothecaries, were estimated by drams, ounces, &c.

DUTCH DROP. Gin

TO FIRE A SLUG. To drink a dram.

FLANNEL. See 'hot'.

FLASH. Gin

FROG'S WINE. Gin.

GENEVA. Gin.

GIN SPINNER. A distiller.

HOLLANDS. Gin.

HOT. A mixed kind of liquor, of beer and gin, with egg, sugar and nutmeg drunk mostly in night-houses, but when drunk in the morning, it is called flannel.

JACKEY. Gin.

JENNY PISSPOT. Gin.

KING THEODORE OF CORSICA. Gin.

KILL GRIEF. Gin.

KNOCK-ME-DOWN. Gin.

LADIES DELIGHT. Gin.

LADY DACRE'S WINE. Gin.

LAST SHIFT. Gin.

LIGHTNING. Gin. A flash of lightning; a glass of gin.

MAKE-SHIFT. Gin.

MAX or MAXIM. Gin.

MOTHER'S RUIN. Gin.

MY LADY'S EYE-WATER. Gin.

OLD TOM. Gin

PARLIAMENT GIN. Gin, made pursuant to the Gin Acts.

PUNCH. A liquor called by foreigners Contradiction, from its being composed of spirits to make it strong, water to make it weak, lemon juice to make it sour, and sugar to make it sweet.

RAG WATER. Gin, or any other common dram: these liquors seldom failing to reduce those that drink them to rags.

RAW. Undiluted gin.

ROYAL POVERTY Gin.

SHOVE IN THE MOUTH. A dram.

SKY BLUE. Gin
STRIP ME NAKED. Gin.
TAPE Blue or white tape; Gin.
THUNDER and LIGHTNING. Gin with bitters.
TOM ROW. Gin.
WHITE RI[B]BIN. Gin.
WHITE TAPE. Geneva.
WHITE WOOL. Geneva.

Slang and other words associated with drinking, as defined in Grose's Classical Dictionary of Vulgar Slang:

BARREL FEVER. He died of the barrel fever; he killed himself by drinking.
BINGO. Brandy or other spirituous liquor.
BLUE FLAG. He has hoisted the blue flag; he has commenced [being a] publican, or taken a public house, an allusion to the blue aprons worn by publicans.
BLUFFER. An inn-keeper.
CHIMPING MERRY. Exhilarated with liquor.
COGUE. A dram of any spirituous liquor
CORNED. Drunk.
CUP-SHOT. Drunk.
CUT. Drunk. A little cut over the head; slightly intoxicated.
DAFFY'S ELIXIR. A proprietary remedy described as 'the soothing syrup'.
DISGUISED. Drunk.
DOCTOR. Milk and water, with a little rum, and some nutmeg; also the name of a composition used by distillers, to make spirits appear stronger than they really are, or, in their phrase, better proof.
DROP IN THE EYE. Almost drunk.
FLAWD. Drunk.
FLICKER. A drinking glass.
FLUSTERED. Drunk.
FOXED. Intoxicated.
FUDDLE-CAP; a drunkard.
GO SHOP. The Queen's Head in Duke's court, Bow Street, Covent Garden; frequented by the under players: where gin and water was sold in three-halfpenny bowls, called Goes.
GROG. Rum and water. Grog was first introduced into the navy about the year 1740, by Admiral Vernon, to prevent the sailors intoxicating themselves

with their allowance of rum, or spirits. GROGGY, or GROGGIFIED; drunk.

GUN. He is in the gun; he is drunk:

GUZZLE GUTS. One greedy of liquor.

HALF SEAS OVER. Almost drunk.

HARE. He has swallowed a hare; he is drunk.

HICKEY. Tipsey; quasi hiccupping

HOCKEY. Drunk with strong stale beer, called old hock.

HUM CAP. Very old and strong beer, called also stingo.

KNOCK ME DOWN. Strong ale or beer, stingo.

LINE OF THE OLD AUTHOR. A dram of brandy.

LUSH. Strong beer.

MANUFACTURE. Liquors prepared from materials of English growth.

MAUDLIN DRUNK. Crying drunk: perhaps from Mary Magdalene, called Maudlin, who is always painted in tears.

MAULED. Extremely drunk, or soundly beaten.

MELLOW. Almost drunk.

MONKEY. To suck the monkey; to suck or draw wine, or any other liquor, privately out of a cask, by means of a straw, or small tube.

MOP UP. To drink up. To empty a glass or pot.

OLD HARRY. A composition used by vintners to adulterate their wines; also the nickname for the devil.

PIN. In or to a merry pin; almost drunk.

POGY. Drunk.

PURL. Ale in which wormwood has been infused, or ale and bitters drunk warm.

PURL ROYAL. Canary wine; with a dash of tincture of wormwood.

RED RI[B]BIN. Brandy.

ROT GUT. Small beer; called beer-a-bumble—will burst one's guts before it will make one tumble.

RUM NANTZ. Good French brandy.

RUMBO. Rum, water, and sugar;

SHAFTSBURY. A gallon pot full of wine, with a cock.

TO SHOOT THE CAT. To vomit from excess of liquor; called also catting.

TO SOAK. To drink.

STEPNEY. A decoction of raisins of the sun and lemons in conduit water, sweetened with sugar, and bottled up.

STEWED QUAKER. Burnt rum, with a piece of butter: an American remedy for a cold.

STINGO. Strong beer, or other liquor.

STIRRUP CUP. A parting cup or glass, drunk on horseback by the person taking leave.

SUCK. Strong liquor of any sort.

SUCKY. Drunk.

SURVEYOR OF THE HIGHWAYS. One reeling drunk.

SWILL TUB. A drunkard, a sot.

TAPE. Red tape; brandy.

TOP HEAVY. Drunk.

TOSS POT. A drunkard.

VICE ADMIRAL OF THE NARROW SEAS. A drunken man that pisses under the table into his companions' shoe.

WATER BEWITCHED. Very weak punch or beer.

WET QUAKER. One of that sect who has no objection to the spirit derived from wine.

WIBBLE. Bad drink.

WORD OF MOUTH. To drink by word of mouth, i.e. out of the bowl or bottle instead of a glass.

WRAPT UP IN WARM FLANNEL Drunk with spirituous liquor

Appendix 2

Early recipes for Gin cocktails

From Jerry Thomas's book *How to Mix Drinks: Or, The Bon-vivant's Companion:*

Gin Punch
Half pint of old gin
One gill of maraschino
The juice of two lemons
The rind of half a lemon
Four ounces of syrup
One quart bottle of German Seltzer water
Ice Well

Gin Cocktail
3 or 4 dashes of gum syrup
2 ditto bitters (Bogart's)
I wine glass of gin
1 or 2 dashes of Curacao
1 small piece of lemon peel;
Fill one-third full of fine ice; shake well and strain in a glass.

Fancy Gin cocktail
This drink is made the same as the gin cocktail, except that it is strained in
a fancy wine glass and a piece of lemon peel thrown on top, and the edge of
the glass moistened with lemon.

Gin Crusta
Crusta is made the same as a fancy cocktail with a little lemon juice and a
small lump of ice added. First, mix the ingredients in a small tumbler, then
take a fancy red wine glass, rub a sliced lemon around the rim of the same
and dip it in pulverised white sugar so that the sugar will adhere to the edge
of the glass. Pare half a lemon the same as you would an apple (all in one
piece) so that the paring will fit in the wine glass and strain the crusta from
the tumbler into it. Then smile.

Hot Gin Toddy (Use small bar glass).
One teaspoonful of sugar
Half a wine glass of boiling water
One ditto gin
Stir with a spoon and sprinkle with nutmeg.

Gin sangaree
The gin sangaree is made with the same ingredients as the gin toddy,
omitting the nutmeg and with cold water. Fill two-thirds full of ice, and dash
about a teaspoonful of port wine, so that it will float on the top.

Gin sling
The gin sling is made with the same ingredients as the gin toddy, except you
grate a little nutmeg on top.

Gin Fix: (use small bar glass)
One table-spoonful of sugar
Half a wine-glass of water

Quarter of lemon
One wine glass of gin

Fill two-thirds full of shaved ice. Stir with a spoon, and ornament the top with fruits in season.

Gin sour

The gin sour is made with the same ingredients as the gin fix, omitting all fruits, except a small piece of lemon, the juice of which must be pressed in the glass.

Gin and Pine: (use a wine glass)

Split a piece of the heart of a green pine log into fine splints, about the size of a cedar lead pencil, take two ounces of the same and put into a quart decanter, and fill the decanter with gin. Leave the pine soak for two hours and the gin will be ready to serve.

Gin and Tansy: (use wine glass)

Fill a quart decanter half full of tansy, and pour in gin to fill up the balance one-third tansy to two-thirds gin. Serve to customers in a wine glass.

Gin and wormwood: (use small bar glass)

Put three or four sprigs of wormwood into a quart decanter and fill up with gin. NB this drink is not much used except in small country villages.

As a supplement to the book on mixing cocktails, there was a section by Christian Schulz, being 'A Manual for the Manufacture of Cordials, Liquors, Fancy Syrups etc etc'

To make ten gallons of Domestic Gin: three drachms of oil of juniper; dissolve in five and a quarter gallons of alcohol, 95%; add four and five-eighths of water and one-eighth of a gallon of white plain syrup

To make ten gallons of English Gin: three drachms of oil of juniper; one drachm of oil of turpentine. Dissolve in five and a quarter gallons of alcohol, 95%, add four and three-quarters gallons of water.

To make ten gallons of Holland Gin: Two and a half gallons of Holland Gin, three and three-quarters gallons of alcohol, 95%; three and three-quarters gallons of water, mix together.

To make ten gallons of Gin, London Cordial: three drachms of oil of juniper; one drachm oil of angelica, 10 drops of oil of coriander. Dissolve in five and a quarter gallons of alcohol, 95%, add half a gallon of white plain syrup and four and a quarter gallons of water. Filter.

From Harry Johnson's book *The New and Improved Illustrated Bartenders' Manual:*

Silver Fizz: (use a large bar glass).
Half a table-spoonful of sugar;
2 or 3 dashes of lemon juice;
1 wine-glass of Old Tom gin, dissolved well, with a squirt of Vichy;
one egg (the white only);
three-quarters of a glass filled with shaved ice.

Shake up well with a shaker, strain it into good-sized fizz glass, fill up the glass with Syphon Selters or Vichy Water, mix well and serve. This drink is a delicious one and must be drunk as soon as prepared, as it loses its strength and flavour.

John Collins
Three-quarters of a table-spoonful of sugar;
2 or 3 dashes of lemon juice;
4 or 5 small lumps of ice;
1 wine glass full of Holland Gin.

Pour in a bottle of plain soda, mix up well, remove the ice and serve. Care must be taken not to let the foam of the soda water run over the glass while pouring it in. This drink must be taken as soon as mixed, or it will lose its flavour.

Gin Julep: (use a large bar glass).
Three-quarters of a table-spoonful of sugar;
or 4 sprigs of Mint;
Half a wine glass of water.

Dissolve well, until the essence of mint is extracted, then remove the mint. Fill up with fine ice; add one and a quarter glass of Holland Gin. Stir up well with a spoon, ornament it the same as you would with a mint julep, then serve.

Old Tom Gin Cocktail: (use a large bar glass).
Fill the glass with fine shaved ice;
2 or 3 dashes of Gum syrup;
1 or 2 dashes of Bitters (Boker's genuine only);
1 or 2 dashes of Curacoa or Absinthe if required;
One wine glass of Old Tom Gin.

Stir up well with a spoon, strain into a cocktail glass, twist a piece of Lemon peel on top, and serve.

Gin and Molasses: (use a whisky glass).
Pour into the glass a small quantity of Gin, to cover the bottom of it, then take one tablespoonful of New Orleans black molasses, and hand with a bar spoon and the bottle of gin to the customer to help himself. Hot water must be used to clean the glass afterwards as it will be impossible to clean it in any other way.

Gin and Milk: (use a whisky glass).
Hand the bottle of gin, glass and spoon out to the customer to help himself, fill up the balance with good rich ice-cold milk, stir up with a spoon and you will have a very nice drink.

Bibliography

Anonymous: *Presentment of the London grand Jury*. J. Roberts, London, 1736.

Anonymous: *Presentment of the Middlesex Grand-Jury*. J. Roberts, London, 1736.

Anonymous: *'An Elegy on the Much-Lamented Death of the Most Excellent, the Most Truly-Beloved and Universally Admired Lady, Madam Gineva'*. London.

Anonymous: *The Gin Shop*. London, 1836. Available online via Hathi Trust.

Anonymous: *Low-life, or, One half of the world, knows not how the other half lives*. Printed for T Legg, London, 1764. Available online via Hathi Trust.

Berlin, Michael: *The Worshipful Company of Distillers*. Phillimore & Co, Chichester, 1996.

Boothby, William Thomas: *The World's Drinks and how to mix them*. San Francisco, 1908.

Bradstreet, Dudley: *The Life and Uncommon Adventures of Capt. Dudley Bradstreet, Etc*. Dublin, 1755.

Clark, Peter. 'The 'Mother Gin' Controversy in the Early Eighteenth Century', *Transactions of the Royal Historical Society*, vol. 38, 1988, pp. 63–84. JSTOR, www.jstor.org/stable/3678967.

Cooper, 1736. *Historical Texts / Ecco*. Web. 22 Feb 2015.

Craddock, Harry: *The Savoy Cocktail Book*. Constable, London, 1930.

Defoe, D.: *A brief case of the distillers: and of the distilling trade in England*. London: T. Warner, 1726.

Dickens, Cedric: *Drinking with Dickens*. London, Elvendon Press,1980.

Dickens, Charles: *Sketches by Boz*. John Macrone, London, 1833.

Dickens, Charles: *Barnaby Rudge, A Tale of the Riots of Eighty*. Chapman & Hall, London 1841.

Dickens, Charles: *Bleak House*. Bradbury & Evans, London, 1853.

Dillon, Patrick: *Gin: The Much-lamented Death of Madam Geneva*. Justin Charles and Co, Boston, 2002.

Eboranus: *A Proposal to Prevent The Common Tippling of Spiritous Liquors in Such Manner As Shall Not Any Ways Prejudice the Public Revenue*. London, 1736.

Edgar, John: *Digest of Evidence before the Committee of Parliament*, Belfast, 1835

Fearon, Henry Bradshaw: *Sketches of America. A Narrative of a Journey of Five Thousand Miles through the Eastern and Western States of America.* Longman, Hurst, Rees, Orme, and Brown, 1818.

Fielding, H.: (1751) *An Enquiry into the Causes of the Late Increase of Robbers.* London, 1751 (Repr. AMS Press, New York, 1975). Available online.

Forsyth, Mark: *A Short History of Drunkenness.* Viking 2017

Glauber, Johann Rudolph: *A description of new philosophical furnaces or, A New Art of Distilling.* London 1651. Available online.

Grose, Francis: *A Classical Dictionary of the Vulgar Tongue.* S. Hooper, London, 1785.

Hales, Stephen: *A Friendly admonition to the drinkers of gin, brandy, and other distilled spirituous liquors.* B. Dod for the SPCK, London, 1751.

Harrison, Joel, and Ridley, Noel: *The World Atlas of Gin.* Mitchell Beazley, London, 2019.

Haywood, Eliza: *A Present for Women addicted to drinking.* W. Owen, London, 1750. (Available online).

Holden, A.: *The Trial of the Spirits.* T. Cooper, London, 1736.

Johnson, Harry: *New and Improved illustrated Bartenders Manual, or, How to mix drinks of the present style.* New York, 1882.

Kirton, John William: *The Gin Shop* (illustrated by George Cruikshank). S W Partridge & Co, London, 1869. Available online via Hathi Trust.

Loftus, William R.: *Loftus's New Mixing and Reducing Book for the use of Publicans and Spirit Dealers and Retailers in General.* London, 1869.

Mandeville, Bernard: *The Fable of the Bees, or, Private Vices, Publick Benefits.* London, 1714.

Melville, Herman: *Redburn.* New York, 1850.

Miege, G: *The Present State of Great Britain and Ireland.* J. Brotherton, London, 1748.

Ryan, Michael: *Medical Jurisprudence.* Philadelphia, 1832.

Sabourn, Reay. *A Perfect View of the Gin Act, with its unhappy consequences; Containing Not Only an Inquiry into, but also a Full Account of the Power of the Justices of the Peace, as limited by that Law.* London: Printed for W. Thorne. 1738. (ECCO/ Historical Texts).

Sipsmith Ltd: *Sip - 100 Gin cocktails with only three ingredients.* Mitchell Beazley, London, 2019.

Thomas, Jerry: *How to Mix Drinks: Or, The Bon-vivant's Companion.* Dick & Fitzgerald New York, 1862.

T. S.: *A Proper Reply to a Scandalous Libel, Intituled 'The Trial of the Spirits'*. J. Roberts, London, 1736.

Turner, Thomas. *The Diary of Thomas Turner, 1754-1765*. Ed. by David Vaisey. Oxford: Oxford University Press, 1984.

Vizetelly, Henry: *Glances Back Through Seventy Years: Autobiographical and Other Reminiscences*. London, 1893.

Williams, Olivier: *Gin Glorious Gin: How Mother's Ruin Became the Spirit of London*. Headline, London, 2014.

Wilson, T.: *Distilled Spirituous Liquors - the Bane of the Nation*. J. Roberts, London, 1736. (Available in digitised format as part of the Wellcome Collection).

Wondrich, David: *Punch: The Delights (and Dangers) of the Flowing Bowl*. Penguin Group, 2010.

Online resources

Old Bailey Online https://www.oldbaileyonline.org/forms/formMain.jsp

By the Dutch https://www.bythedutch.com/about/

Difford's Guide for Discerning Drinkers. https://www.diffordsguide.com/producers

Pepys, Samuel: *Diaries* https://www.pepysdiary.com/diary/

The Gentleman's Magazine. Hathi Trust. https://www.hathitrust.org/digital_library

The Gin shop 1836 Hathi Trust https://babel.hathitrust.org/cgi/pt?id=hvd.32044105550396&view=1up&seq=7

White, Jonathan: *Luxury and Labour: Ideas of Labouring-Class Consumption in Eighteenth-Century England* (thesis for Warwick University). http://wrap.warwick.ac.uk/36401/1/WRAP_THESIS_White_2001.pdf

Poli Grappa Museum, Schiavon: https://www.poligrappa.com/eng/affinity/discovering-grappa-web-serie.php

Credits & Acknowledgements

Text Images by Page Number

38. Detail from *Distillatio*, attributed to the workshop of Philips Galle. Rijkmuseum.

39. Eighteenth-century Trade card for George Browne, Distiller & Tobacconist. Lewis Walpole Library, Yale University, lwlpr20865.

45. Thomas Rowlandson's *Holiday at Tyburn*. In public domain, per Boston Public Library.

47. Extract from *The distillery of Deacon Giles seen as the work of the Devil*. Wood-engraving after G. B. Cheever, ca. 1835. Wellcome Library.

54. Thomas Rowlandson's *Naval Officers and a Bowl of Punch*. In public domain, per Google Art Project.

55. *Man with glass and bowl*. Andreas van der Myn, after I. van der Mijn, 1724 – 1800, per Rijkmuseum.

66. Extract from *A Parody on Milton!* by Thomas Rowlandson, 1807. Lewis Walpole Library, Yale University, lwlpr10948.

67. *Refreshment at St Giles* by George Townly Stubbs. Lewis Walpole Library, Yale University, lwlpr37517.

75. Thomas Rowlandson's *A Tub Thumper.* In public domain, per Google Art Project.

77. R Dighton's *Vill you give us a Glass of Gin*. Lewis Walpole Library, Yale University, lwlpr07729

86. *A View of the Frost Fair on the Thames, 1814* Library at Yale University, lwlpr33651

88. Illustration showing the Gordon Riots, in *Chronicles of Newgate* by Arthur Griffiths, 1884, via Gutenberg.

98. Extract from caricature by Richard Newton Lewis Walpole Library, Yale University, lwlpr08594.

99. *Miseries of London* by Thomas Rowlandson, 1807. Lewis Walpole Library, Yale University, lwlpr35435b

107. W P Carey's *A sketch from Nature*. The Metropolitan Museum of Modern Art.

109. Illustration from *The Gin Shop* by George Cruikshank, 1829. In public domain.

123. *A busy Gin Palace with customers buying drinks* by George Cruikshank, 1842. Wellcome Collection. 4.0 International (CC BY 4.0).

125. *A still house in a distillery.* Wood engraving, late 19th century. Wellcome Collection 4.0 International (CC BY 4.0).

129. Extract from *The Lancet*, 1868. In public domain.

140. Quinine plant. Wellcome Collection, 4.0 International (CC BY 4.0).

141. *Victory* paddle steamer shown courtesy of Linda Hall Library of Science and Technology.
149. The drunkard's progress, 1832. Lewis Walpole Library, Yale University, lwlpr13571.
151. Woman's Holy War, Grand Charge on the Enemy's Works. Library of Congress.
155. Temperance Battle card Advertisement, The Workers Onward. January 1915.
163. The Savoy Cocktail Book, first-edition, 1930.
164. Cocktail photograph by Nikita Tikhomiro, Unsplash, in public domain.
174. G&T photograph by Jez Timms, Unsplash, in public domain.
175. Gin palace exterior from *The Gin Shop*, 1836. In public domain.
180. *The Drunkard's Arms* by Carington Bowles, 1785. Lewis Walpole Library, Yale University, lwlpr05680
184. Victorian era advertisement for 'Old Tom'. In public domain.

Plates

1. Distillation apparatus for aqua-vitae, from *Liber de arte Distillandi*, by Hieronymus Brunschwig 1512. In the public domain, per Wikimedia.
2. Distilling Oven, circa 1500. Wellcome Collection 4.0 International (CC BY 4.0).
3. Frontispiece to Pierre Morel's *The expert doctor's dispensatory: apothecary's shop.* Engraved 1657. Wellcome Collection 4.0 International (CC BY 4.00).
4. *Distillatio*, attributed to workshop of Philips Galle after Jan van der Straet, c. 1589 – 1593, Rijkmuseum.
5. From Diderot's Encyclopaedia *Distillateur,* 1751. In public domain.
6. *The English Physitian* dated 1652, by Nicholas Culpeper. In public domain.
7. *Distillery of an Apothecary* Johannes Jelgerhuis, 1818. Rijksmuseum.
8. *The Alchemist in his laboratory.* Oil painting by a follower of David Teniers the younger. Wellcome Collection 4.0 International (CC BY 4.0).
9. *L'alchimiste* by David Teniers the Younger. In public domain per Wikimedia Commons.
10. Plague doctor outfit, Wellcome Collection 4.0 International (CC BY 4.0).
11. *The Funeral Procession of Madam Geneva,* 1751. Lewis Walpole Library lwlpr01509.

12. Hogarth's *A midnight modern conversation*. Metropolitan Museum of Modern Art.
13. Hogarth's *Gin Lane*, 1751. Metropolitan Museum of Modern Art.
14. Hogarth's *Beer Lane*, 1751. Metropolitan Museum of Modern Art.
15. One man sits soundly sleeping as his drunken companion offers him another drink. Etching by T. Sandars, 1773, after J. Collier. Wellcome Collection 4.0 International (CC BY 4.00).
16. Thomas Rowlandson's *Rum Characters in a shrubbery drinking Gin*. Metropolitan Museum of Modern Art
17. *Doctor Drainbarrel conveyed home in order to take his trial for neglect of family duty* by Thomas Rowlandson, 1806. Wellcome Collection 4.0 International (CC BY 4.00).
18. *The gin shop displayed* by Carington Bowles. Wellcome Collection 4.0 International (CC BY 4.00).
19. *The Battle of A-GIN-COURT* by T McLean. Lewis Walpole Library lwlpr14144.
20. *Gin Juggarnath* by George Cruikshank, 1835. Yale University Library.
21. *I want a small glass of Gin*. Etching, 1830. Wellcome Collection 4.0 International (CC BY 4.00).
22. *The Gin Shop* by George Cruikshank, 1829. Lewis Walpole Library lwlpr13337.
23. *The Drunkards Children* by George Cruikshank, 1846. Wellcome Collection 4.0 International (CC BY 4.00).
24. *The Drunkards Children* by George Cruikshank, 1848. Wellcome Collection 4.0 International (CC BY 4.00).

Index